D0753722

IN MY FATHER'S HOUSE

THE STORY OF THE LAYTON FAMILY AND THE REVEREND JIM JONES

MIN S. YEE & THOMAS N. LAYTON

WITH DEBORAH LAYTON, LAURENCE L. LAYTON AND
ANNALISA LAYTON VALENTINE

BERKLEY BOOKS, NEW YORK

FOR LISA PHILIP LAYTON
1915–1978

FOR MY FRIEND
Through Winter and Summer,
Who gave me Spring and Fall

M.S.Y.

This Berkley book contains the complete
text of the original hardcover edition.
It has been completely reset in a type face
designed for easy reading, and was printed
from new film.

IN MY FATHER'S HOUSE

A Berkley Book / published by arrangement with
Holt, Rinehart and Winston

Holt, Rinehart and Winston edition / May 1981
Berkley edition / July 1982

Copyright ©1981 by Min S. Yee and Thomas N. Layton.
This book may not be reproduced in whole or in part,
by mimeograph or any other means, without permission.
For information address: Holt, Rinehart and Winston,
383 Madison Avenue, New York, New York 10017.

ISBN: 0-425-05387-3

A BERKLEY BOOK ® TM 757,375
Berkley Books are published by Berkley Publishing Corporation,
200 Madison Avenue, New York, New York 10016.
PRINTED IN THE UNITED STATES OF AMERICA

Contents

*All was silent after that. No, I heard
someone crying....I listened carefully,
and I noticed that it was my own crying.*

—Ryunosuke Akutagawa, *Rashomon*

Authors' Notes

This book is based upon the compilation of an enormous family record—literally hundreds of pounds of documents that included letters to and from each other, diaries, baby books, introspectives, and, for more than a year following the tragedy in Guyana, tape-recorded telephone conversations. Thomas Layton and I have supplemented that record with interviews and exchanges, mainly with Dr. Laurence Layton, Annalisa, and Debbie, also with a number of family relatives and friends.

As some of their statements in the Afterword indicate, the Layton family is not happy with this book. That was not unexpected, given a family story based on the memories and perspectives of six different people, as well as the viewpoints of friends and relatives. With some minor exceptions, what finally appeared in this book is what I thought should be there. The names of seven persons—one important to the narrative and the others with very minor roles—were changed for considerations of privacy.

I was fortunate enough to have enjoyed a great deal of help and guidance in the course of researching and writing this book. First and foremost, my gratitude goes to Don Hutter, Executive Editor at Holt, Rinehart and Winston, for being a most understanding and helpful editor. His sensitivity and guidance carried us all through some difficult moments. Jessie Wood provided research and editorial assistance for much of the book, particularly for chapters 6, 8, 9, and 10. Nancy Spiller provided research and editorial assistance on chapters 5 and 6.

I especially want to acknowledge the contribution of my co-author, Thomas Layton, who worked tirelessly in gathering and organizing the primary source material, conducted interviews with family relatives, and wrote the original drafts for many of the vignettes in this book.

MIN S. YEE
Mill Valley, California

My contribution as co-author of this work has been as researcher, documenter, and interviewer, in part drawing upon my collection of documents dating from the present back to 1820 for the family of my mother Lisa Philip Layton, and to Quaker Pennsylvania of 1685 for my father's family. Only a small portion of this large body of information, most of it dating from the time of the American Civil War to 1980, has actually been incorporated into this manuscript. While I vouch for its authenticity, the choice of the information included, and the voice, style, and manner of its presentation, are not my own.

Perhaps because I am an academic, I have misgivings about this book. It tells a story—a true one—but it is not scientific; it describes rather more than it explains. For the Layton family, it is simply too soon to attempt an analytic study. For us, the events described here are still unfolding. Larry's legal problems are unresolved; we have yet to hear his story.

Many people have contributed to this book. First I would like to thank Grace Corse and Ethel Wright for providing the hiding place for my sister Debbie immediately after her escape from Guyana. The first formal interviews leading to this book were conducted in the refuge of their house. Thanks also go to Doctors Philip Rasch, David Nasatir, James Freeman, and Linda King for encouragement and advice; to Ernst Hochfeld, Lisa Hirsch Burnham, and Julie Dewey for assistance in translation; to Alan Leventhal for covering my classes at San Jose State University during my absence in Guyana; to a number of wonderful relatives who contributed information but who wish to remain anonymous; and to Larry's attorneys Rex McKay and Jainaraine Singh in Guyana and Tony Tamburello in San Francisco. Finally I thank Bertha Klausner, my literary agent, and Donald Hutter, Executive Editor at Holt, Rinehart and Winston, for their efforts in bringing this book to completion.

THOMAS N. LAYTON
San Jose, California

Prologue

Monday, November 13, 1978, was a cool, crisp day in the nation's capital. Orange and red leaves swirled across government lawns. The air held a threat of snow, a blue-gray hint in the skies over the Capitol's dome. Below, on C Street, a black Chrysler limousine bumped over the pavement's edge and coasted silently down into the basement garage of the Senate Office Building.

The car stopped, and the driver and four others got out. The driver stood about six-foot-two and had the broad shoulders of a football player. He approached the slender young woman who had stepped out on the other side. Because he towered over her, he had to bend down to put both his arms around her. He gave her a big fatherly hug.

"Don't worry, Debbie," he said. "Everything is going to be all right."

The woman nodded, her large dark eyes reflecting doubt.

Congressman Leo J. Ryan gave her shoulder a final pat, smiled reassuringly, and walked briskly away to his private car.

As a member of the House Committee on International Relations, Ryan had invited Deborah Layton Blakey to fly to Washington to meet with his staff and State Department officials. He had asked for the meeting because, six months earlier, twenty-five-year-old Debbie had escaped from Jonestown, Guyana, and a few weeks after that had made public an eleven-page document entitled, "Affidavit of Deborah Layton Blakey Re the Threat and Possibility of Mass Suicide by Members of the Peoples Temple."

The sworn document, dated June 15, 1978, had been sent to officials of the State Department and to various members of Congress, and it had been widely reported by the news media. Reaction had been skeptical. In its thirty-seven clauses, the affidavit revealed the appalling conditions in Jonestown under the maniacal tyranny of the Reverend Jim Jones. It also expressed Debbie's deep concern for the safety and well-being of the Temple members she had left behind. Even as she was saying good-bye to Ryan, her husband, Phil Blakey, her mother, Lisa Layton, and her brother Larry were still living in the jungle settlement. Debbie knew that Jim Jones regarded her family as hostages to her silence about the conditions at Jonestown.

In the six months since her escape, her life had not been easy. No one wanted to listen to the tragedy she was foretelling: the self-annihilation of more than nine hundred followers of a religious cult. Her letters to the State Department and Congress had remained unanswered until Ryan had contacted her a month ago. He believed her story, and he wanted her to tell it to officials at the State Department. But even now, after two days of meetings, the State Department officials still didn't seem to care. Ryan himself had had to insist that they take notes while Debbie described the substance of her affidavit. It had been pointed out that the United States had no jurisdiction in foreign countries to deal with such questions. But when the meetings were over, Ryan seemed buoyant and hopeful. His staff and aides were excited over the congressman's impending trip. Debbie, however, was depressed. She had warned them all of possible violence. She would be afraid to return to Jonestown, she told them, even under the protection of a congress-man.

Debbie went up to Ryan's office to retrieve her suitcase, walked out of the Senate Office Building, and met the ride that would take her to Dulles International Airport. Settling back into the front passenger seat of the automobile, she leaned her head against the cool leather of the headrest. As the car eased out into the evening traffic stream she closed her eyes. But the images would not go away.

She thought of her mother, the beautiful and cultured Jewish girl from Hamburg who had escaped the certainty of one con-centration camp only to end in another, lying cancer-ridden in the Guyanese jungle, waiting for Jones' ultimate cure. Lisa Philip Layton had left her husband—the brilliant and eminently successful research scientist, Laurence Laird Layton—to join the Peoples Temple, had devoted five years to the cause, and had donated more than a quarter of a million dollars.

She thought of her brother Larry, the Quaker radical without a cause until he met Jim Jones and how Jones had emasculated his psyche by having sex with both his first and second wives, ridiculing and taunting him in public. Larry had returned from each humiliation with undiminished devotion to Jones.

And she thought about herself. Her own life had been aim-less until she had joined the Peoples Temple. Jones had taken her precocious body and underdeveloped mind, defiled one and filled the other with a wonderful and almost holy vision of heaven on earth. "Thank you, Father," she had said to Jones after the beatings. "Thank you, Father," she had said after he raped her. Jones had trusted her; he had sent her to Central America and Europe carrying huge amounts of Temple money to be deposited in secret accounts. How good and hopeful it had all seemed in the beginning; how grim and evil it had become.

The car glided to the curb. Debbie got out. An attendant helped her with her bags. She checked in and boarded her return flight to San Francisco.

The following morning, Congressman Leo Ryan boarded a plane for Guyana.

PART ONE

Oh as I was young and easy in the mercy of his means,
Time held me green and dying
Though I sang in my chains like the sea.

—Dylan Thomas, "Fern Hill"

1

The Laytons: Roots in the Virginia Frontier

In the bituminous coal country of south central West Virginia the town of Boomer nestles snugly along a gentle bend of the Kanawha River. Around the turn of the century, the coal, the town, and its inhabitants were essentially the chattels of the Mark A. Hanna Coal Company. In 1902, when the mines were first opened, the company built eight hundred homes in Boomer to house the miners and their families. Each house was like all the others: a four-room cottage, raised about eighteen inches from the ground and supported by a series of spindly posts. There were no foundations or basements. There were no bathrooms. The streets were unpaved. There was no sewer system.

Sheldon Thomas ("Tom") Nutter (1862–1940) collected the rents for the coal company. In fact, as general manager for outside operations, he ran the place. Stern, with deep-set blue eyes and a tall, lean frame that he held stiffly upright, Nutter had been a circuit-riding preacher, Baptist and Methodist on alternate Sundays, in the hills of Virginia, West Virginia, and Kentucky.

Although Nutter considered himself above everyone else, he tried not to show it, living modestly and frugally in a four-room cottage like other folks. He had chosen the most conveniently located house for himself, however.

And maybe Nutter was right to feel superior. His influence was certainly felt in this rough mining town. He had organized the building of a nondenominational church, and he had been one of the town's first schoolteachers. One of his students in the one-room schoolhouse had been Rosa Etta Huddleston, the granddaughter of three of the wealthiest families of antebellum Virginia. In 1888, a couple of years after her graduation, Rosa and Tom were married.

The town of Boomer had been named after Rosa's Uncle John Boomer Huddleston, and had been a corner of the family estate from 1765 until after the Civil War. Uncle Boomer's original house, built around 1800, had served as a hospital when Robert E. Lee and the Army of Northern Virginia had tried to hold that part of the state. After the Confederates lost the battle of Carnifax Ferry and Gauley Bridge and retreated across the Alleghenies into the Shenandoah Valley, the family lands were occupied by Union troops. The invading Union Army destroyed the crops, slaughtered the animals, and freed the slaves, although the slaves would remain friends of the family for generations. With the defeat, Confederate money became worthless, so the Huddleston family land was sold for Northern money or traded off for food.

With his marriage to Rosa, and since he was the only educated local resident, it seemed natural that when the Mark A. Hanna Coal Company moved into Boomer in 1902, Tom Nutter was picked to run the place. It was he who convinced the coal company to build the eight hundred houses. A carpenter and shipwright, he trained his teenage sons and their cousins as jackleg carpenters, then hired them to build the houses.

Tom Nutter was Laurence Laird Layton's maternal grandfather.

Laurence Layton's paternal grandfather, John Finney Layton (1865–1946), was the third of three sons whose father died young in a mine explosion. Their mother remarried and the family moved to Richmond, Virginia, where the Layton boys were pretty much left to raise themselves. John Finney, having no particular skills, moved to West Virginia, to the coal mining country of the upper Kanawha River Valley, where he met and married Bertha Jarrett (1876–1910), the fourteen-year-old daughter of a wealthy and landed family. Furious that she had married beneath herself and against his wishes, Bertha's father, Bentley Jarrett, refused to accept John into the family and disinherited Bertha, leaving her one dollar in his will.

Bertha had long straight black hair and high cheekbones. People said that she had Cherokee blood through her mother, whose ancestors had moved to the Kanawha Valley from the Cherokee country of North Carolina. John Finney and Bertha had eight children, of whom John Wister Layton, Laurence's father, was the eldest.

John Finney was an alcoholic who worked irregularly, when he worked at all. As the story goes, he was drunk on the steps of the church at his wife's funeral, and relatives had to step over him to view the corpse. After her death, John Finney put little or no effort into raising his eight children. John Wister left school when he was thirteen to support the family by working in the coal mines.

John Wister Layton hated his father. He once told his uncle, Hartford Jarrett, "I wish I could jump into that coal stove over there, and burn out all the Layton, and leave only the Jarrett." He was determined to overcome his father's reputation. He would do all the correct things. And so he neither drank nor smoked. He dressed neatly and stylishly. He associated only with proper girls from good families. He was also very ambitious. By the time he was twenty-three, he was a self-educated but well-paid electrical engineer on the staff of the largest mining company in the state. All who knew him recognized his precocity, and many spoke of him as a genius.

In those turn-of-the-century Horatio Alger days, John Wister Layton modeled himself after Thomas Edison, earned an electrical engineering certificate through the International Correspondence School in Scranton, Pennsylvania, and before his early death in 1922 had invented the circuit breaker, the automatic boxcar coupling lock, the illuminated signs used on top of taxicabs beginning in the 1920s, an automatic trapdoor to confine mine explosions, and a number of other electro-mechanical devices.

John Wister met Eva Nutter at a church service in 1911. Through her mother, Eva was a member of the prominent and landed Huddleston family; and through her great grandmother she was John's third cousin. Eva had been raised from the age of four by her grandmother, Sarah Beirne Huddleston.

Eva had never been allowed a life of her own. At first she wasn't even allowed to go to school, although her father was a college-educated teacher and minister. She was taught at home by her Aunt Edna Huddleston. So when Eva reached the age of sixteen, she was damned well determined to escape from the farm.

Eva's father, Tom Nutter, was by 1911 a prominent businessman and church leader, as well as general manager of the coal company. So when John Wister Layton took an interest in Eva Nutter, her father was annoyed and her brothers resented him. Up to this time, Eva had been keeping house for and nursing her paralyzed and bedridden Grandmother Huddleston. The family saw that they were about to lose the free services of a domestic—and to an uppity nobody, at that. Their resentment was intensified by the fact that John Wister, although from a poor family, was brighter, harder working, better educated, cleaner living, and better paid than were Eva's brothers. The Nutter brothers had great pride of family that, juxtaposed against their own lack of accomplishment, made them defensive and arrogant.

Matters came to a head one evening in 1912 when John was walking Eva home after church. Her brother Vernon had been drinking, and his resentment against John Wister boiled out of control. Vernon approached the couple and said, "I'll take my sister on home." "No you won't either," John replied; "I started with her, and I'll take her." Vernon suddenly swung at John. John, apparently prepared for such an attack, deftly sidestepped the blow, pulled out a revolver, and smashed Vernon in the face with its butt.

A few days later John left town to return to a job in Columbus, Ohio, and Eva's father swore out a warrant for his arrest. Since there was no secret about where Layton had gone, he was soon arrested and brought back to Boomer to stand trial. But once Tom Nutter heard John's and Eva's side of the story, apologies were made by both sides and the matter was dropped, never to be mentioned again.

John and Eva were married on January 18, 1913. Eva was only seventeen years old. Before the wedding Eva's father took Layton aside and asked him, "Can you provide for her?" "I can provide as good as she's had," the young man replied tersely. There would never be any warmth between the Nutter family and John Wister Layton.

John and Eva's first son, Laurence Laird Layton, was born in his grandfather's house on March 8, 1914. A few months later John took his wife and new son to Raleigh County, West Virginia.

Those were good times for John and Eva. Two more children were born, Rosemary in 1916 and Sheldon Thomas in 1918. John not only enjoyed his work, he even constructed a laboratory at home so that he could work at night and still be close to Eva. He was an affectionate husband. His salary was good. Books lined the walls and expensive walnut furniture filled the house. The Laytons were the first family in town to own an electric washing machine and to have a ceiling fan over the dining-room table. The marriage was a happy one, and although he was a loving father to all three children, John was particularly close to his eldest son, Laurence Laird. Laurence, for his part, modeled himself after his father—he would be a scientist. One Christmas he asked for a chemistry set, so he could do experiments "just like daddy."

If Laurence came by his scientific talent legitimately, his attitudes toward women and sex were even more predetermined, by both John and Eva.

"When I came along I was to be perfect. Mother really wanted a girl, so I had bobbed hair and wore dresses when I was little. Her grandmother's influence and her father's influence came out of the eighteenth- and nineteenth-century frontier right down on me.

"I was taught that women are at a terrible disadvantage in life, that women are innocent victims. They got pushed around by men, and men were selfish bores. I was not permitted to date, and my mother taught me that I should never put my hand on a girl and should be very careful not to insult them. To insult a girl would be to say something that had anything to do with sex. I was quite careful not to do any of those terrible things when I was young, so I grew up a very artificial person in the real world. I never learned to recognize my own sexuality, and I didn't even know that women had any desires.

"As I grew older I was taught that sex was men taking advantage of women, exploiting them. Women were to be treated in one of three ways. You ignored them. You exploited them. Or you cherished them. I was taught to cherish them or ignore them, one or the other, and I did only those two things."

Laurence's mother was a fanatic about germs. To her, all germs brought disease. Whenever the family traveled on the train, which was fairly often, Laurence was cautioned by his mother about the danger of infection, especially when he went to the toilet. Until he was six years old, however, young Laurence was not tall enough to clear the toilet seat when he urinated, and after one occasion when he came in contact with the seat, he developed a mild inflammation. His mother went wild with fear that the boy had caught a "bad disease."

His father took him to a good physician (not a coal-company doctor), who decided that Laurence needed only to be circumcised. The doctor added that the minor operation could be performed immediately. Father and son walked to the hospital. It was the first time Laurence had been in a hospital; it was the cleanest, brightest place he had ever seen. A nurse quickly undressed him, washed him, and helped him onto the operating table.

What followed was the most frightening experience of his life. His hands, arms, and legs were tied down so that he could not move. The surgeon smeared the inside of his mouth and around his lips with Vaseline, put a device like a dog muzzle over his nose and mouth, and poured ether over a wad of cotton gauze onto the muzzle. Laurence felt that he was dying. First he sank into a pit. Then he was in a great hallway or corridor lined with white marble tile. The corridor had the height and width of a railway station, but was very long. He could still hear the conversation among the surgeon, the father, and the nurse, but the sound re-echoed down the great corridor in a most horribly unfamiliar way, as if they were yelling down a great pipe.

His face felt furry, and every breath he took brought that hot burning odor of ether into his throat and lungs. He was being held down, his hands especially. The fact that his hands were tied down frightened him most. The nurse told him to count after her. He couldn't resist. He heard himself repeating the numbers as if it were someone else, but it was his own mouth, operating slowly, like a mechanical robot...one... two...three...four...five...

Laurence awoke to nausea and a feeling of dullness. His father was smiling and talking to him. Laurence did not smile back. He had acquired his concept of death and dying. To die was to suffer that terrible fear of being bound helpless in a great cold corridor where his screams would only re-echo and bounce back to him. No one there but Laurence and a vaguely perceived evil presence.

When Laurence was eight years old, his father died suddenly. Working as an electrical engineer for a coal company, John was repairing a motor when an electric pole, like a trolley-car pole, fell and struck him on the cheek. The wound developed a staphylococcus infection, and he died within days. He was thirty-one years old.

"I was eight years old and my sister and brother were six and four. The infection was just a sore place on his cheek, a little bit like a boil, swollen, and it hurt, and then three days before he died he started having terrible headaches. I remember there was a revival meeting across the street in the school. My dad never went to church, but he did go over to that revival meeting just the week before he died. He and my mother went over there, and he came home so pleased; he really had enjoyed it and said he wanted to go again the next Sunday night.

"But the next Sunday was the day before he died, and he wasn't able to get out of bed. I went over to the meeting myself. I called in to him, 'Good night, Daddy, I'm going to church.' And he didn't answer. All day he had been moaning, 'Oh, my head, my head.'

"That evening he was out of his mind. He acted as if he

didn't know where he was or what was going on. He couldn't talk. When I got home from the revival meeting Dr. Gordon was there, and Mother sent me off to bed. At four in the morning, my mother woke me and Rosemary up. She said we must pray to God to save Daddy. We got out of bed and clasped our hands and prayed with Mother. While we were praying the door opened. Dr. Gordon stood there. He said, 'He's gone.' Mother cried, I cried, and because we cried so did Rosemary. It was 4:30 A.M.

"At daylight Daddy was taken away in a wagon. The next day they brought a casket into the living room, or as Mother called it, 'the parlor.' The casket was opened and I looked at my daddy. He looked like a boy, just a big boy. His hands were forced out of shape. He had clenched them in dying, and despite all attempts to straighten them the knuckles remained in a closed fist.

"March 23 was a cold dark day with a few snowflakes flying. My dad was to be buried in the old Huddleston cemetery at Boomer. At the funeral there were only Huddlestons, Nutters, a few Laytons, and some Huddleston ex-slaves. My dad's father was there. He was crying, and as he passed the open casket he bent over and kissed my father's forehead. We all went up the hill to the open grave and watched the casket being lowered into the grave; then we went back down the hill to Grandpa's house. I never saw my grandfather Layton again after that day."

Although John Wister Layton had made a good salary, there were no savings and no insurance when he died. Eva Layton returned to the house of her father. As a destitute twenty-seven-year-old widow with three small children, back in her father's house, Eva was at last defeated. She resumed her duties as the family domestic, keeping house for her father and eldest brother, who was living there at the time. Essentially, Eva was demoted in status to that of a child. Whenever she or her children wanted anything, they had to ask her father. If the children misbehaved they were told that "Pa," their grandfather, wouldn't like that.

All connections with John Layton's relatives were broken as Eva, overcompensating for whatever loss of status might be attached to the Layton name, raised her children to be "better" than everyone else. Laurence was not allowed to play with "trash," which was defined by Eva Layton to include most of the eligible playmates around town. His surrogate father was a minister, and Laurence was raised a preacher's kid. His younger sister, Rosemary, and brother, Tom, rebelled, but he did not. Laurence was extremely obedient. Having suffered an immense loss when his father died, Laurence tried doubly hard to please his grandfather. Sheldon Thomas Nutter, however, was not an affectionate man, and his interest in Laurence was at best perfunctory.

Laurence was never physically comfortable in his grandfather's house. In winter, the cold would seep in through the walls, the doors, the windows, and the uncarpeted floor. A glass of water would freeze on a bedroom dresser. The kitchen, heated by the cook stove, was the only warm place in winter, but it was stiflingly hot in summer. There was no hot-water heater. Cold, untreated river water was piped directly through the kitchen wall over a sink that had no drain because the town had no sewer system. The bathroom was an outdoor toilet located about a hundred feet from the back door of the house. The Nutter household did not have a bathroom until Laurence was almost twenty years old.

Emotionally, Laurence's life was not easy either. In expiation for the "bad blood" and sins of the Laytons, Laurence was inculcated with an extremely strict and rigid version of early American fundamentalist morality, reinforcing his parents' early training. Sex was sin. There were only two kinds of women: the good and the fallen. Laurence was raised to believe that women didn't like sex, that they were easily offended by even the most innocent of male advances. As a result his early sexual energies were sublimated into his studies. He would prove he was superior to everyone else. He would win affection and recognition from his grandfather through outstanding academic achievements and through adherence to the strictest of moral codes.

"When my father died and we went to live with my grandfather, it was pointed out to me who I couldn't associate with. When those boys wanted to play with me, I explained to them that I couldn't play with them because they were trash. So they beat the hell out of me. After that happened a few times, I kept my mouth shut about how much better I was than they were.

"My best friend in high school was of a family who thought

they were aristocracy. But when you talked to *my* folks about them, they'd say, 'Oh, when that family came out of the woods in 1870 they had lice!' That was a family that didn't have good blood, in spite of the fact that two of them were my best friends. One of those friends went insane, and so did his sister—she burnt their whole house down, and she's still completely insane.

"That family has had only tragedy. The reason was said to be sin being visited from the fathers onto the children in the third or fourth generations: It's in the Bible. And there is also such a thing as hereditary defect. Bad blood means just that; there's something wrong with the blood in the family."

For Eva Layton's children, families who had "bad blood" were easily identified.

"They were lazy, indigent people, and you could often tell by looking that there was something wrong. They were always on charity, or they were always dirty. They had deformed children, or had harelips or club feet, or the women were loose. These were all supposed to be signs of bad blood. If you saw a family that produced a number of retarded children in various generations, or insanity in the family—bad blood. If you knew that there had been a history of murder, or criminal activity, then watch out."

For six years Eva Nutter Layton kept house for her father and her three children, and there were no young men in her life. Eventually, however, she met Charles Fredrick Chandler, a handsome brown-eyed blonde, very debonair, very gregarious, who boarded at the house next door. Fred ran a coal-cutting machine, and made more money than anyone else in town. He was pretty well able to conceal the fact that he had no education, that he couldn't even read.

"Fred decided that he wanted to get acquainted with my mother, so he would come over and sit on the porch and talk with us. They never went anyplace because there was no place to go. So we'd just sit on the porch. In February of 1928, they informed us that they'd gotten married. So that was it. They were now married." It was a month before Laurence's four-teenth birthday.

Fred Chandler, Jr., was born in November of 1928. Laur-ence was delighted, and spent much of his free time with his infant half brother. Two years later, Fred, Eva, Rosemary, Tom, and Fred, Jr., moved to Pennsylvania, leaving Laurence, then sixteen, to take care of his grandfather. Laurence and Grandfather Nutter kept house together off and on for the next ten years, until his grandfather's death in 1940.

Laurence Layton did not date until after he entered college. He was too shy, and he had little money. But in the summer of 1933, after his freshman year at New River State College, Mildred Arthur came to Boomer to visit relatives. She was the most beautiful girl Laurence had ever seen. She was sixteen, he nineteen. He fell madly in love. "At the same time," he recalls, "I was taking a course in differential calculus, and I spent eight hours a day in the classroom working out calculus problems on the blackboard. I finished the year's course in two weeks. I was terrifically impressed with mathematics, but I was even more impressed with this beautiful girl."

Laurence rented a boat from a neighbor and rowed Mildred up and down the Kanawha River, admiring her "just sitting there being beautiful." Eventually he discovered that he enjoyed kissing Mildred. "I would hold her and kiss her and think, Oh my God! But it had no conscious sexual implication."

Laurence Layton had never given a party; his grandfather did not approve of parties. Nevertheless, he decided to invite his new love, Mildred, her sister Opal, and a male friend of his for an evening of candy making. "I had planned that we would just sit on the porch at my grandfather's house and make candy. That was the first time I had ever invited a girl to my house. I prepared some sandwiches and nonalcoholic drinks, and they came—not three of them, but four. A friend of Mildred's had shown up from Pikeville, Kentucky, a fellow by the name of Hatfield. I was crushed, destroyed. Here on my porch was this handsome Hatfield boy, and Mildred had known him back there in Kentucky. Now even though I had a block against sexual involvement, I feared that for her that might not hold, that there might have been intimacies. In other words, as far as I was concerned this boy might be her lover. In fact, he wasn't even her beau, but I thought he was. I was able to hide my feelings and bear up that whole evening. I entertained them all and was very pleasant, but after they left I went to pieces." This first relationship with a girl ended just as it had begun: innocently. After two days of deep depression,

Laurence decided he had to get out of town. He quit college and caught a bus for Scranton, Pennsylvania, where his mother and stepfather had moved three years earlier.

Laurence was lonely in Pennsylvania. The YWCA was only a block from his mother's house, so one day he walked over and sat in on a meeting of the Young People's Socialist League. "They were all Jewish people," he remembers, "I was the only WASP. All the young socialists were much better informed than I was, even though I was the only one with a year of college. The girls were not as beautiful as Mildred, but they were nice girls. I became terribly excited about socialism and what it might mean."

Layton soon became a leader of the group. "Here I was, a hillbilly majoring in mathematics, getting into this group of first-generation Americans, all my age, all Jewish, all very bright and very friendly. Of course, their brightness was what caught my interest, because I had always admired brains. I stayed in Scranton and associated with them for about a year, and by that time I was cured of my infatuation with Mildred, even though I never dated any of the girls."

While in Scranton, Laurence received a letter from his math professor at New River State, telling him that under a grant from the National Youth Administration he could become a teaching assistant at twenty dollars a month. He accepted the offer and returned to college as a sophomore. He had missed a year and a half of school.

No sooner had Laurence returned to school than he fell in love with Constance Jeffries, a seventeen-year-old poet whose intelligence he admired. Again, no sex was involved. Laurence believed that what attracted Constance to him was his Huddleston family background. They dated for one semester, and then Constance left for nursing school in Charleston, while Laurence finished college at New River State. The following year he began studies for his master's degree at West Virginia University. In the course of his research, he invented a molecular still. Local newspapers reported this invention by a very young scientist and ran a photo of Layton alongside the article. Two weeks later, Constance killed herself. "I had the guilty feeling that she had read this article and then committed suicide. We had separated. We both had gone away to school, and she had become a nurse, while I was still a graduate student. When

I got this newspaper clipping that she was dead I went into mourning. I always had the feeling that whenever I was involved with women there were personal disasters." This would not be the last suicide for which Laurence Layton would feel responsible.

Laurence was an exceptional student. Although his special areas at New River State had been mathematics, chemistry, and physics, he was also interested in economics, history, and sociology. His unabashed goal was to become one of the world's great scientists. This seemed a reasonable objective, since he was usually the highest-ranked student in whatever school he attended.

After graduating with honors in mathematics from New River State in 1937, Laurence had soon discovered that there was no employment for a math major with a bachelor's degree. He managed to get a job digging ditches and shoveling quartzite for five dollars a day, a hundred dollars a month. The job lasted two months, until November, when a recession forced the company he was working for to lay off all the new hires. This didn't bother Laurence too much, because watching the straw bosses lean on sticks while he was digging ditches had already convinced him that he should prepare for a better job. In any case, he did not want to stay on as the best-educated ditchdigger in the county.

He contacted a number of universities, and West Virginia University was the first to respond, with an offer of a half-time job as teaching assistant. It would pay thirty dollars a month, and he would be able to pursue his studies. He traveled by bus to Morgantown and found a place that offered room and board for twenty-five dollars a month. With some money he had saved, and a hundred dollars borrowed from his grandfather, Layton enrolled as a student and simultaneously became a teaching assistant in quantitative analysis.

Morgantown proved to be an unpleasant environment. Layton's teaching supervisor was a cantankerous old professor who didn't believe in universities helping students through school, and who treated the teaching assistants as charity cases. Although Layton remembers coming close to a physical breakdown from starvation, he performed well—so well that he was one of only three out of forty graduate students to pass the qualifying examinations for a master's degree in chemistry. He was offered a full scholarship for his doctoral work.

Suddenly, to Laurence's amazement, Grandfather Nutter took notice of him. Persuaded finally of Laurence's brilliance and character, Sheldon Thomas Nutter told his grandson, "I'll let you have the money to go to Harvard or any other university you choose to take your doctor's degree." Laurence was accepted by several universities, but chose Pennsylvania State, then the country's leading university in chemistry.

2

The Philips:
Roots in Jewish Banking

Lisa Philip's ancestors had lived in Hamburg for many generations. They were descendants of the Sephardic Jews who migrated across North Africa into Spain and Portugal in the Middle Ages. Almost eight centuries after their initial settlement in Spain they were forced out by the Spanish Inquisition. Moving to more tolerant lands, they founded the Jewish communities of Amsterdam, London, Hamburg, and New Amsterdam (New York City).

Lisa, the first child of Hugo and Anita Philip, was born on July 14, 1915; her sister, Eva, was born two years later. Hugo Philip, the son of Max Philip, a successful banker and stockbroker, was a handsome, gregarious man, athletically inclined and musically talented. A skilled mountaineer, he returned to climb the mountains of Northern Italy every year until 1967, when he was eighty-five years old. Although Hugo's ambition was to become a professional violinist, his father insisted that he join the family firm—a decision he regretted for the rest of his life, even though he managed to become known as the best amateur violinist in Hamburg.

Hugo was closer to his father than to his mother, whom he described as demanding, sharp-tongued, and self-centered. He told his children and grandchildren the story of the time that his mother had insisted that his father dance with her at a party. His father had complained that he didn't feel well, but she prevailed on him to dance with her anyway. He danced a few steps and then fell at her feet, dead of a heart attack.

Lisa's mother, Anita Lea Heilbut, the daughter of a wealthy stockbroker, was educated in private schools, including two years at an English boarding school, and graduated from a Hamburg college with a degree in home economics. For the next four years, until her marriage to Hugo, Anita did volunteer work for an agency helping young girls to find positions.

Attracted by Anita's classic beauty—for he was a man who "loved beautiful things"—and possibly because he hoped for a deferment from fighting in World War I, Hugo married Anita on June 14, 1914. The marriage was not a happy one—temperamentally, the partners were not well suited: Hugo was loud, outgoing, and demanding; Anita was reserved, cool, and somewhat distant. Anita took frequent vacations from Hugo, traveling alone or with her daughters for extended stays at various health spas in southern Germany. Apparently she wanted a divorce, but was either too proud to let it be known, or was talked out of it by her mother, to whom she complained bitterly about Hugo's treatment of her, especially about his affairs with family friends and with the family's live-in maids.

Financially, however, the 1920s were good to the Philip family. As a stockbroker, Hugo represented such firms as I. G. Farben and the chemical giant Siemens and Halske. His banking business also flourished, and the family lived well. Like everyone in Germany, the Philip family suffered during the inflationary period following World War I. The situation got so bad that Hugo and Anita went out one evening and spent all the money they had saved for Lisa's dowry on an elegant dinner. They figured they might as well get some good out of the money before it became totally worthless. But Hugo managed to recoup his sizable fortune in a relatively short time. By 1927 he had enough cash on hand to hire the noted architectural firm of Bloch and Hochfeld to design and build an ultramodern house in Hamburg. It had such then-unheard-of features as a sunken bathtub, stall showers, built-in cabinets and closets, and even built-in furniture.

Hugo especially valued the large music room, the humidity-controlled vault in which he kept his tobacco and fine cigars, and the special built-in cabinets for his rapidly growing collection of etchings. He liked to support developing young artists, and his collection included works by the German expressionist Emil Nolde, the sculptor and painter Käthe Kollwitz, and the impressionists Edgar Degas and Max Liebermann.

In spite of the parents' marital tensions, the Philip family vacationed together often in the Austrian Alps, in resorts along the Baltic seacoast, and at the Attersee lake resort in Austria. Anita was always concerned about the health of her children, and when Lisa developed a kidney disorder at the age of eight, Anita took her, Eva, and a nursemaid to Sestri Levante on the seacoast of northwestern Italy for the winter.

On Sundays, Lisa and Eva often spent the day with their maternal grandparents, the Heilbuts, in Blankensee, down the Elbe from Hamburg. The children also enjoyed frequent weekend outings with their parents to the country home of friends, where they played at being American Indians. Their parents helped them make Indian clothing, and they had great fun scrambling around in the bushes.

At home in Hamburg there were frequent and elaborate musical evenings, when Hugo indulged his passionate interest in music. He often subsidized struggling young musicians, who in exchange for their stipend would join Lisa's father and other friends for evening performances at the Philip home. Lisa grew up in a rich atmosphere of dinner parties, concerts, operas, and plays.

Both Hugo and Anita were modern and progressive in their attitudes about education. Lisa and Eva attended the private *Lichtwarckschule,* a coeducational school that stressed critical freethinking. Lisa, an outgoing and athletic teenager, enjoyed the open atmosphere, in which subjects like architecture, sociology, and geography were taught by means of week-long field trips all over Germany.

The Philip children were raised as Germans. They were

citizens of Hamburg, as their ancestors had been for generations. They had never been to a synagogue; they had never
received Jewish religious instruction. In fact, religion played
no role at all in their lives. The Philip family celebrated Christmas and Easter; they did not observe any Jewish holidays.
Although Hugo's father had been a religious man, Hugo never
went to temple, and he let his membership expire in a Jewish
society he had joined to please his father. Hugo believed that
children should not be pushed into any religion, but should be
free to make their own choice as adults. So Lisa and her sister,
Eva, grew up with no religion at all.

The girls left the *Lichtwarckschule* at the end of 1931, and
Lisa took a job as an assistant in the decoration and poster-
drawing department of a large store. But after less than a year
on the job, she received a letter to the effect that although she
was an honest and hardworking employee, she was being laid
off because of "changes in our organization." She wasn't sure
at the time whether or not she was being discharged because
she was Jewish.

After losing her job in the department store, Lisa enrolled
in a trade school in Altona, a suburb of Hamburg, where she
learned to design clothing, weave and dye cloth, and repair
fabrics. On Sunday, July 17, 1932—a few months before Lisa
had enrolled in the school—the Nazis, under police escort,
staged a march through Altona; in the riots that followed, 19
persons were shot dead and 285 were wounded.

By this time, the Nazis were firmly entrenched throughout
most of Germany. In the elections of 1930, Hitler's National
Socialist Party had emerged as a major force, with 107 seats
in the Reichstag, up from their previous 12. Their popular vote
jumped from 800,000 to 6,500,000. The Communist repre-
sentation rose in the Reichstag from 54 to 77. Reflecting the
general world economic situation, Germany was in the throes
of a depression that ground on and on, hopelessness and despair
growing ever deeper.

Using his mesmeric oratorical skills, Adolf Hitler denounced
the Treaty of Versailles as a humiliation, and the Weimar Re-
public as an exercise in futility. He ranted against Marxists,
Bolsheviks, communists, and socialists. But most of all he
denounced the Jews. In speeches against unearned incomes,
war profits, land speculation, the power of great trusts and

chain stores, high interest rates, and unfair taxes, he blamed all of Germany's problems on the Jews. In anti-Semitism, Hitler found the lowest common denominator whereby he could appeal to all parties and all classes. On the political right, Jewish capitalists were anathema; on the political left, Jewish communists and revolutionaries were a horror.

But in spite of the rise of National Socialism, and nearly oblivious to it, Lisa and Eva were leading an almost normal life. In 1933, when Lisa was seventeen and Eva fifteen, their parents allowed them to take unchaperoned trips in groups with boys. Just before Lisa's eighteenth birthday, she bicycled more than sixty miles from Hamburg to Priwall on the Baltic Sea. Hugo would give his daughters money and say, "Now, this is for your trip. If you want to spend it all in a fancy hotel, you'll have to come home tomorrow or the next day. If you want to conserve it, you can stay as long as the money lasts." So the girls would ride their bikes, cook for themselves, and stay in hostels or at farms where they would be allowed to sleep for free in the barn, above the hogs and horses. At this point Lisa already had two boyfriends, Theo and Wolfgang. Lisa and Wolfgang, along with Eva and some school friends, took a skiing trip in the Harz mountains over Christmas vacation in 1933.

But even though Lisa was raised in a permissive atmosphere, her parents were also prepared to say no to her. When she was seventeen, Lisa wanted to attend the annual Arts Ball with her friend Wolfgang, but her father refused to allow her to go because the masked ball had the reputation of being a rather loose affair. In spite of the entreaties of both Wolfgang and Lisa, Hugo would not relent.

Three months later she asked her parents for permission to visit her other boyfriend, Theo, at his home in Frankfurt, in southern Germany. Again her parents refused, stating that seventeen-year-old girls simply did not travel five hundred miles alone to visit their boyfriends.

This time, however, Lisa was undeterred. After persuading Eva to cover for her absence from the dinner table, Lisa pedaled her bicycle to the nearby elevated train station and took a train to the nearest truck depot. From there she hitched a ride with a truck driver bound for Frankfurt.

"Dear Parents," she wrote the day she left, "When you get

this letter I will be on a truck heading for southern Germany. There I shall remain a few days, and then I will come back home—and everything is for free! I would like to see something of this world just like father. Man wills his own heaven. 1000 Kisses, Lisa. P.S. I will write while traveling later. I have no time now."

The "few days" turned into two weeks. Although she never told her parents, years later she confided to her husband that during this trip she had to appeal to the truck driver's honor as a Nazi to prevent him from raping her. But her letters home at the time were enthusiastic. Everything was "beautiful" and "truly lovely." With Theo she visited cathedrals and museums "to look at pictures, Raphael, da Vinci, Dürer, Rembrandt, Botticelli, Grünewalde, and of all things a Madonna by Botticelli which was extremely beautiful."

Soon, though, the visit took on more political overtones. She and Theo went sightseeing with another couple, returned to Theo's house, and "there we started talking about politics and what is going to happen to us younger generation. The girl had just been fired from her job, and Eric is not able to study further at the university. So that concerns us all."

Less than three months earlier, Adolf Hitler had been named Chancellor of Germany. Six weeks before Lisa's trip, part of the Reichstag building had burned down during a violent election campaign, and Hitler blamed the fire on communists and Jews. And on March 23, 1933, only three weeks before Lisa wrote to her parents from Frankfurt, the Reichstag and the Reichsrat had passed the Enabling Act, which gave the government, in the person of Adolf Hitler, dictatorial powers. This act firmly established the Nazi dictatorship, and coincided with a national boycott of all Jewish businesses and professions.

Lisa wrote once again about her Jewish friends. "Unfortunately many of them are 'on vacation.' Mrs. Cahn [Eric's mother] went to Zurich and came back yesterday. She told us she saw an awful lot of friends in Zurich with blue eyes and blond hair; but then on the other hand you don't know for sure. I am convinced that things are going to get better, but I will talk to you about that when I see you."

The "friends" did not, of course, have blond hair and blue eyes; they were Jewish friends. And they were not "on vacation"; they were unofficially emigrating from Germany.

Lisa hitchhiked back to her home in Hamburg on April 25. When she returned from this adventure, she was not punished; her father was proud of having such an independent, intelligent, and clever daughter.

Lisa continued to attend the trade school in Altona, but the emphasis of her studies shifted from fabrics to gymnastics, physical education, and physical therapy. "She is well talented for the specialty of gymnastics and body workings," the director of the school wrote. "She is always interested and busy. Her behavior is without fault."

In November 1935, Hugo was prohibited from taking his seat on the Hamburg stock exchange. After that, Hugo and Anita were forced to sell their dream house and move into a much smaller rented house. He was still allowed to perform some banking services for his clients, but a drastic curtailment of Jewish financial activity was under way.

As the year ended, Lisa took a position as a housekeeper in the home of some close family friends in Hamburg. She was planning to take physical therapy training in Berlin, and wanted to save on room and board. At the same time, in an effort to meet some nice young men, she joined a choral group—one of the many "underground" ways that Jews continued active social lives during this period of increased oppression. At choir practice she met a young physician, with whom she fell in love. Their romance was brief. Within weeks, the doctor was to emigrate to India to practice tropical medicine. Along with many other Jews with good sense, he saw that it was time to get out of Germany.

In her diary Lisa wrote, "It became clear that the time had come that I had to meet a nice person and therefore I got the idea to sing with Frau Trude. . . . The long and the short of it is I went there with the best intention of looking at Dr. B. and Mr. W. I arrived before the others. When Dr. B. came I opened the door for him. I looked at him and answered my own question immediately. His nose is very much like that of Erik S. So he's out as far as I'm concerned. Too bad. Now, I had to see about Mr. W. He came a little later, a 20-year-old young one— boring, a little bit too soft, impossible, out of the question. Again, bad luck."

After the choral group had met several more times, and had begun attending dancing parties together, Lisa took another

look at Dr. B. This time, she was in a better frame of mind.
"B. came up to me," she wrote. "We ran into each other almost
as if we had planned it. And then we danced and we danced
awfully well together. We both were in a wonderful mood, and
we danced once, and we danced twice, and three times and on
and on. And then we sat down and chatted awhile and we
laughed a lot. We were silly and danced some more. In the
midst of it all, he lifted me up over his shoulder and let me
down on the other side of him as you do with little children.
That was fun. A friendly strength and a basic feeling was in
this."

Within a week she was in love. But Dr. B. was leaving.
"Right now," she wrote, "I'm in the midst of it all, and only
one more week. Then he will leave forever. Forever. One can
hardly visualize what the word means—Forever. The feeling
that he's only going to be here one more week, and perhaps
once or twice will I be with him. It tightens my heart. It's like
a cramp in me. I feel as full as after eating a rich dessert, but
at the same time I feel an emptyness. When I have bumped
myself somewhere I run around the room and rub myself where
it hurts. Now, I fall on my knees, or I press myself against the
wall and cover my face with my hands.

"Everything that comes toward me I feel strongly. I'm happy
and full of love for the flowers, for the world, for mankind
because of him. I am looking forward to the next time I can
see him, and I think with pleasure of the last time that we were
together. Everything is different because he is going away. I
cannot imagine how it would be if he were staying. If my
feeling would be just as strong I do not know. I do not know
him well enough. With me it takes so long. We were together
in the afternoon and it was a little painful already. When the
concert was over, I went up to the coat room, put on my coat
and stood in front of him. And then for the first time in my
life I did something without thinking, and without being very
clear in my mind of what I was doing. Suddenly, I had my
arms outstretched and threw them around his neck. And he
kissed me and he kissed me and kissed and kissed and he smiled
as happy as a child. He didn't think. He only smiled. And
there was so much in this smile, words and complete understanding without anything being said. All difficulties, problems, suffering—everything was wiped out, and there was just
happiness. And that was one time."

Dr. B. left for India, and on August 1, 1936, he wrote Lisa from Hyderabad. He asked how she was and how she was enjoying her massage course. But there was no hint that he would return, and no suggestion that she join him. Lisa waited.

"Love is a strange thing," she wrote introspectively. "One lives days, weeks, and months. One is happy. One is sad. One looks forward to this and that. One waits and hopes. This is what I do anyway. Sometimes I am really happy and delighted. I love my life, I could shout with joy, ready to kiss everything."

A childhood friend recalled that "Lisa was a very romantic girl. She loved to see the flowers, the landscape, the clouds. Often, when she was at Büchen [about thirty miles east of Hamburg by train], we lay on our backs in the grass and looked up to the sky and followed the moving clouds with our eyes. And we dreamed and we discussed about all things under Heaven. Our hearts were so full of hope, even in the first years of the evil Nazi time. We children were educated very freely and world-wise and so looked with criticism at everything that belonged to the Nazi regime.

"We went swimming at the canal. We swam naked. She enjoyed it very much and liked to feel the sun on her skin. She was the most beautiful girl I ever saw."

Lisa's romanticism was, indeed, unbounded. "I am lying on my back and staring into the sky," she wrote later in that summer of 1937. "There are soft white clouds shimmering in the bright sky and the light is coming through. I am lying on my back and I watch. Not to the right and not to the left, not behind me and not ahead of me, only into the clouds. They are far away, yet they seem close. I am so happy to be so close to them. Nobody can talk to me about it. I am feeling the huge stillness that comes into me from these clouds and it touches my soul.

"You know how it is when one is troubled. There is a pain inside me and it does not leave. It is not getting bigger and it is not getting smaller, but it is there. Now it is a little less. What a lovely mild evening . . . And the air is aromatic. There is a fragrance and warmth, yet now I want to forget it all. Now I would like to go away, to be carried away by something that loves me, the great mother."

At a time when almost every Jew who could was leaving Germany, it seems odd that Lisa, given her family's affluence, lingered there so long with so much hostility all around her.

"Look here," she wrote to a friend in mid-1937, "we humans have many, many possibilities to achieve what we dream. It is all within us, and if we really want something from deep in our hearts we must try it until we achieve it. You may not give up until you have really tried everything. It is never too late. Perhaps you have not used all your strength and all the possibilities. I'll be glad to help you, if my help can be of use to you."

While offering help to a friend, Lisa continued her own search. "I could cry, cry, cry because I too am looking for that happiness. I am searching for love, but I too carry this love within me. Yes, it should always be awakened, but I hope that he will come, he for whom I am waiting to be something for. And he should not notice how much I would love him. My dear, dear God. Do help me, please."

By late 1937, the Philip family was making plans to leave Germany forever. Lisa's younger sister, Eva, was already living in Austria, where she was completing training as a pediatric nurse. Hugo and Anita wrote to Bernhardt Berlin and his wife, family friends living in Philadelphia, and the couple agreed to sponsor Lisa. She received her visa from the American Consulate in Hamburg on April 23, 1938.

Lisa sailed from Hamburg on May 6, 1938, aboard the S.S. *Manhattan*. Her passport, like that of all Jews leaving Germany, was stamped JUDEN. Writing home from aboard ship, her tone was giddy. She hadn't laughed so much during the past year as on this voyage. She swam, she chatted, she danced, and she met interesting young men.

She was met in New York by the Berlins and several of her German friends who had preceded her, including an old boyfriend named Franz. That same day they drove down to Philadelphia, where she would share a room with her sponsors' twenty-year-old daughter, Ruth. Of America, she wrote to her parents, "Everything is very natural and without restrictions. Everybody does as he pleases. Clara's [the Berlin's other daughter] fiancé and others come and go as they wish. Sweet parents, there is so much new that one can only stand here with open eyes and mouth.

"You know," she added, "I have a feeling that life is open for me and that I am free more than ever. You should see these

Americans here. It seems that they all live by the basic concept, 'keep on smiling and everything is so much simpler that way.' They understand how to live, and I will try and do my best to copy this."

She added as a postscript, "By the way, they have named me Li or Lis because Lisa they say is like a Negro name, Liza. You have to address your letters to Li, Lis, or Liesel."

Lisa's sister, Eva, arrived in the United States in December 1938, to live with a sponsor in Houston, Texas. Hugo and Anita, however, could not get American visas, so they fled to Merano in northern Italy, near the Austrian border, and rented a large house where they intended to take in boarders—quite a step down in the world for a wealthy German stockbroker and his aristocratic wife. Returning briefly to Hamburg, they shipped their household furniture to Italy, including their Steinway piano and Hugo's library and art collection. They arrived in the south Tyrol in June 1938, but in September Italy promulgated a new law that gave all aliens six months to leave the country. The Philips managed to stay in Italy for another year, but when the war began in September 1939, they were given five days to leave the country. Although Austria had become part of Hitler's Third Reich on March 13, 1938, and even though Italy and Germany were allies, the borders were closed. When Anita and Hugo reached the Italian-Austrian border, Nazi guards there told them that they had to return to Italy. But the Italians maintained that the Philips had been deported, and refused them reentry. Since they were carrying German passports, they had to return to Germany.

Certain that they were facing a hopeless future and bound for a concentration camp, the couple purchased enough Veronal for a relatively painless death. Suicide would be preferable to life in a Nazi concentration camp. They took the Veronal as the train traveled through the Austrian countryside. When the conductor discovered them unconscious near Lienz, about thirty miles inside Austria, they were removed from the train and taken to a Catholic hospital there. The local officials, all Nazis, inquired daily at the hospital about their condition. The Philips, the Nazis told hospital officials, were not Austrian Jews and therefore had no right to remain in Austria; they wanted to make certain that Hugo and Anita continued their journey back to Germany as soon as they recovered sufficiently to travel.

During their stay at the hospital Hugo became friends with a supervising physician. Both men were music lovers, and Hugo had with him his magnificent violin, which had been crafted by Guadagnini, a student of Stradivarius. Like Hugo, the doctor was an excellent musician. The two played duets together. Each day the doctor made excuses to the police about why the Philips were not yet healthy enough to travel, thus prolonging their stay at the hospital for several weeks. These were critical, almost frantic weeks during which Hugo, Anita, and their physician friend tried desperately to make contact with Aryan friends in Vienna. This was no small task since Aryans who were openly friendly to Jews drew strong and ugly attention to themselves, even in Austria.

Finally, contact was made with two couples living in Vienna. Leo and Asta Dukes were old friends with a common interest in music. Having visited with the Philips in Merano earlier in the year, the Dukes were aware of their predicament. Then there were the Kalchers, Walter and Helene, friends of Anita's sister who had already departed Vienna. The Kalchers were an Aryan couple who were actively helping Jews in the Austrian underground by securing passports, protecting property transfers, arranging for Catholic "baptisms," and even concealing refugees in their home. With the help of the hospital physician and the Kalchers, Hugo and Anita traveled to Vienna. These sponsors told Austrian officials that the Philips had other sponsors in the United States and were simply waiting for notification of their visas. It would be only a matter of weeks, they argued, but in truth they had no idea how long it would take. Actually, almost every Jew in Austria then wanted a visa, and quotas were being filled from long waiting lists.

By the time they reached Vienna, Hugo and Anita had no money left. They carried with them the family silver as a last desperate capital resource. The Dukes, the Kalchers, and others assisted the Philips with ration cards, money, and food during their frightful wait in Vienna.

Their stay lasted four months, and during that period the Philips were cared for by the Vienna Gildemeister Committee and the refugee committee of the American Society of Friends. They lived in a boardinghouse and, for Anita especially, the times were dreadful. "You hardly saw any well-dressed women and men in the streets," she wrote later, "but there were many men in Nazi uniforms. Those who wore no uniform usually wore the swastika in their buttonhole, men as well as women. Jews were not allowed to wear the swastika, so you could see who was Aryan and who was not. All non-Aryans were not allowed to go out of their house after 6:30 P.M. There were food tickets, dress tickets and coal tickets. The only thing that was sufficient was bread. Meat, fat, eggs and everything else was given in small quantities. The non-Aryans had a mark on their tickets and were not allowed to buy their food at the same time as the Aryans. When we went to market, everything that might have been there—vegetables, fruit, etcetera—was sold out. We were not allowed to buy fish or fowl."

During the four months that the Philips waited for their American visas to come through, men from the Gestapo visited the boardinghouse repeatedly to ask how long they expected to wait for their visas. On March 20, 1940, as Hugo and Anita embarked on the S.S. *Conte di Savoia* from Genoa, Italy, bound for the United States, they cabled a message to their daughter Lisa:

> LEAVE GENOVA BY CONTESAVOIA 20 MARCH
> INFORM EVERYBODY. HURRAY.
>   HUGO ANITA PHILIP

Anita's parents, the Heilbuts, did not fare as well. They were living in Norway, and in the summer of 1939 an article was published in an Oslo newspaper congratulating Anita's father, Julius Heilbut, on his fiftieth anniversary as a banker with the firm of L. Behrens & Sohn. Julius Heilbut was made an honorary citizen of Norway on that occasion. Hitler invaded Norway on April 9, 1940, but Lisa, Hugo, and Anita continued to receive letters from the Heilbuts until August 1942, when all communication abruptly stopped. After the war, the Red Cross notified the Philips that the Heilbuts and nine hundred other Jews had been deported to Poland on the S.S. *Donau* in November 1942, and had been gassed.

Lisa had been accepted by the Johns Hopkins University nursing school, but canceled her plans when her parents received their visas. She had lived with the Berlins in Philadelphia for

The Reverend Sheldon Thomas Nutter, grandfather of Laurence L. Layton, about 1910

At left, John Finney Layton, Laurence's grandfather and husband of Bertha Jarrett Layton

Boomer, West Virginia, in 1931

Bertha Jarrett Layton, about 1890

John and Eva Layton, Laurence's parents, 1913

Laurence (CENTER) with his sister, Rosemary, and brother, Tom—July 4, 1922

John Wister Layton, Laurence's father

Laurence in Boomer, July 1938

Max and Nanny Philip, Hugo Philip's parents, in 1900

The Philip family (left to right): Hugo, Eva, Anita,
Lisa, and Grandmother Nanny Franck Philip

Eva and Lisa Philip

The house Hugo Philip built for his family in Hamburg, upon its completion in 1927

Lisa Philip as a teenager

Hugo and Anita Philip in Merano in October 1938, just prior to being deported

several months, but found herself increasingly unhappy there. As time passed, she felt more and more confined. She wrote her parents that she had to be "on the watch all the time so they don't take advantage of me."

In late 1939, Lisa accepted a position as governess with the family of the Reverend Galen Russell, a Congregational minister in Chappaqua, New York. It was the first time she really felt at home in the United States. She and the minister's wife, Buddy Russell, shared an interest in gymnastics and massage. Continuing the same bent that she had developed in Germany, Lisa exercised in the privacy of the Russells' garden, joined by Mrs. Russell. She was also quickly adjusting to life in Protestant America. To her parents, Lisa described the Congregational Church as "a very progressive church in this country," and wrote that Mrs. Russell "is explaining to me about the church community in New York."

"Today was Sunday," she wrote, "and I went to the church with them. That I have to do."

What little there had been of Lisa Philip's Jewishness had ended for her within months of her arrival in the United States. She had left it behind her in Philadelphia in 1939.

Courtship, Marriage, and Career

Lisa often hummed and sang to herself the refrain from a German children's song: "Everywhere I have searched for my beloved. He's not here. He's not there. Probably he's in America." *Ist nicht hier. Ist nicht da. Ist wohl in Amerika.*

Lisa was depressed; she had not found her beloved. In contrast to her almost hysterically cheerful letters to her parents, her letters to her best friend, Annelise Schmidt, expressed feelings of worthlessness and loneliness. Annelise wrote back, "You don't have anywhere to go when you are terribly lonesome, but Lisa, you must not give up the longing for something beautiful if you want to climb the mountain. A strong love would be the most cleansing thing for you. When one is far away from one's feelings one needs great strength to come back to all the good things. The memories of the past are there, and you feel that you have been plucked from your past, but I am sure that you will rebuild your roots. If you have a devil within you, don't hide him but put him in front of your wagon so that he will use up all his strength by pulling you forward."

In September of 1940, while her parents were trying to regain livelihoods for themselves—Hugo investigating possibilities in Cambridge, Massachusetts, and Anita in Philadelphia working at the Kingsley Settlement House—Lisa Philip was working as a physical therapist at the hospital at Pennsylvania State College, where Laurence Layton was a graduate student. Laurence too was lonely, finding it difficult to meet people, particularly "acceptable" young women. So he went to the dean of the graduate school and suggested that the university support his efforts to organize a graduate club. The college officials liked the idea, so Layton—with the help of other young faculty and graduate students—formed the Graduate Club of Pennsylvania State College and became its first president.

Laurence's loneliness and his unbending rigor in moral matters were clearly stated in a letter he wrote at about this time. When his brother, Sheldon Thomas, married in November 1940, Laurence wrote to Grandfather Nutter, "I certainly was glad to hear of Tom's marriage. The girl, I think, is respectable, which is more than some are. I don't think he will regret it from that point of view." On the same day, he wrote to his mother, "How do you like your new daughter-in-law? She is a nice girl so Tom is lucky he doesn't have a drinking, smoking, wild wife. I feel he can trust her...I surely wish I were settled down with a family and a good income and a happy home life. I often feel desperate. I've never even met anyone satisfactory to me." Laurence was looking for a wife, but he was being very circumspect about it. He seemed to envision a family and a happy home life, but with no mention of a partnership, a fulfilling marriage, or even a wife. On December 12, 1940, a few days after these letters, Grandfather Nutter died.

Laurence and Lisa Philip were introduced early in 1941 by a mutual friend, Franz Werner, the boy from Germany who had met Lisa's ship when she arrived in the United States. Laurence's doctoral studies required that he master German, and he needed help; the beautiful young woman offered to tutor him. During their first sessions together, the two discovered that they had a common interest in philosophy. Layton decided that she was "a very, very lovely person." When Lisa did not see Layton for some weeks during the spring of 1941, she wrote a poem that she sent to him in the hope of seeing him again.

It was not an easy situation for Layton. Lisa was very popular. She dated frequently. In fact, she was dating Franz Werner, who in his pursuit of a doctoral degree in physics had also become a friend of Laurence Layton.

Then too, Laurence had heard stories about Lisa that filled him with misgivings—like the time, on a ski trip, when she decided to take a snow bath. She took off all her clothes, ran outside, and rubbed herself with snow. Such goings-on were shocking to Layton. Still, he was lonely, and when he confided this feeling to his friend, Franz surprised him by suggesting that he date Lisa. Layton decided that he ought to at least try to become better acquainted. "When I did get acquainted with her family, I found that, by God, she came from a fabulous family," he recalls. "Down home we're always interested in 'blood lines,' but the fact that she was Jewish didn't bother me. She told me that Dr. James Franck, winner of the Nobel Prize in 1925, was her father's cousin, and that she was related to a Spanish cardinal who was confessor to Charles the Fifth in the sixteenth century. Brains and money all over the place. I found her intellectually stimulating. I wasn't interested in money, but I was interested in her. She was very beautiful, and she had such a pretty accent. She had a lot of Spanish blood. In fact, I always thought of her as Spanish in appearance and temperament. And she was interested in philosophy."

The couple read together constantly—works such as Will Durant's *Story of Philosophy*, and textbooks on philosophy—and for the first time Layton "began to realize that girls were interesting as people, as individuals, for something other than taking walks with."

The young couple also found a common interest in Quakerism—Lisa from her mother, and Laurence from his Virginia forebears. They began regular attendance at the State College Friends Meeting.

Lisa had fallen in love—she had found her beloved, and she wanted to marry him. Layton was amazed that beautiful, exotic Lisa had chosen *him*. Moreover, he had deep misgivings:

about himself, about his work, about marriage, and about life in general. He wasn't interested in getting married yet. Lisa told Laurence that life without him looked black.

The couple continued to read together and to take long walks. In June, Lisa's mother, Anita, came to visit, and found young Layton very likable. In July, Laurence told Lisa that he was fairly certain he should not get married, that he didn't really want to get married. Lisa's reaction, an outpouring of gloom and depression, suggested that she might commit suicide. Laurence took her in his arms and tried to comfort her. After all, he thought, why not? She was far more beautiful and more intelligent than any other woman he knew. Nor, he felt, would many other women ever look at him closely enough to really get to know him; and if they did, they probably wouldn't like what they saw.

One evening in August they were visiting a friend, Gaylord Whitlock. They were sitting on the porch swing when Whitlock said, "Larry, why don't you marry Lisa? Lisa, why don't you marry Larry?" Larry was embarrassed, especially when Lisa replied, "My mother said the very same thing." Layton insisted that he didn't know Lisa well enough, he didn't want to "get committed," and besides, he was still in school and penniless. But Lisa continued to bring up the subject of marriage, and finally Layton agreed to take her home to West Virginia to meet his family.

The family liked Lisa very much. In deference to her wishes, Laurence saw no reason to tell them about her Jewish ancestry. The young couple decided to return by bus to Pennsylvania by way of Washington, D.C., where they spent the night together for the first time. This was Layton's first sexual experience, and it came only after his family and friends had met Lisa and approved of her.

Having spent the night with Lisa, Laurence felt honorbound, committed. He agreed to marry her.

Lisa had become a member of the State College Friends Meeting, and the Quaker rule was that a young couple planning marriage should notify the Meeting six months in advance; that is, there should be a cooling-off period before the Meeting would solemnize the marriage. Lisa did not want to wait six months; she did not want to wait six weeks; she wanted to get married immediately. She had searched for the Beloved since she was a child; now that she had found him, she didn't want to wait any longer.

Although Laurence's Huddleston ancestors had been Quakers in Bucks County, Pennsylvania, he had been raised a Methodist by Grandfather Nutter; so it was natural that they be married by the Campus Methodist minister in his study on October 18, 1941. The witnesses were fellow students Gaylord Whitlock and his own new bride, Margaret.

On September 15, a month before they were married, Lisa wrote to Laurence on the subject of religion in the first of a mutual lifetime exchange that included letters, diaries, and introspective notes.

"Dear Larry: Here I am sitting, in a nonbelligerent attitude with the sincere intention of writing a letter to you. After all, there ought to be cooperation! To come back to the old question of religion. . . . One has to think about it and deal with it and come to at least some conclusion, in order to have peace of mind. Or else ignore the question as much as possible by letting things go as they are. Perhaps accepting a traditional code of religious concepts as our fathers and forefathers believed in them. And comforting yourself with emotionally accepted pictures like: angels that guard your life and the life of your family; God, who as a kind father forgives you your sins, who guides you in times of doubt and insecurity, and who finally takes you into his kingdom of heaven after you die, to a place where there is eternal peace and harmony, and where you'll be united with the people you love after they have died."

There is no doubt that Lisa was well aware at this point of Laurence's rigid moralistic upbringing. She continued, "All those beliefs are accepted by most people that go—and even do not go—to church every Sunday. They were inspired by those 'pictures' when they were little children. . . . It is a funny thing how much the happenings we lived through, and the surroundings we lived in, in our childhood, influence our later life.

"Many people that like to accept tradition as it is, without ever questioning it, are religious in this superficial, conventional way. There are so many that simply don't have the desire to search, and to get to the bottom of things. They merely accept a picture they have in their imagination, colored with the strange and sweet feeling of memory from childhood and early youth. When it comes to accepted pictures—it is never going to be questioned. Or even ever can be questioned. Because it has been accepted as a picture, or a feeling. It is living somewhere back in our unconscious mind and shows up in everything we 'feel' toward other people, situations and ourselves.

"This picture memory plays the most important part in the religious concept of most people as they are nowadays. And it is a dangerous one, since it is not questioned and newly accepted through independent thinking. Of course, the memories and pictures in our minds will always influence our final decisions. And I do not believe that we ever will be able to free ourselves from them. Just as much as we can't free ourselves from the physical and mental disposition we partly inherited from our parents.

"As far as I am concerned, I do know what I believe in, when it comes to my own personal conduct of life. But I do not know what to believe in when it comes to the question of authority on the happenings in our lives, and the life of nature. I agree with you, that it is essential for us to be happy. For all of us human beings. But aside from the fact that there are so many different ways in different people to achieve happiness there is this fundamental question at the end: 'What for?' . . .

"[Happiness] includes satisfaction of accomplishment through work, through good deeds, and productive thinking. It also activates our positive inclinations. A happy person loves and does not hate. A happy person is tolerant and generous toward others. But happiness does not produce all those attitudes as it might seem to do. It is exactly the other way around. We have to try to understand and love. We have to try to tolerate. We have to try to overcome our own weaknesses. We have to try and try and try again. All our lives.

"And we will be happy. And we will find ourselves in a position where we don't hate, and don't feel discontented. And it seems to me that this might also be a way to approach religion. Maybe we will never be believers by thinking alone. Because belief comes to us through experience and life. And the thinking about it will be fruitful once life is lived fully in a positive way. The way one wanted it.

"I do not have a belief or a religion yet, which means that I still hope to find it. I have the unpleasant picture in my mind that I, as a believer in nothing, have a vacuum within myself that has to withstand continuous pressure from the outside, and therefore never can escape my fundamental consciousness. While once I put a hypothesis in place of this vacuum, I could be at ease with myself in the hope that I will find a basic belief or religion some day."

Morality, religion, happiness, tolerance, God . . . and the largest question of all: What for? For Lisa, it was a matter of living her life and slowly, gradually, filling in that "picture." For Laurence, the picture had long ago been filled in, by his family and his childhood experiences.

As the couple grew closer, Lisa told Laurence about her past—that she was not inexperienced, she had had lovers—but insisted she had put it all behind her. Laurence could not allow that. At first, his reaction was, "It didn't even click as to what she was telling me." But it bothered him. And he knew that it bothered him because of his background.

"My puritanical upbringing," says Layton, "has messed up a lot of things. Possibly the whole family. Before we were married, Lisa had known three very fine men. Two of them had doctoral degrees, and the third was a graduate student in physics who happened to be a friend of mine. All very high-class people. So she wasn't a guttersnipe or a streetwalker or anything like that. But it bothered me, because of my puritanical background, coming up against the realization that there were men around who had had sexual intimacy with this woman, my wife.

"If I had had time to think about it, I wouldn't have gotten married. And this knowledge bothered Lisa because she was a very honest person. She began to feel the guilt that she carried for the next thirty years. It was a very difficult subject to talk about, and it always developed into a crying spell on her part. She would cry and feel bad and I would be blue and low, and we never got it worked out. She claimed later that she carried it continuously as a burden on her heart. And she tried to convince me that I really was the only one that mattered to her; that these other relationships had been incidents—accidents—in her search for the Beloved. I could understand that; but because of my own rigid upbringing, I found it a difficult and recurring struggle to accept the facts of her life."

Laurence had married because he "thought it was the right thing to do. It was not that I wanted to get married. I suppose I felt trapped—not trapped in an ugly way, but as if I didn't know how to handle this new kind of situation."

Lisa had married because for years she had fantasized her Beloved and had wanted to be married and to have a home. Laurence appealed to her because he was interesting, intelligent, well educated. Lisa was also eager for security and a comfortable financial status, although she had achieved that fairly well on her own. Laurence was rather firm and demanding; she thought she wanted that then. Finally, he was a Gentile, a white Anglo-Saxon Protestant; Lisa had long ago decided that she did not want her children to be Jewish in a non-Jewish society.

Even though they were well aware of the cultural differences, Lisa's family was delighted. They were impressed with the fact that Laurence was well educated, and that he would become a university professor and would be able to provide security for their daughter.

Layton's grandfather, Sheldon Thomas Nutter, had been born on Lincoln's Birthday, February 12, 1862. Layton decided that he and Lisa would conceive a son on the eightieth anniversary of his grandfather's birth. Thomas Nutter Layton was born nine months later on November 13, 1942.

Laurence discovered that he had to teach his Lisa everything about housekeeping and cooking. After all, cooking and cleaning had not been part of her upbringing. On his side, Laurence had been doing these chores for his grandfather for years. Lisa dressed tastefully, but the color of her clothes tended toward the drab. Laurence changed all that with suggestions that she buy or sew more colorful attire.

Even after marriage, Layton was puritanical about sex. Somehow it was still "sinful." He had been brought up to believe that sex was something to apologize for. It was "of the flesh," and therefore ugly, bad. To a limited extent, the couple did enjoy each other sexually, but Laurence always felt a bit ill-at-ease. Even if he wanted to make love, he would not disturb her or wake her up. He was ashamed to. Lisa could not understand or accept his attitude. Laurence knew absolutely nothing about foreplay. He had never heard of it. He didn't know anything about a woman's orgasm. Neither did Lisa. She was as shocked as Laurence when she experienced her first orgasm.

Laurence was preparing for his doctoral examinations when the Japanese attacked Pearl Harbor on December 7, 1941. Fearing that Laurence would be drafted, Lisa wrote to her father's cousin, Dr. James Franck, the Nobel laureate who was now professor of physics at the University of Chicago. Dr. Franck arranged a predoctoral appointment in physics for Layton at Chicago. But then Layton received a student deferment, and he decided to finish his doctoral work at Pennsylvania. (If he had gone to Chicago, he discovered later, he would have been working on the Manhattan Project, developing the first atomic bomb. Lisa was horrified when she learned this.)

Layton's first job after receiving his doctorate was with the Eastman Kodak Company in Rochester, New York. While working on his master's degree at West Virginia University, he had concentrated on a newly discovered process called molecular distillation. He had been working with a method of isolating free radicals by applying this new technique, which had been pioneered by Dr. Kenneth Hickman at Kodak. Layton wanted to work with Dr. Hickman.

Laurence and Lisa arrived in Rochester in early September of 1942. America was at war. That summer, the naval battles of the Coral Sea and Midway were fought, resulting in decisive U.S. victories. By September, the Marines had captured the Japanese airfields on Guadalcanal.

Lisa was radiantly pregnant; she carried the baby well, easily in fact. She had designed and made some pretty dresses for herself, and she was happy about having a baby.

The couple had made the trip to Rochester by train, and they arrived without a place to stay. Lisa was tired. Laurence had to carry the suitcases, almost had to carry her too. They took a streetcar, then a bus, winding their way out toward the lake. They spent the night in a hotel. The following morning they walked around the neighborhood near Lake Ontario to look for rental vacancies. They asked a gray-haired woman who was sitting on a porch if there were any in the neighborhood, close to the lake and close to the Kodak laboratories. The woman, at first cantankerous and suspicious, said she didn't know of any, then finally said that she was willing to rent them a single room. The Laytons accepted the offer of a sleeping room on the second floor.

Laurence worked every day. Lisa took walks. She walked in the yard, walked around the neighborhood, walked down to the lake. She was waiting for the baby.

When the time came to go to the hospital, the maternity ward was full. There was a rush at that time to have little "weather strips," as folks said then, "to keep Papa out of the draft." Thomas Nutter Layton was born in the hallway of St. Mary's.

The baby came in the middle of the night. Dr. Layton, who had been waiting at the hospital, was not pleased with his initial glimpse of his newborn son. "When I first saw him, I thought, gee whiz, if I had taken him to a Hindu hospital he would have looked like a Hindu. Because I took him to a Catholic hospital, and he certainly looked like a Latin or an Italian. So much so that I was upset. I wondered whether they had switched babies on me. Why would one of my babies look like an Italian? Of course, he was all shriveled up, his hair started about his nose and went back over his head, and I was not used to new babies. My mother's children had been blond and they weren't shriveled by any means. They were pretty babies. In any case, I had the feeling that Tom would be a shriveled-up little Italian-looking guy, maybe four feet tall, and I just couldn't see him spreading out, filling out, and being the beautiful baby he was a month later."

Lisa herself was appalled. "Little Thomas is so ugly," she wrote her mother three days after his birth. "His nose is bent very much and broad (like that of a little Turk). He has hardly any temples. He's got black hair growing down his cheeks and on his head. His eyes are a dirty bluish-brown color. As a whole, his little face is squeezed together and puffed up. He is ugly, and if he ever changes he simply has got to get prettier. There is no other chance for him!—and yet I love him so much."

She also commented to her mother on her perception of Laurence's reaction: "Larry was so disappointed that he looked so ugly that he almost cried."

In the meantime, Lisa's father, Hugo, excited by the prospect of greeting his first grandchild, had moved to Rochester and been settled in an apartment chosen and furnished by Laurence and Lisa. The rules of the hospital were that only the father and maternal grandmother could visit the mother and new baby, and Anita was still working in Philadelphia. Hugo was not about to be stopped by "stupid rules or stupid people." He purchased flowers and went to the maternity ward demanding to see Lisa and his new grandson. He was refused admittance. He reasoned, "There is no Grandma here, I am the only grandparent, I demand to see my daughter." He began to raise his voice; he spoke a wild mixture of German and English, pushed the nurse aside, and went looking for Lisa. Lisa was embarrassed at the commotion created by her father. For his part, Hugo was pleased with himself. He was ecstatic when he saw Lisa nursing the "dream child—Thomaskind." For the next year he spent hours every day with the "Wonder baby." This affection for his "first son" continued for the remaining thirty-six years of Hugo's life.

After mother and baby came home, Laurence showed Lisa how to change diapers, and convinced her that even if one held a baby up by the heels to change its diapers, the baby would not break. Tom's crying, however, upset the landlady. "How can I stand that racket?" she would lament in a loud voice. She told her children how afraid she was of Dr. Layton because he was from the South. Whenever Layton came down the stairs, she would yell over the telephone to her daughter or son that she was afraid, and ask whoever she was talking with to stay on the phone to listen and be sure that nothing happened to her. Layton decided that it was time to move. He found a more pleasant apartment along the shore of Lake Ontario. Laurence and Lisa started a victory garden, where they raised broccoli and beans.

On the eve of their first wedding anniversary, Lisa had written another letter to Laurence. She was still optimistic about the marriage, but not quite as much as she had been.

"I do think that we have become happy with each other," she wrote. "At least I feel happy with you. And I hope with all my heart that it will stay this way between the two of us for years to come. Both of us have learned a lot during this first year. I have noticed you change very much from being a strong individualist (in the bad sense of it, where the egotistical element comes in) to a person with more concern for others. An individualist in the 'better' if not good sense. (I did not mean to say that there is no room left for further improvement) . . .

"I am looking so much forward to our first child to be born. It will do much to give our lives the strong foundation we both want. I do believe that this foundation, that so many people find in their religion, will come to us as we are growing older and more mature and are getting settled in life. Both of us have been wandering around a great deal. Perhaps away from ourselves seeking happiness. And it seems to me now as if we are finding our way back and are coming home."

This feeling would change drastically. If the marriage of Lisa and Laurence had started on shaky ground, in less than two years, even with the baby, it was very nearly on the rocks. Lisa believed that Laurence could not forget her premarital relationships, let alone forgive them, that he perceived her as soiled, one of the fallen, and had given way to passion when he married her. For years he had desperately wanted a family, if only to fill the void in himself and thereby make his own life more meaningful. But now that he had one, he found that he had married a woman whom he deemed morally unfit to raise his children.

In a depressed mood, she wrote in her diary in 1943, "There is one thing that is causing me to be more desperate and unhappy than I thought I ever could be, living as well as I do, having a perfect little son, and a good husband. It is the opinion another person one greatly cares for has of one. As a woman, even more depends on the opinion such a person has of one, trying to either live up to it, or improve it. But, what if the opinion of one is poor. What if one is put in a class with the lowest creatures in the opinion of that person? It is terribly hard to keep a countenance of self-respect then. One cannot possibly be at peace with oneself, more so if one thinks that the person thinking such about oneself is right. . . . How horrid this idea is and how the knowledge of my husband's knowledge will not let me come to peace anymore. . . .

"I would have repented and tried to be as good a person as

I could. But now things seem to be pulled out from under me. There is nothing I seem to be able to stand on. Is there anything I can be proud of? Is there anything in my person that I can build on? Nothing. There is to my knowledge nothing. No stray faith in God. No love great enough to make me forget myself. Nothing enough to look forward to and work for to forget the wretchedness of my existence. . . . To whom do I mean anything, and who am I able to help to be a happy person? Nobody. My little boy would be better off not to be around me. Larry's life I make miserable, and I know that another woman could make it happy for him provided she is the right person. There is nobody else who either suffers or profits from my existence except for myself. And there is no profit or anything positive as far as I can see—Why don't I then take my own life? I know that I would not do that because I couldn't. . . . I can imagine that there would be unusual circumstances where I would, if there would be no way out anymore. But as long as there is the faintest spark of hope anywhere I have to try. There must be sparks left, I am sure. . . . I sense there must be something to live for and something that will help me to become an upright human being again. I cannot live with nothing to pride within myself. How can anybody live without pride? I dread and despise the idea of a mere vegetating and bare existence, just drifting along despite everything that is against oneself. I cannot live that way and I will not. The only thing that I will be able to build up on is in the potentialities of that which I may be able to do in times to come. I have to pull myself up on the right things I want to do every day as every day comes along. I must start to live every day and plan every day and try to do things right every day. I may not give in to moods of inferiority and despair. I must think of the good things I will do, and do the things that ought to be done. I must think of sadness and gloom as something sinful in itself because it takes the strength to be the way one ought to be. I must, and must forget myself as a wicked person and know my sins and things of the past that have to be overcome.

"Please God give me the strength to carry on what I ought to do."

After a while Lisa couldn't contain her feelings of desperation any longer. On September 9, 1943, a month before their second anniversary, she wrote to Laurence: "Dear Larry, I am at a point now where I can't know where to go. Tnere is neither a going back to, nor a future. All I have ever hoped for seems to be denied to me. . . .

"I want a home and children. I want to feel part of you. Or at least that there is something that belongs to both of us, that is our relationship to each other. I know what you are thinking now. And I am not able to do anything about that which has happened. I know that a true relationship to a person one truly likes will be stronger than anything else. Or perhaps I should say, I thought and hoped would be stronger. But it has not proved to be so. Those ugly thoughts come to you and blind you to all that could make you happy. . . . When you say that you love Tom desperately, it is self-pity and self-concern that makes your love to be mixed with desperation and sadness. I can tell simply by looking at myself. When things are all right between the two of us, my love for Tom is happy, and it fills me with contentment and a feeling of security to see him play and feel good. But when things are the way they have become now, my love for him is not a real, true and unselfish love, because I try to regain from my love for him what I have lost in you. And since this is not possible, or only possible to a very small extent, my love becomes desperate. And seeing him happy is more liable to bring tears into my eyes than make me laugh and be happy too. . . .

"You cannot believe my feeling toward you, because you cannot feel it. You are a prisoner of yourself, because selfishness prevents you from overcoming your limits. And there seems to be no way of my helping you because all I have to offer is my affection toward you and it doesn't seem to reach you. It comes back to me unwanted. . . .

"I wouldn't ask you to come back if I thought it would be better for you to leave me. I do not believe that your possibilities for happiness are greater away from me. I truly believe that you can be happy if you once make that jump beyond that which is imprisoning you now. And I know you can if you really want to.

"Please Larry. I will wait for you.

"Your wife Lisa."

Layton was also having his troubles at work. It turned out that his boss at Kodak, Dr. Hickman, was interested in ideas that came from one source only—himself. Layton was coming up with too many suggestions that Hickman thought crossed over into his own private preserve. One sketch sheet that Layton turned in had to do with thermal diffusion in the purification of chemicals. Layton didn't know it at the time, but the Manhattan Project had already been set up and Kodak was involved in it, using a similar process in purifying uranium isotopes at its plant in the remote town of Kingsport, Tennessee. This process was an area that Hickman felt was his. The company's assistant director of research approached Layton and suggested that he just hold off on his own ideas until Hickman had tired of the subject.

Layton didn't like that idea, so he began looking for another job. In November of 1943, after a little over a year with Kodak, he took a position as assistant professor of chemistry at the University of Maryland. Although he soon tired of university politics, he taught there for three years.

Annalisa and Laurence John were both born while the family was living in the Washington suburb of College Park. Annalisa Laird Layton was born on September 9, 1944, a lovely baby who would grow into a beautiful woman. She was named after her mother's friend Annalise Schmidt who, along with her own young daughter, had been killed in a British bombing raid while walking in the woods near Hamburg. After Annalisa's birth, as she had done for Tom, Lisa kept a baby book for several years in which she recorded her child's growth and development, and to which Laurence occasionally contributed.

When Annalisa was thirteen months old, Laurence made the following entry, addressed to his daughter: "I wonder when you will read this, sweetheart (sometime when I am physically no more). Oh that you should know and respond to the deep love which I bear for you. Oh Annalisa, my child, lead a good, clean, decent life, <u>above</u> the <u>standards</u> of your day. The pendulum swings but it does have a so-called rest point. Read history; try to live according to what you really admire in human character. Live privately as you would like the best people to believe you live. <u>Your father is a most unhappy man because he betrayed himself and compromised ideals</u> which he cannot and would not discard. I shall elaborate on these matters later in this book. With love, Laurence Laird Layton."

Lisa, of course, must have read these thinly veiled lines as commentary on her own morality. But she made no reference in her later entries to what her husband had written.

The first three Layton children were born with almost mathematical precision. Boy, girl, boy—one about every year and a half. Unfortunately, by the time the third baby, Laurence John, came along on January 11, 1946, his parents' enthusiasm for and ability to concentrate on newborns had diminished. His own baby book seemed like an addendum to the fat and chatty tomes that his parents had lovingly prepared for Thomas and Annalisa.

"Laurency," as he was affectionately called, had the earmarks of a loner from the beginning. Even in the Maryland hospital where he was born, he arrived with a minimum of assistance from the staff. The attending physician gave Lisa an injection to induce labor and then left. So did the nurse. When Laurency decided to make his appearance, it was just him and Mom together against the world. He was showing his head when a student nurse happened by and the obstetrician was summoned. Later, it was questioned by both Lisa and her husband whether the attending physician had arrived in time to deserve the seventy-five-dollar delivery fee.

"After he had nursed for a few times to get the colostrum," Lisa wrote in his baby book, "Laurency was put on a bottle because his mother wanted it that way. With a three-year-old brother and a one-year-old sister there simply would not have been enough peace and quiet for nursing. However, Laurency did just as well with the bottle. He hardly cried, gained weight and seemed content."

From his birth, his parents saw in Laurency an "unbelievable" resemblance to his great-grandfather, the stern Sheldon Thomas Nutter. Laurency had the large blue eyes, fair skin, and facial idiosyncrasies ("like pursing his lips and trying not to laugh") of the self-controlled Methodist minister of Boomer, West Virginia. He was a quiet child, not demanding much attention, content to play alone in his playpen and happiest whenever anyone picked him up. His mother's hands, however, were already full. She was busy keeping track of his two ambulatory predecessors. As a result, Laurency was left alone in his playpen a great deal more than the two older children had been, and a great deal more than his mother would have liked.

Lisa thought this might have been one reason why Laurency was slow in learning to walk and talk. Tom had been running around before he was eleven months old; Laurency did not acquire that skill until he was more than sixteen months old.

In 1946, Dr. Layton became interested in the phenomena associated with aging in animals and human beings. He had read an article by Alexis Carrel, recipient of a 1912 Nobel Prize in physiology and medicine for his work in suturing blood vessels, in transfusion, and in the transplantation of organs. Carrel hypothesized an aging substance, something that built up in the blood with age and prevented the cells from behaving as they had when the person was younger. He thought it was a lipid—a fatty acid or fat-soluble toxin of some sort. Although Dr. Layton had not formally studied cell biology, he found Carrel's reasoning persuasive, and decided that he would like to work in this obscure area of medicine.

Layton placed an advertisement in a professional journal and was hired to do research on aging at the Johns Hopkins University in Baltimore, where he would also teach biochemistry. The family moved to Baltimore, and Dr. Layton entered the department during a period of transition. Dr. E.V. McCollum, who had isolated vitamin A and had discovered vitamin D, had just stepped down as departmental head to concentrate on research. His place was taken by Reginald M. Archibald of the Rockefeller Institute of Medical Research. It was Archibald who hired Layton, but it was McCollum who became his new confidant and father figure.

It took Layton two years to discover that Carrel's hypothesis on blood and aging was wrong. He carefully repeated many of the Nobel Prize-winner's experiments and gradually came to the conclusion that Carrel's work had not been sufficiently controlled. Although he was a great surgeon, Carrel was a poor chemist. What he thought was an aging factor in blood was merely an artifact, a poisonous or toxic material that was formed in the test tube by the chemical manipulations of the experimenter, Carrel himself. In short, Carrel had created his own aging process in a test tube, mainly through bad chemistry.

Layton then turned to another obscure area of research,

attempting to develop a technique for diagnosing cartilaginous cancer. He made several major discoveries, which he wrote up and published in the medical journal *Cancer*. Through these discoveries, he became interested in the action of cortisone, and his research led to applications in wound healing and the treatment of arthritis. The publication of this discovery in 1951 made medical headlines, and Layton was invited to lecture on his work in Great Britain, West Germany, and Switzerland.

Within months of his arrival in Baltimore, on March 30, 1947, Laurence wrote again in Annalisa's baby book: "Getting back to the children, they are already showing signs of great or even noble character traits, especially Tommy who reasons and considers every action. He constantly considers the meaning of ideas and actions in their relationship to other people, to God, to right and wrong. He is a little minister."

Still, he could not let the past die. "I hope," he wrote of Annalisa, "she is intelligent rather than intellectual. Intelligent girls, properly reared, rarely become unhappy due to moral transgressions, which they carefully avoid. Intellectual women very easily fall into moral decay due to the abandonment of the concepts of right and wrong evolved by society. This, in my experience and observation, always leads to unhappiness of the most hopeless nature, because hope itself is abandoned during the process of decay. Hope, once abandoned by the intellectual, can never again be found. Intellectual 'disillusionment' is an incurable and always fatal malady. But more on this matter at a future date. L.L. Layton."

Another entry three weeks later: "I have just read the first few pages of this book—very interesting, isn't it, Annalisa? At present I'm reading *Anna Karenina*, an interesting account of a very foolish woman who was to die as a result of her indiscretions in shame and horror—a suicide."

In response to those two entries in Annalisa's baby book, Lisa wrote Laurence a formal letter begging him to let her past "die a natural death." She wrote, "This thing that has been standing between us and keeping us from being happy and our true selves has been bothering me as much as it has you. Please Larry, let's bury it. I am not any more Lisa Philip no matter how you may look at it. I am really and truly your wife and the mother of Tom, Annalisa and Laurence who are our children. Whenever I think of myself, that is whom I am thinking of, and I want you so much to feel the same way. Without you and without the children everything important to me would be lost."

After Laurence received the letter, he and Lisa discussed the problem and he wrote down his thoughts, suggesting obliquely that he might improve "with age."

"Dear Annalisa: Tonight I was talking to your mother about certain rather odd attitudes that I have. For example, I feel very much a father to you children but I have never felt much of a husband! Lisa suggested that it was because of my not remembering my mother as anyone's wife. At Grandpa's house (where we children were reared) Uncle Ara was a brother of Mother's, Grandpa was her father, etc. Your mother may be correct; in any case it is a most unfortunate situation for us, but maybe I'll improve with age? . . . Happiness is all that matters really—Happiness and pleasure are different and are often antagonistic in the narrow view. Pleasure may destroy <u>all hope</u> of happiness; especially has this been proven true in the realm of sex and morals. In any society the moral standards to choose and to live by are those that over the last two thousand years have made the <u>most</u> people <u>happy</u> for the <u>greatest number of years.</u> More on this subject later—I must not leave this issue indefinitely, I shall tell you definitely my ideas on a moral code for all time even though civilization may well have destroyed itself ere you should have read these lines—Love Dad."

That was the last entry dealing with morality. By this time Tom was four, Annalisa two, and Laurence John was sixteen months old. Years later, however, the children recalled that Laurence often joked that Lisa had proposed to him and that she, not he, was the one eager to get married. He told Tom that it might be good if he were to wait until he was thirty-five before marrying. Tom took this to mean that if his father could have done it all over again, he would have married someone else. Yet there was never any mention of divorce; Laurence often spoke about how bad it was for children when their parents divorced. Tom took this to mean that his father was sacrificing his life to keep the marriage going for the benefit of the children.

Lisa believed that Laurence considered his children to be the only ones who really deserved his affection. She was always afraid that he might reveal some embarrassing detail of her past to the children. This led her to fear rejection by both her children and her friends. The couple entertained extensively, and even when Lisa was in her fifties she was always under nervous tension when guests were in the house for fear that Laurence would bring up her past or otherwise insult her in their presence. The fact that it never happened did not reassure her.

During the family's stay in Baltimore, Layton spent most of his time busily conducting his medical research, developing his career while Lisa stayed home with the children. He worked six days a week and far into the night teaching graduate students, studying medicine, and conducting a research program on the healing powers of cortisone. Sunday was a day of rest, spent with the family in worship at the Homewood Friends Quaker Meeting, sometimes picnicking in the country or on the Chesapeake Bay beaches.

There were no children of Laurency's age for him to play with in the neighborhood. Tom and Annalisa considered him too much of a baby, so he was left to his own devices. Only at the Quaker meetings did he find friends to play with, and even then his father observed that "Laurency could not defend himself against aggressive children, and would cry or be moody."

About this time Layton began to be unhappy at Johns Hopkins. Many of the other scientists were prima donnas; Layton considered himself "just another hardworking guy." In 1951, deciding that there was not much of a future for him at Johns Hopkins, he resigned and took his family to Woods Hole, Massachusetts, where for several past summers he had been doing research at the Marine Biological Laboratory. As the season wore on, however, he began to be anxious about where he'd be working the next academic year.

While lecturing in Europe on wound healing, cortisone, and sulfates, Layton had received a letter from the chief of chemical warfare of the U.S. Army, offering him a job as chief of biochemistry in the Chemical Warfare Division at the Dugway Proving Grounds in Tooele, Utah. The offer jolted him into a search of his conscience. The Laytons were a Quaker family, and he had misgivings about being associated with war in any capacity. Also, in the past he had refused all offers of government positions because he looked down on government workers as nonproducers.

However, Layton was promised that at Dugway he could do research on wound healing, and particularly the study of flash burns from atomic devices and from chemical warfare agents. He began to view government research in a different light: He would have an opportunity to do a great deal of medical research, not be required to teach, and he would earn a salary far in excess of what he had been making at Johns Hopkins. He would not be directly involved in research that would hurt anyone. Also, having precipitously quit Johns Hopkins, he badly needed a job. After discussing the matter with Dr. McCollum, he decided to accept the offer.

Lisa was very upset with the decision. As a Quaker, she found warfare of any kind, especially chemical warfare, repugnant. The couple discussed the job offer with friends at the Homewood Friends Meeting House in Baltimore—the one church group where the Layton family as a whole every really felt at home. Lisa loved the friends she had made at the Quaker meeting. In later years she considered it a great tragedy in her life that she had had to leave that warm circle in Baltimore for the cold proving grounds of the salt flats of Utah.

Laurence drove out to Utah by himself in the family Nash. He arrived at the Dugway Proving Grounds on November 5, 1951. Within a month he had purchased a house and some Montgomery Ward furniture. Lisa and the three children arrived in Salt Lake City by Vistadome train just in time for Christmas.

4

A Quaker as Chief of Chemical Warfare

Between the Dugway Mountains and the Stansbury Range, eighty miles southwest of Salt Lake City, lies the Dugway Proving Grounds. Like more than half of Utah, the area in prehistoric times was covered by Lake Bonneville. Now the flat, dry lake bed encompasses thousands of square miles. During World War II, Dugway was the testing site for various types of incendiary weapons. Field and laboratory tests of toxic gases and chemicals were also conducted there.

When Laurence Layton arrived at Dugway in the fall of 1951, his title was Chief, Biochemistry Branch, Chemical Warfare Division. As the chief, he directed the work of eight other chemists and biochemists, a team that performed toxicological and pharmacological investigations of various toxic agents and how these agents affected animals in field tests. The research team also studied the effects of various chemical warfare agents on blood and nerve enzymes. All of their work was classified Secret or Top Secret.

Four months after his arrival, Layton's responsibilities expanded greatly when he was named chief of the entire Chemical Warfare Division. By the spring of 1952 he was directing all the activities of the division, including the research, development, and testing of all chemical items and toxic agents by the division's five branches: analytical chemistry, biological chemistry, organic chemistry, physical chemistry, and the field-test branch. According to an unclassified government report, he "was responsible for the publication of ten classified reports on research aspects of chemical warfare agents, and more than 100 reports on chemical weapons systems."

Layton's personal research consisted of subjecting chickens to thermal burns in order to study the healing process. At the same time, officially, he was devising tests to calibrate the effects of nerve gas. He and his team of researchers would go out to the salt flats, pour a certain amount of nerve gas, or G-agent, on the ground, and let the wind carry it over their monitoring devices and to test animals dispersed at various points in the area.

Later, the team engaged in actual bombings by chemically armed jet planes, and they simulated bombings by throwing the chemical agents from a high tower. Grids were set up around the tower, along with experimental animals and radio-controlled sampling devices to measure and analyze the effectiveness of aerial chemical attack.

What the team discovered was that chemical warfare is the most ineffective type of warfare, because its effectiveness depends so much on which way the wind is blowing. The men joked that their work was essentially meteorological warfare.

Layton found himself split on the moral aspects of his job. On the one hand he was against all warfare; on the other, he considered chemical warfare to be a less inhumane type of weaponry. "You can blow people to bits with bombs, you can shoot them with shells, you can atomize them with atomic bombs, that's all considered moral, but the same people think there's something terrible about poisoning the air and letting people breathe it. Anything having to do with gas warfare, chemical warfare, has this taint of horror on it, even if you only make people vomit. It's all right to kill somebody in war, but it's not all right to make him vomit, or make him silly. Actually, it's one of the most humane types of warfare, if you want to compare it to other types. I'm not apologizing for chemical warfare. I'm just saying that the prejudice against chemical weapons and in favor of conventional and atomic weapons is absurd."

Layton's work caused his family a great deal of anxiety. Lisa kept bringing up the moral implications, and the children asked a lot of questions. Layton answered as best he could, but Lisa kept saying, "I feel it's a terrible mistake, our coming out here with the Army."

Lisa's mother, Anita, who had become a devoted Quaker because of the Friends' stand against war and violence, was even more upset than Lisa. The thought that her son-in-law was the chief of chemical warfare at Dugway—that his job was conducting research on how to kill more people with chemicals—troubled her greatly. Her marriage to Hugo was not going well. The country was in the middle of the Korean War. Anita's letters to the family in Utah reflected what appeared to be an increasingly paranoid outlook. She thought she was being spied upon.

Actually, there was a basis for Anita's fear. For all officials in high and sensitive positions, the FBI conducts a very thorough security investigation, and Dr. Layton was no exception. And because he was a Quaker with foreign in-laws, the investigation included Hugo and Anita Philip. Unknown to Dr. Layton or to themselves, Anita and Hugo were thoroughly investigated, and found to be loyal. However, during their investigation the FBI agents questioned Anita's Quaker friends in New York without informing them of the investigation's purpose. These friends warned Anita that the FBI was asking questions about *her*. Anita was gripped with a horror and fear that only a refugee from Nazi Germany could know. What did they suspect her of doing? What treason would they accuse her of? She wrote to Lisa that she was being followed. Lisa and Laurence, not knowing anything of the routine procedures of the FBI, thought that Anita was becoming paranoid. Anita, her self-confidence destroyed, wrote a farewell message to her loved ones.

On May 10, 1952, just two months after Layton was named chief of the Chemical Warfare Division, Anita Philip committed suicide by jumping from the window of her New York apartment. The suicide note she left behind was written in German, and translates roughly as follows: "My friends, know that I, free and proper, am a good American. But I was a gossip and have been entangled in a network of intrigue. I no longer have the strength to free myself from it. Forget me not my beloved children and family. And you, Hugo, forgive me. Live well. All of you loved mankind so well!" She signed the note with the single letter "A." She was sixty-one years old.

After Anita's death, Laurence decided that a lengthy visit by Hugo might ease his father-in-law's pain. Spending time with his grandchildren might help him get over his wife's suicide. Laurence invited him to Utah, and Hugo accepted.

Grandfather Philip was a difficult guest. As the eldest member of the family, Hugo naturally assumed that he was in charge, even in his son-in-law's home. The fact that he was highly opinionated and extremely demanding made matters worse. One evening at dinner he stated loudly in his thick German accent that the youngest child, Laurency, was always getting the smallest share of everything, whether food or clothes or toys. Laurence strongly disputed this, but Hugo continued the argument for days. Finally Hugo made his point by dumping his own dinner onto six-year-old Laurency's plate. A loud argument flared between the two patriarchs and became so vehement that Lisa took the children out onto the lawn where they listened and waited until quiet was restored. Hugo left the house the next morning and did not return for twenty years.

Layton had not wanted his family to arrive in Utah at Christmastime. He had felt that the winters there were too harsh and so preferred that they arrive in the spring. But Lisa had pleaded with him in a series of letters, and finally he had agreed that they should join him as soon as possible. For one thing, Lisa felt that the children—and five-year-old Laurency in particular—needed their father. The problematical nature of this father-son relationship was first broached by Andrew Simon, Laurency's Sunday-school teacher at the Homewood Friends Meeting in Baltimore.

When Layton had been in Utah for several weeks, Lisa wrote to him about a conversation she had had with Andrew Simon. "Andrew stayed for a while and we had a long talk. He is concerned about Laurency because he loves him. He thinks that when he—Laurency—starts to whine for instance, you should pick him up and love him and never become impatient with him. . . . He said that Laurency needs <u>consistent</u> love from his Daddy. I said that you give him a great deal of love, but Andrew said that, according to his observations, your love is not consistent enough in its manifestations for Laurency's needs. Well, I am just passing this on to you. Andrew brought up the subject and did all the talking. He is such a good man. . . ."

When the rest of the family moved out to Utah, Tom had just turned nine, Annalisa was seven, and Laurency was almost six. Layton had purchased a newly constructed house in Tooele, a small Mormon community about fifty miles from his laboratory at Dugway. When Lisa and the children arrived just before Christmas, Laurence met them at the train depot at Salt Lake City. "It was the most beautiful family you could imagine, just absolutely adorable," he recalled.

After the move to Utah, Laurency seemed even more lonely. He attached himself to any stray mutt that passed through the yard, exhibiting little interest in anyone or anything else. The two older children chipped in their allowances to buy him a puppy. He named the dog Goldie, and the two were inseparable.

Tom and Annalisa, however, had a more sophisticated request: They wanted Mom and Dad to give them a little sister.

Actually, Lisa had already decided that at the age of thirty-seven she wanted to have one more child before it was too late. Deborah June Huddleston Layton was conceived the week of Anita Philip's death, and was born in February of 1953. Tom and Annalisa were just as proud as their parents when Lisa brought home their very own baby sister that cold wintry day. Laurency, however, had a harder time adjusting to the newcomer; he announced that he hated her. He also told his mother that a bone had fallen out of his neck while she was in the hospital. But everyone was too busy with the new baby to pay Laurency much notice.

His father thought it was typical sibling jealousy. Taking the boy aside, Dr. Layton told him how much he loved him. Laurency, however, remained unconvinced. His dog Goldie mirrored the boy's jealousy, demanding attention and whining. Whenever Lisa tried to breast-feed Debbie, the dog had to be locked in a separate room. Several weeks after Debbie was born, Goldie escaped from the house and tried to follow Laurency to his first-grade class. The dog was running after him when it was struck by a car and killed. The boy was stricken with a grief of such duration and intensity that the family wondered if he would ever recover.

Debbie quickly became the family marvel, walking and talking before she was a year old. By the time she was two, she had discovered that she could always get her father's attention by doing something daring. In their yard at that time was a garden swing suspended on steel bars. She quickly learned to swing under her own power to the most extreme height that the swing would go. "She would smile a devilish smile," her father recalls, "and watch me show fear that she would fall. She enjoyed seeing me squirm. She continued in this attitude for the next fifteen years."

Debbie was not one to suffer passively the pangs of inattention. She got what she wanted. She was doted upon. She was everyone's darling. Laurency withdrew further, and began to suffer severe asthma attacks.

After almost two years at Dugway, Layton decided he had had enough of the Proving Grounds. For one thing, he could not bring himself to participate in the cliquish backbiting and politicking that went on there. He felt that the post commander was "the most disgusting and arrogant and profane person I'd ever met." Layton wanted no part of the professional jealousy and paranoia of his colleagues. When a friend from Washington, D.C., visited the Dugway facility, Layton confided his unhappiness, and the friend suggested that he apply for an opening at the Naval Powder Factory (later more accurately named Propellant Facility) at Indian Head, Maryland.

Layton arranged for an interview, put in for some vacation time, took a train to Washington—and was immediately offered a job as associate director of research and development. He didn't feel fully qualified for the position, but working with ballistics, rockets, ICBMs and the new Vanguard satellite program seemed an interesting challenge. Also, he would be leaving behind the unhealthy politicking at Dugway. And his family would be happy with the move back to Maryland.

In a conscious effort to show partiality to Laurency and

strengthen the bond between himself and his youngest son, Layton took Laurency with him in the family's new Cadillac for the drive east. It was planned that when the two got to West Virginia, Laurency would stay with his Aunt Rosemary in Boomer to finish the second grade. The rest of the family would stay behind in Utah until housing was found in the Washington area.

The two Laytons, father and son, took their time driving through the Southwest, learning about geography and stopping at various Indian reservations along the way. Laurency celebrated his eighth birthday on the road in New Mexico. According to his father, it was a delightful trip. Dr. Layton recalls that Laurency "seemed happy to have all of his father's attention, and chattered away much of the time. When we arrived in the East there had been an ice storm from Missouri to New England, so we drove very carefully and I asked Laurency to keep quiet so that I could give all my attention to driving. This request for silence seemed to break his spell of happiness."

When they reached Boomer, West Virginia, Laurency was left in the care of Dr. Layton's sister, Rosemary, while he went on to Indian Head to assume his new duties as the Naval Powder Factory's associate director of research and development. Laurency, now beginning to be called Larry, stayed on for three months with Rosemary and her four boys, one of whom was about the same age as he, and finished the second grade. Laurence and Lisa had decided that this would be the easiest way for Larry to handle the transition from Utah to Maryland. Tom and Annalisa were more resilient and thus better equipped to shuffle through different schools and living quarters; and Debbie, not yet in school, was oblivious to changes of residence.

Rosemary remembers Larry as "a very retiring boy, very quiet but also very loving. He was never demanding and would always go along with what other kids wanted rather than exert his individuality. He got along well in school and mingled easily enough with the other children in the neighborhood, but being the new kid on the block kind of held him back. Friendships didn't come all that easily. Bedtime stories, any kind of stories, were what really captured his imagination. He'd get carried away with fantasies, asking questions, getting excited until you had to remind him that it was a story and not reality."

Compared to Rosemary's own all-American hellions, Larry

was "exceptionally well behaved and well trained. He'd go to bed without an argument while my kids would typically beg and plead to watch just one more TV show. He wasn't a child you had to spank either. My punishment for children was an hour or a half-hour sentence to the corner chair. Larry was so meek about it, so good, he always obeyed the rules."

In April, Larry's grandmother Eva drove him to Washington to rejoin his family.

"Unfortunately, he didn't join," Dr. Layton recalls. Larry was withdrawn. He suffered worse than ever from asthma. The entire household lay awake at night, listening to Larry wheeze in his bedroom.

Dr. Layton had taken psychology courses while at Johns Hopkins, and had been reading about psychotherapy in his spare time. He decided to try his knowledge on his son. Appreciating that Laurency had a great deal of faith in his father, he hoped to cure his asthma with the power of suggestion.

Sitting on the edge of the bed, Dr. Layton took the boy on his lap and said, "Dad thinks that he can help your breathing trouble." Dr. Layton described to Larry the time that he had been left in his playpen and "was so good that Mama became busy with his wild brother and sister and forgot he was there, and then it was hard for him to breathe." He connected himself with the problem. "I suggested that Daddy had given him attention when he couldn't breathe, and that might be related to what was happening at that moment. I told him that I could cure his asthma if he would help me. I stroked his head and back and suggested that this was helping the asthma disappear—that *we* were doing this together and that we could always do it, even when he was by himself. His asthma ceased that night and never returned during the remainder of his childhood and, so far as I know, even into his adult life."

It is Dr. Layton's belief that this incident profoundly affected their relationship. To Larry he, the father, had become "bigger than life."

But Dr. Layton's healing powers were not much help with Larry's problem as the low kid on the sibling totem pole. When his older brother Tom entered junior high school, he couldn't be bothered with a baby brother in the third grade. Larry wasn't especially welcome around Tom's group of prepubescent friends.

The older Layton children were fiercely competitive to stay

on top both academically and socially. At age eleven, Annalisa showed strength in both fields. She was not above cruelly putting down another child to build herself up. "We children were unforgiving of people's differences," Annalisa recalls. "It is really painful now to think of how mean I was to some kids. I remember once even joking about a girl whose sister had died of leukemia. I don't remember any lectures from my parents about being nice to the less fortunate, but maybe they didn't know how nasty we were."

This attitude extended to her brother, as illustrated in Annalisa's crayon interpretation of their roles circa 1954: Larry is lying prostrate while Annalisa triumphantly stands with both feet planted firmly on top of him. Evidence of her successful attempts to manipulate Larry include a signed document in which he pledged, "On my honor, I sware not to ask Mama if I can use the suit case Annalisa wants to use." In exchange, Annalisa promised that she would "not try to draw any of Laurence's friends away from him."

Larry's asthma may have gone away, but he was having a lot of trouble in school. He seemed to have a learning disability, which his father believed to be the result of "internalized feelings of inadequacy or a problem aggravated by the move from Utah to West Virginia to Maryland all in the same school year." Larry was having difficulty identifying the simplest words. At about that time, Lisa read the best-seller *Why Johnny Can't Read,* and she set to work correcting what she identified to be dyslexia, as well as a lack of attention, in her youngest son. Armed with all the recommended workbooks, she taught Larry the phonetic system of reading.

Earlier, when the family had arrived in Utah in the middle of the school year, they had discovered that Tom was not as well prepared as the other fourth-graders and had some catching up to do. His father had tried to tutor him in mathematics, but Dr. Layton had not been the most patient of teachers, and was quickly annoyed by Tom's inability to follow his instructions. "The more frustrated and annoyed Dad got," says Tom, "the more uptight and blundering I became." Dr. Layton decided that Tom should be held back a grade.

Lisa tried to avoid these mistakes with Larry. She rewarded him with treats for good performance. He began to sound out words that he had never heard before, and his spirits rose along with his self-esteem. By the beginning of the school year he was reading third-grade material with ease. All the same, as with Tom in Utah, it was decided to hold Larry back a grade.

Friends of the Laytons would often mention, in a kind sort of way, that Larry did not seem quite normal. "Your son Larry seems to be carrying on a silent mental conversation with himself," a colleague of Dr. Layton's observed after dinner one evening. "I was talking with the children, and Larry would enter in as if he were in the middle of his own unspoken thoughts. He seems partially aware of the conversation going on around him but is carrying on an internal conversation only somewhat related. He will even begin to speak in the middle of these mental sentences."

Dr. Layton noticed that "this was actually true. Larry seemed to confuse fantasy with reality as if he were dreaming while awake." The father observed that his son's tendency to dreaminess continued into adulthood. Dr. Layton never spanked Larry "because I knew he couldn't take it." Larry did not fight back when challenged, and he never instigated trouble. He would come home and break into tears, but rarely had anything to say. Misfortunes and disappointments were swallowed without comment. A naturally stern expression masked his timorousness and sense of inferiority.

When confronted with unavoidable aggression, however, Larry proved on at least one occasion that he could handle it in a firm, albeit passive, fashion. His father later described it as "a strange performance." The incident took place when Larry was eleven years old. A neighborhood bully repeatedly lunged at Larry, who stood calmly with his fists balled up and his arms outstretched. Each time the assailant charged, he ran into Larry's unmoving but stiffly outstretched arms, knocking himself down. For Larry's part, he was acting nonviolently.

Even at that young age, the pacifism that would develop for Larry into deep political and philosophical convictions was taking root. As soon as he learned to read in the third grade, he became passionately interested in the news, and especially in politics and race relations.

In 1957, Dr. Layton accepted a position as research scientist at the U.S. Department of Agriculture's Western Regional Research Laboratory near Berkeley, California. Lisa was greatly relieved; they would finally leave warfare behind them. The children too were enthusiastic—not because of the warfare issue, but because California sounded like utopia.

With the family preparing to move once again, Laurence and Lisa had at last attained a balance of sorts in their own relationship: As far as their marriage was concerned, they lived for their children. And Lisa had apparently accepted her husband's moral code, for herself as well as for her children. She was a quiet, competent, and dutiful wife.

The Laytons moved west in July of 1957.

5

Coming of Age
in the Sixties

During the late 1950s, the San Francisco Bay Area was in the middle of a population explosion. Housing tracts and subdivisions couldn't be fabricated fast enough. Thanks to the Korean War baby boom and the G.I. Bill, instant communities were dividing and subdividing like amoebas in a pond of green algae.

For lack of time to find anything better, the Laytons first moved to El Sobrante, a lower-middle-class working community. On any given weekend the place looked like a truckers' convention. The local school district was broke, and the kids attended half-sessions. Annalisa, now thirteen, spent an inordinate amount of time in the front yard trying to attract the attention of the next door truck driver's son.

"A lot of the parent-teenager conflicts began here," Annalisa recalls. "Dad was always obsessed with virginity, even for his sons. He wanted everything I did and everything I wore to be above reproach. He controlled who I associated with so I wouldn't be exposed to the wrong things. He often told me how it would destroy my life if I had any serious relations with anyone before marriage.

"I heard about a girl on the next block getting pregnant in high school. I asked Mom why she would want to have a baby while she was so young. I was astounded when Mom told me sex was a drive that sometimes got out of control. I had always thought the sole purpose of sex was to have children and that my parents had only done it four times.

"Straight skirts with a kick pleat were the fashionable thing to wear in the eighth grade. Dad absolutely forbade me to have one because my hips were too broad. I cried and begged for one but he held tight. He insisted that I dress to look good to him and not to fit the latest style."

Dr. Layton knew that this was not the neighborhood or the class of people he wanted for his children. Within a year, the family moved to the Berkeley hills, to a place Layton believed would provide the proper atmosphere for his intellectual dynasty. Their three-story, twenty-five-room house was surrounded by the homes of university professors, three Nobel laureates, the retired Admiral Chester Nimitz, and other similarly successful Berkeley intelligentsia. The new home on San Luis Road came complete with a social community—a circle of homes around a woodsy private park with swimming pool, tennis court, and picnic tables where the Laytons could congregate with their neighbors. It was a visible sign, at least to Dr. Layton, that they had arrived socially. "It was millionaires' row, and we were the only nonmillionaires on it." The country boy from Boomer had made good. Or had he?

Dr. Layton was well aware that the position of research scientist with the Department of Agriculture could, in some ways, be considered several steps down from associate director of research and development with the Navy, but he had wanted to get away from the classified, secret world of the military. He wanted to conduct medical research and to publish his results. He also wanted to be closer to the more intellectually prestigious community of the University of California, where the research was pure and scientists were recognized for their accomplishments. But, as he often told his son Tom, university politics weighed heavily in the awarding of Nobel Prizes, for he considered himself the intellectual equal of most winners of Nobel Prizes in medicine and physics.

For the first year, Dr. Layton's assignment was little more than that of a flunky. "Any technician could have done what the Department of Agriculture set me to work doing. I spent an awful lot of time running taste-test panels to see if atomic irradiation affected the taste of cooked chicken meat. After that we started busily measuring the degree of tension needed to pluck the feathers from a dead chicken."

Because his talents weren't being used to their fullest, Dr. Layton became frustrated and mired in self-pity. The children were growing up, spending more time with their friends, and he took this as a personal affront, a threat to the unity of his family. The Laytons were a nuclear family, but now everyone was spinning out into separate orbits. Dr. Layton had always emphasized the fact that the family was the all-important social unit, and now he lashed out angrily at any hint to the contrary. "Any rejection of the family was considered a personal rejection of Dad," says Tom. "'You children don't care about the family' was a familiar and painful litany of his. I remember trying to prove that I really cared about the family, that I did spend a lot of time at home, but all the other kids were going to see Elvis in *Jailhouse Rock* so please, couldn't I go too?"

This conflict led to many loud confrontations, with Dr. Layton on one occasion threatening to move out and leave the family to their own devices.

Shortly before the Laytons' arrival in Berkeley, Annalisa joined a church young people's group that supplied her with a ready assemblage of giggling teenage girl friends. The social whirl that kept her away from home finally pushed her father too far when she asked permission to attend one slumber party too many. He exploded, told Annalisa she had no interest in anyone but herself, that his wife, Lisa, was supporting her in this antifamily behavior by allowing their daughter to be away so much, and as a result the family was being torn apart. Since no one else seemed to care or take notice, he asked, why should he fight a losing battle against a household of self-centered people? If there was to be no family life, he would rent a room near his lab and live by himself.

The kids were thrown into an emotional hurricane. Tom recalls "being frantic that Dad thought that I did not love him. I was really afraid that he would move out. I wanted to reassure him that I did love the family, but in this case as with future

incidents, no amount of assurance could convince Dad that his
children loved him. Dad wanted to know that he was loved
more than our friends, as much as Mother, and for himself,
not just because he was a paycheck.

"Dad also started talking seriously about his own death
around this time, by natural causes or suicide," Annalisa recalls. "He used to assure me that he would die of a heart attack
before I was twenty years old. This was in 1964. It was frightening. I would cry to myself in bed at night. Other times he
would threaten to take an overdose of pills. One year we went
on vacation to Oregon. Mom didn't come because she was
working. I shared a motel room with Debbie, and Dad shared
one with Larry. At breakfast one morning, he told me that he
had had a heart attack the previous night, but that Larry had
helped him and now he was okay. I felt so sorry for Larry for
having to go through that. It is still very traumatic for me every
time Dad clutches his heart, which is often."

Teenagers of the late 1950s were like some foreign tribe, feared
and misunderstood by the best of parents. The "evil" influences
of popular culture and permissive parenting threatened to taint
the rarefied moral cloud that enveloped the Layton children.

"We were held to different standards than the other kids.
We Laytons were part of an intellectual and moral elite," says
Tom. "After all, we were Baltimore Quakers and thus some
kind of higher life form. From our upbringing we had learned
morality and ethical behavior. We learned to abhor segregation,
inequality, and racism. Yet early on, we knew that we were
better than other people, the people who did things that Dad
didn't approve of and whom he considered to be 'trash.' During
the fifties, trash wore duck-tailed haircuts, blue jeans, and blue
suede shoes. Trash were overly interested in automobiles and
sports, attended too many movies, and suffered brain damage
from watching television and listening to popular music. In
grammar school we developed a love of good books, but would
still try to get ourselves invited to watch 'I Love Lucy,' 'My
Little Margie,' and 'You Asked for It' on the neighbor's television set. I always felt a little guilty afterwards because it was
not an intellectual activity and probably trashy."

The fact that the "boob tube" in their own home was closely

monitored by Lisa set the Laytons apart from the other kids. Layton minds weren't wasted trying to guess the answer to the "$64,000 Question"; instead they were taught the beauty of asking questions themselves. To this day, Annalisa feels that there is something "degenerate" about planting oneself in front of the TV for the evening.

Tom recalls that, "By 1960 Dad and I were reading books like Freud's *Moses and Monotheism*. We would argue over the significance of the Eighteenth Dynasty of Egypt in the beginnings of Hebrew monotheism. We read Tacitus' the *Agricola* and the *Germania,* not to mention Herodotus and Flavius Josephus." Such intellectual exercises more than made up for Tom's interest in rebuilding Model A Fords in the family driveway. He credits them with "preadapting me to a career as an anthropological archaeologist, as opposed to a life in the car-repair business."

In line with Dr. Layton's theories about intelligent rather than intellectual women, however, the girls were not encouraged along such scholarly lines.

"When we were growing up," says Annalisa, "there were always things I wanted to do. I would ask Mom for permission and she would always say it was up to Dad. When he said 'No,' that was the final answer. I felt like there was no democracy. Dad ruled. I see even more clearly now with my own children that there are differing opinions on matters and one parent shouldn't have absolute rule. However, Mom told me that she felt it very important for the husband of a household to be a strong person and the policymaker.

"The whole matter of absolute rule remained a problem in our family. Dad did not have any inclination to be democratic. He laid down the rules."

By 1958, civilization—at least in the casual atmosphere of California—might well have looked in a state of ruin to Dr. Layton, the puritan patriarch. He had always felt that nothing was too good for his children; now nothing was good enough for them. In 1960, when gangs of juvenile delinquents spent boulevard nights in the lowlands of Berkeley, Dr. Layton pulled his kids out of the Quaker church socials because even the Quaker youth were "too liberated to suit me. I saw trashy kids, atrociously costumed and displaying poor manners. I thought my children were too young to participate in this sensual dancing, those kinds of goings-on." The family briefly joined the Unitarians, a group considered to be "more intellectual—but they turned out to be too sexually oriented as well." Tom and Annalisa were allowed to settle at last with the Congregational Church youth group, which appeared to be closely supervised.

For the most part, Annalisa and Tom upheld the "moral code for all time" that their father had inscribed to them in their baby books. It wasn't until Larry and Debbie joined the social revolution of the 1960s that his rules and attitudes were openly defied.

As Annalisa recalls, "We upheld the 'moral code' because those who finished high school before 1963 were on the tail end of a whole generation who at least paid lip service to such things. Larry and those finishing high school in 1964 were the forefront of an entirely new generation.

"Whereas for Tom and me, drugs and premarital sex were frowned upon by peers, the teens of Larry's age were almost required to experiment in both, and peer pressure is probably the strongest pressure of all."

A big change in Debbie's six-year-old life came with the move to Berkeley. She began attending kindergarten at Cragmont Elementary School, three blocks from home. Once Debbie was safely tucked away for a full day of school in the first grade, Lisa reluctantly took a job outside the home—her first since Tom's birth. Lisa was doctrinaire about very few things, but she had always considered it essential that a parent be there when the children arrived home from school. She didn't like the idea of her children being greeted by an empty house; and she had misgivings about the boredom and possibilities for mischief that would present themselves. In Berkeley, it was hard to break that tradition of being there when her children got home from school, but the extra paycheck would help toward sending them to college. Later, Lisa was to blame her afternoon absence from home for Debbie's personal problems.

Rather than spend an hour alone after school in that big house waiting for her mother to get back from her part-time job, Debbie sought the company of the elderly ladies she passed

on the way home from Cragmont School. She established a
circle of such friends, and Lisa would get calls from concerned
neighbors asking if Debbie should be kept home from school
for a day. She could often be seen walking hand in hand with
Admiral Nimitz as he took his afternoon stroll through the
neighborhood.

Life for Debbie was the most idyllic it would ever be. In
the evenings she would climb onto her father's lap while he
sat in his rocking chair, and together they would read poetry.
"He loved to hear me read aloud to him, and it helped me to
pronounce words and read more."

When it came time for Debbie to go to bed, Tom and Larry
would begin "the big count." This was the signal to run upstairs
and hide. After they reached the count of ten, they would make
ghost and witch sounds and go looking for Debbie. After they
had found her, Lisa would pray with her before kissing her
good night.

Tom and Annalisa were always available to take up any
slack in her parents' attention. Debbie was their mascot, their
pet, and was included in activities with their teenage friends,
all of whom would join in the praise of any new achievement.
A properly tied shoelace, a few lines of a nursery rhyme were
greeted with a round of compliments.

Annalisa taught her how to swim. She would jump off the
pool steps and swim out to her older sister. Each time, Annalisa
would move a little farther away. When she was almost to the
other side of the pool, Debbie would swim well over halfway
across, yell out "I can't make it," and turn around and swim
all the way back to the steps.

Debbie fondly remembers Tom and Larry baby-sitting for
her. "The second my parents would leave, they would start
whispering. They'd pretend they were monsters and chase me
up to my room. Before I could get the chain on the door to
keep them out, they'd push it open and grab me. I would yell
and giggle: it was great. After we all calmed down, they'd read
a story to me, or I'd read one to them, and off to sleep I'd
go."

Tom had been tinkering with Model A Fords since he was
thirteen. Once he received his California driver's license he

began to work on them in earnest. It was an activity taken up with capitalistic gusto—buying, rebuilding, trading, and selling Model A's. The Laytons' driveway was usually filled with greasy, albeit well-behaved, young car fanatics. That they were eligible males added immeasurably to Annalisa's popularity with other girls in the neighborhood.

Larry, who had long been a "wimp" in Tom's eyes, had now reached pubescence himself, and with it his brother's judgment of him softened. As a half-a-wimp he could hang out with the older guys on a limited basis. Tom taught him the art of bartering, usually to his own advantage.

At Garfield Junior High School, Larry began to develop his first real friendships outside the family. His best friend, Robert, was the son of a professor at U.C. Berkeley. As Dr. Layton noted with approval, the two boys would spend hours together arguing over ideas, telling jokes, and laughing.

In May of 1962, the graduating class of Garfield Junior High School went on a picnic across the bay in Marin County. Five or six of the boys, including Larry and his friend Bob, took turns to see who could stay underwater the longest in the park swimming pool. Bob never came up.

Larry returned home that afternoon, shocked silent. "Bob got drowned" was all the information he'd volunteer. Dr. Layton had to pry the full story from him. Bob had grabbed onto a grate at the bottom of the swimming pool to ensure his winning. He had passed out for lack of oxygen, and water had filled his lungs. By the time anyone realized that something was wrong, it was too late.

Laurence Layton helped his son compose a tribute to Bob that was sent to the boy's family, but the shock of his friend's death was so great that Larry never quite recovered. Dr. Layton believes that his son did not form another close friendship, "perhaps not even with his first or second wife."

By the fall of 1962, Tom and Annalisa were both attending the University of California at Davis. "It was great being away from parents," recalls Annalisa. "Davis might have been a thousand miles from Berkeley for the number of times we came home to visit." Their absence marked a turning point downward in Debbie's life, but for Larry it was a chance to get out of the shadow of his two older siblings and develop on his own. He was especially relieved to be out of direct competition with

Tom, who, he felt, always did everything better than he could.

Debbie compensated for the loss of attention by seeking it in more aggressive ways. In school, she went from teacher's pet to teacher's torment, and in play with other children she began manufacturing tall tales to impress them. "I got the reputation of being a liar. One of the neighbor girls dubbed me 'Liar Layton.' I got so mad, I threw a handful of gravel at her, but I didn't stop making up stories. Later I began to lie to my parents, and worst of all, I began believing my lies. 'The bus was late, Mom, so I went over to so-and-so's to make cookies,' and I'd get carried away with the details of the story, and she'd cut me off in mid-sentence and say, 'Now Debbie, stop it.' I'd be infuriated because she didn't believe me." As for Dad, he couldn't believe that any of his children would deliberately lie.

Larry was no substitute for the gregarious, outgoing, and affectionate Tom and Annalisa. Debbie would stand, giggling, at Larry's bedroom door while he tried to do his homework. He'd do the old count to ten and tolerantly chase her down the hall before closing his door for the rest of the evening.

Larry entered Berkeley High School in the fall of 1962, and found more important things to do than entertain a ten-year-old sister. He joined the Young Democrats, eventually becoming president of his school's chapter. This recognition of his long-developing social conscience appeared to satisfy his loner's need for close personal ties. His circle of acquaintances, both male and female, grew. He had several crushes and one serious girl friend, a political activist like himself. He was shy with women, but they were attracted to his finely chiseled features, set in a beetle-browed, tough-guy appearance that concealed, they suspected, a tenderness within. It made him seem taller than five-foot-seven. He worked on his machismo by taking up *savate,* the French art of foot-fighting, even participating in competitive meets. *Savate* seemed to provide a pressure valve for the emotions bubbling inside. He might be calmly conversing with someone when suddenly, for no apparent reason, he would kick out at the wall.

During the first two years of high school, Larry often expressed a hope to run for public office someday. His heroes were Franklin Delano Roosevelt and Adlai Stevenson, great men who made a difference in the world. But with the assassination of President Kennedy and the harsh events that followed, he lost his faith in the system, his hope that through politics he might be able to right the world's wrongs. Yet he never lost the feeling that it was up to him to do something about the pain and injustice that he saw all around him.

Larry graduated midyear from Berkeley High School, in January of 1965. He planned to enter Davis as a sociology major that spring. During the break between schools, his father noticed that he seemed even more withdrawn than usual, and he confronted him about it one evening. "I don't understand your lack of enthusiasm about going off to school; nor do I understand your unwillingness to spend time in the company of your family during your last days living at home."

There was a long silence, finally broken by Larry's admission that "I have been in intense pain for years, and now my hemorrhoids are so bad that I can't pass anything but blood. I can't stand it anymore."

Dr. Layton lost no time. Larry was on the operating table the next day. The father felt that during this hospital stay the bonds between them were strengthened. Father and son enjoyed private conversations, and Laurence Layton "realized again our close dependency upon each other," particularly when Larry nearly died twice due to the carelessness of the medical staff. The resident intern mistook dextrin for dextrose in Larry's intravenous rig. The mistake was quickly discovered and corrected by Dr. Layton as his son began to black out from hypersensitivity to the blood extender commonly used in transfusions. Next, Larry began to hemorrhage and was transferred to another hospital "to save his life." The excitement proved to be too much for the father. He fainted, and it was decided that he should be put to bed for heart monitoring. Dr. Layton hoped that this loss of control would convince Larry of his father's true concern and love for him.

Larry started school that January at Davis, where Tom was now a senior and Annalisa a junior. Their father had hoped that the three, together on the same campus, would form close ties; but as in their high school days, Annalisa and Tom remained close, even dating each other's roommates, while Larry was by himself.

At spring break, Larry came home for the week. He discussed some of his classes, including his favorite, psychology. It had opened a whole new world for him, and he had become friendly with his professor. "I learned in the course, Dad, that it's very natural for sons to hate their fathers," he announced.

"It can happen," acknowledged Dr. Layton, "but it doesn't necessarily have to happen. At least it never happened to me, and seems not to have happened with my family."

"You know, Dad," Larry continued, "you are a frightening old man. I must always be careful that you don't cut off support and make me drop out of college."

Dr. Layton thought at first that his son was joking. Then it sank in. He realized that Larry feared him, and that he wasn't secure in feeling loved and supported by his father. Dr. Layton tried to refute the point, to show that Larry simply didn't have any instances to support such fears. However, in the father's opinion, communication between the two suffered significantly from that day forward.

Larry, for his part, admired his father and at the same time feared him. And he felt sorry for him. He recognized that his father had problems of his own, problems that prevented him from accepting his son as he was. Larry also felt that he was a great disappointment to his father because he had no aptitude for science.

Laurence Layton had always tried to show his love for each of his children, verbally and in every other way. He felt now that he'd worn his heart on his sleeve, literally fighting at times to show his love, only to meet with rejection. To make matters worse, the children seemed to have an unspoken love for their mother, a love she had never overtly sought. Was it because he had had to make the unpopular decisions over the years, to say "no" when less concerned parents were saying "yes"—or even worse, "I don't care"? Laurence Layton cared more about his children than any other father he knew, and yet he could not fathom what was happening to his family. Annalisa recalls, "Whenever Mom reminded me of Dad's love, it was like a burden on me, something I was expected to live up to."

With Larry away at college, Debbie considered herself an only child, alone in that cavernous house with only her parents for company. Her teacher reported disciplinary problems, and her grades in her first year at Garfield Junior High School were disappointing. Her seventh-grade report card showed a C average, and cited poor attitude, poorly prepared homework assignments, poor test scores, poor study habits, and poor class participation.

Actually, Debbie had given up on school for the most part,

had lost interest in tests and learning several years before. When tested in the fifth grade, her I.Q. had registered at the dullard level, somewhere below 100. Her parents had been shocked, and refused to believe that their daughter was anything less than very bright. She was retested. The second results weren't much better, but her score did register slightly higher and set her parents' minds somewhat at ease.

Debbie felt unwilling and unable to maintain the level of her three studious siblings. Tom, Annalisa, and Larry had all been meticulous about their schoolwork. Debbie found her friends far more interesting. Lisa continued to believe that Debbie's problems were caused by her not being home when Debbie returned from school each afternoon.

Her parents' concern about her grades added to Debbie's own fears, some from outside the home, that she was less than perfect. She worried that she might be what her father referred to as "trash."

A certain neighborhood family was considered trash by Debbie's father. They had money enough to live in a large house near San Luis Road, but near the wrong kind of money. They owned a nightclub in San Francisco, where women dressed in brief costumes and danced to "wild" music. These neighbors were suspect in the moral eyes of the Laytons, and Dr. Layton decreed their children unfit playmates for Deborah.

The Laytons had always been open about the facts of life with their own children. Reproduction had been scientifically explained to them from the time they were old enough to ask. The man put the seed in the woman's abdomen, and there it grew. "How it got there was left rather vague," Debbie recalls.

One day Debbie explained this matter to the neighbor's children. The next day the mother appeared in Debbie's third-grade class, identified herself as a "friend of the family," and demanded to see Debbie privately. The two were left alone, and the mother gave little Deborah a tongue-lashing that, to this day, Debbie finds difficult to talk about. "She claimed that I was a bad influence on her children, telling them the dirty facts of life, and that I was never to play with them again." School officials apologized to Lisa, but the incident left the little angel of the Layton household feeling that she possessed "a filthy mind" and was, indeed, trashy herself. Soon, at the instigation of the angry mother, there were other incidents of parents in the neighborhood slighting Debbie. She never reported any of them to her parents.

In the sixth grade, much to her mortification, Debbie began to develop physically. "I would wear the tightest T-shirts to bind my chest in," she recalls. In seventh grade she began to menstruate. Animated educational films in her hygiene class had primed her on what to expect—"don't take a shower in ice cubes, don't take a bath in boiling water"—but didn't help her emotionally. "I didn't tell my mother for four months. I felt guilty and scared. I was afraid of upsetting her, that I was growing up. I wouldn't be the perfect little girl ever again."

It was also in the seventh grade, at Garfield Junior High School, that Debbie took her first drink. She discovered that getting high that way, escaping reality, was something she liked just fine.

The Berkeley school system had three junior high schools. One was mostly black and another was mixed, but Garfield was mostly white. That is, it was until 1965, when federal regulations required desegregation. That year, Debbie's first in the school, black students were bused in. It was the year of the march on Selma and the riots in Watts. "There were racial tensions, some violence. The safest place was in the middle. I had friends on both sides."

Debbie's parents didn't like the look of things. Her grades were miserable, her attendance record poor, and she was beginning to cut classes. They equated bad grades with bad company. It was decided that in order for her to meet the family's standards—those easily met by Tom and Annalisa—she should be sent to a private school. In the eighth grade, she was accepted at a stringently traditional private school in Berkeley.

"Annalisa," she wrote to her sister, who was traveling in Europe before her first post-college job, "what am I to do? No child has parents like me, and they all think Ma and Pa are unfair. It's just awful. How do they expect me to hang on to standards no other kids have? Dad this summer told me to my face that they wished they never had me because I didn't pass their qualifications. Sometimes I hate both Mom and Dad." She begged Annalisa to get an apartment when she returned so that she could come live with her. "I'll help cook, clean house, do my share, and I'll try to help pay for the apartment."

The cloistered atmosphere of her new school was depressing

for Debbie after the excitement of public junior high. The brown-shingled, two-story house, converted into a school back in the 1920s, was located on a secluded residential street near the university campus. Academic standards were high, and the imported British headmistress maintained order of the stiffest kind. Berkeley kids with real prestige went to Anna Head School or to one of the Catholic schools. Debbie's new school, however, took kids with discipline problems, and operated on the theory that hard, boring schoolwork would keep the students in line.

Although banned in public school, the Lord's Prayer was recited every morning in the hallway that served as a chapel, with the headmistress checking that young ladies' skirts reached the floorboards while they knelt in prayer. She would scratch their legs to check for nylons. Any footwear except short socks and oxfords was forbidden: so was makeup. Sexual education and social lives were left up to the parents. The emphasis here was college prep, with sights set on the Ivy League schools of the East.

A schoolmate of Debbie's categorized the students who attended this school as: (1) antisocial bookworm types; (2) children with health problems; (3) kids (especially boys) on the brink of getting in trouble with the law; and (4) children who had attended private schools all their lives and were so institutionalized that they would have been ridiculed in a public school. One student was a kleptomaniac. Another stuttered badly and enjoyed torturing his pet bat; he also dreamed of letting all the inmates out of the insane asylums.

The Laytons expected the children Debbie met here to be of the highest intellectual order. Not surprisingly, she had trouble adjusting. She did, however, make one fast friend, Arlene Blake. Arlene had the right pedigree. Her father was a historian and professor at the university; her mother was a physician. The Laytons could approve.

Debbie's grades still didn't improve, although her behavior during school did. In an eighth-grade class of ten students, it was difficult to get away with much. Arlene felt that Debbie's inability to get any homework done or to study for tests was due to the fact that "she was upset at home, and she was upset with herself. It was next to impossible for her to think about anything else."

Other friends of Debbie's worried about her relationship

with her parents. One of them, Diane Saksa, contrasts Debbie's situation then with her own. "I was timid about defying my parents," she says, "and underneath my Mom's difficulty in allowing me to make my own mistakes, I was secure in knowing my parents loved me. That was the difference. Debbie loved her parents so much, but she was never sure they loved her because of their actions. Debbie used to pray a lot, and I mean a lot.

"Sometimes, she prayed before bed in a way that was a conversation. She did it in total seriousness, like it was comfortable for her to do so. She prayed that her parents would understand her, that she could measure up to their standards, that they would trust her, and that she would get good grades. She believed that if she prayed hard enough and believed enough, it would have to come true.

"She felt God knew her intimately and could understand her motives. It was all in her prayers, and in this belief was also the innocent notion that if God was good, He could help her, and therefore everyone was basically good. She believed that the worst characters had redeeming qualities because God governed what people did, just as she felt He was instrumental in guiding her to a better life. Debbie always looked for the good in people."

Diane observed that Debbie's fears revolved around Dr. Layton. Permission to do anything outside the house came from the father. Diane remembers times when Lisa Layton would grant her daughter permission to do something, only to have that permission revoked after a telephone conversation with Dr. Layton. All rights and permissions were dispensed by the father.

"When Dr. Layton came in for dinner," Diane recalls, "Mrs. Layton didn't really say much. He was the center of the family, and when he was present, everything revolved around him. Mrs. Layton didn't express opinions. With her soft voice and German accent, she was always polite, but quiet and unassertive."

Diane could sympathize with Debbie because her own mother, like Lisa Layton, was older than the mothers of most of their friends. The wrenching changes that were taking place so quickly in American society during the 1960s, particularly in Berkeley, were very frightening to older parents. Such mothers, who were not involved in clubs or civic or social activities, either did not understand or didn't want to understand what their children were going through.

Lisa had a private fear, as well. She feared that Debbie's rebellious nature mirrored her own, which she had repressed so long ago; and that she was somehow responsible for Debbie's transgressions—and for her pain.

During this time, Debbie retained a deep respect for her father, "like he was a god," another friend recalls. When Dr. Layton spoke, it was frequently in such a tone of voice that even a simple question sounded like a demand. Only once did her father hit her, but thereafter she was always afraid that he'd hit her again. Although he never did, just the thought was scary enough. Debbie even felt guilty about developing large breasts. She thought she was going to contract breast cancer.

Several times she packed her suitcases with the thought of running away. But there was no place to go. Making decisions was difficult because all her life her parents, especially her father, had made them for her, and appeared ready to continue to do so even as she approached adulthood.

It was after school and on weekends that these frustrations were vented. Arlene's house in Point Richmond was considered an acceptable destination, and visiting there was often used as an excuse for inexcusable activities. Arlene and her brother, Peter, also a student at the school, were definitely not innocent young children. Just over the hill from their upper-class home was a community of tough young kids whose parents worked at the Standard Oil refinery. These were kids with whom they could smoke pot, drink wine, and take drugs—speed, Seconal, whatever—after a day in the cloistered atmosphere of private academia.

Arlene's parents were much more permissive than the Laytons. They saw that their children were on drugs, and they didn't let it bother them. Peter recalls passing out once at the dinner table from having taken too many reds (Red Devils, another name for Seconal). His mother, a physician, "just leaned over and patted me on the back, and asked me how many had I taken this time." Dr. Layton, on the other hand, simply refused to let the thought that any of his children might be on drugs, be members of the "drug culture," enter his mind. On one occasion he came to pick Debbie up at Arlene's house while she was "rather loaded" on reds. "I just told him that I was really tired, that was all. He believed me."

Arlene and Debbie commiserated together over their problem parents—Arlene's lacking in control, Debbie's unbending in their demand for total control. Debbie's friends thought that her parents were exceptionally strict and that her father seemed to be around only when it came time to lay down the law. Lisa and Debbie shared a closeness, however. They would go for hikes together, take weekend trips, talk with each other.

The parental pressures brought to bear in demands for exemplary grades and model behavior made Debbie feel unworthy, and by extension unwanted. Negotiations in the battle continued to break down, to the point that Debbie felt the only way to get a response from Dad, something that would, however indirectly, reassure her that she indeed did belong to him, was to make him angry.

A few times, hanging out at the Point with her friends, Debbie let her feelings about her parents spill out uncontrollably. One night remains vivid in Arlene Blake's memory. "We all smoked pot, we all took speed. Debbie had taken 'Christmas trees,' a pill much stronger than Bennies. She had planned on spending the night, but for some reason the story had changed and she had to go home after all. She was too high to face her folks when the time came for her to go. She freaked out and ended up running from one end of the school yard near our house to the other. For three hours this went on, her panicking that she was too loaded to make it home on time, able only to run in circles. She'd sing, then she'd go into a crying jag over her parents, then she'd remember that she had to go home and plead hysterically, 'I've got to go home, I've got to go home, what am I going to tell my parents?' I chased after her all night, worried that she might collapse from the combination of speed and exertion."

Debbie hated the restrictions of private school and begged her parents to let her go back to public high school. She promised to mix with the right kids, not to go back to the old crowd and the old ways. Of course, they weren't aware of just how bad her ways had gotten. They wanted to be able to trust their Deborah.

In the fall of 1967, Debbie got her way—she entered ninth grade at Berkeley High School's West Campus. The school had previously been all black; it had now become fully integrated and was the only public-school ninth grade in the district. The neighborhood was low-rent, on the freeway side of the railroad tracks. The school faced onto University Avenue, with its liquor stores, gas stations, and hamburger hangouts. It was close enough to the university campus to be influenced by political activists there, students who were involved in the last days of the Free Speech Movement and the beginnings of the Vietnam War protest. It was also close enough to Telegraph Avenue to get the drift of the street scene and its attendant drug culture.

For a child in need of attention, it was not a good place to be. Debbie had moved from a private school class of ten students to a public school grade with more than a thousand. The school was crowded with several hundred students over capacity. The campus was "open," providing drug dealers easy access to a lucrative market. Kids could come and go as they pleased; they could take "lunch" in the neighborhood, or the neighborhood could bring "lunch" to them.

Debbie spent her lunch money, her weekly allowance, and her baby-sitting income on experimenting with highs until she found the one she liked best. Sniffing glue made her dizzy and made her ears ring. Marijuana made her hungry, an undesirable side effect given her constant struggle against an expanding waistline. Speed helped curb her appetite, but the rush could get crazy and the comedown was depressing. Chugging Red Mountain burgundy brought on the Technicolor yawns. Red Devils were just right. They were like getting drunk without getting sick. They became her passion.

"I loved getting stoned, not being aware. I loved having everything subdued. And I think one of the biggest things was that I got attention that way."

Once high, students could easily disappear into the surrounding landscape. Debbie would take reds nearly every day before homeroom period—sometimes as many as seven or eight—check into that one class, then take off, mentally and physically, for the rest of the day. If she chose to go home, she could disappear into her room, easily avoiding her parents' scrutiny.

"People at school would come to me and say, 'Oh, Debbie, let me take care of you, let's go to this place or that place.' Teachers would beg me to come to class just to sit there so they would know where I was and that I was relatively safe. If people hadn't doted on me at school when I was there and drugged, I wouldn't have done it."

Sometimes she'd skip school and take the bus to Arlene's house in Point Richmond; other times she'd walk a block down University Avenue to Burger Towne. That was where the really "bitchin' crowd" hung out. These were the hoods, the real greasers, definitely not of the Peace-and-Love-Flower-Child ilk. Dashikis be damned. Peg those black jeans and rat that hair. "If your boyfriend hit you, you really knew he cared." They even had a Hell's Angel. "At least he said he was a Hell's Angel." They'd sit around sipping Cokes and playing knuckle-bashing card games while waiting for a drug dealer to come, or the drugs to take effect, or the night to fall.

Some days Debbie and a few friends would cut school and head for the Jay Vee Liquor store just a block away. They'd try to score some wine or beer and take it to a nearby house. A Mexican girl they all vaguely knew lived there, and she'd let them sit and sip booze and smoke cigarettes until oblivion set in. "I did it all to extremes. I'd get falling-down drunk." She earned a reputation for drinking anything that was put before her, taking any pills that were handed her. Becky tells the story of someone handing Debbie a bottle of mouthwash, late into an evening's party, and she downed it as if it were Ripple. Of this period, Debbie says, "Some kids were hippies, but I was a hood."

As part of her arsenal of self-hatred, sex became repulsive to Debbie; to indulge in it was to be a whore, to be trash. Perhaps it was something trashy in herself that made her attractive to men and brought out perversions in them, or so she thought when strange men made off-color remarks to her, laid their hands on her thigh, or laughed as they deliberately brushed against her breasts. Incidents like these would leave her upset for days.

A counselor at West Campus, a black woman, took note of Debbie's troubled behavior and told her, "Debbie, if you're having problems you can always come and talk to me." The counselor promised that she would not tell anyone, that Debbie could count on that. By then Debbie wanted to tell everything; she wanted someone to know. At last an adult had reached out to her. "I just opened up, about my taking drugs, about the kids I was hanging out with, the things we did together. I wasn't happy about any of it. The counselor immediately called my parents and told them everything. I felt betrayed."

That was when Laurence and Lisa first became aware of the

extent of their daughter's troubles. When the counselor telephoned Layton, he was suffering a prolonged attack of severe ulcers. The counselor called almost daily. One day she said that the Laytons should take their daughter to get a pelvic examination; she thought that Debbie was pregnant. Dr. Layton got in his Cadillac and drove down the hill to look for his daughter. His first stop was Burger Towne, where he was directed to a Mexican boy named "Shockey," a high school drop-out he knew Debbie had a crush on. (Earlier, because Shockey's family was poor, Debbie had asked that her father help him out financially to go to college.) But Shockey didn't seem the least bit interested in helping Dr. Layton find his daughter. The next stop was the school. Dr. Layton was appalled to see the school that Debbie had begged him to allow her to attend. "I thought I was in the Congo. That's when we decided that we were not going to be sending her to Berkeley High School the next year."

The greatest fear that Debbie expressed to her friends was that if the full extent of her misdeeds were known, she'd catch hell from her father. She was scared that he'd spank her. That one spanking had occurred when she'd received an F in physical education at West Campus, along with the usual C's and D's. Dr. Layton had wondered aloud how anyone could get an F in P.E. without trying very hard. Thinking he wasn't looking, she rolled her eyes sarcastically. He caught her at it and put her over his knee.

"I deserved that whipping. . . . I would have beaten a kid like me to death. I was an atrocious child, just horrible."

After that spanking, Dr. Layton felt so guilty for having resorted to physical punishment that he broke down and cried. Joining in his tears, Debbie comforted him, assuring him that she had deserved it.

But when he found her that day, there were no cathartic spankings. "What will we do with you, Debbie? We just can't seem to handle you anymore," was all he said.

With Debbie the only child still at home, the whole Layton clan seldom got together anymore. In April of 1966, however, Larry, Debbie, Annalisa, and Tom joined their parents and Grandmother Chandler at a barren, ten-acre plot near Vacaville, in the farming country fifty miles northeast of San Francisco.

Dr. Layton had purchased the property as a family estate, two and a half acres for each child. He envisioned a gracious Southern manor house of his own design to be built there, which they would all enjoy. The day was overcast. Larry wore sunglasses because, as he confided to Tom, his pupils were dilated from having taken acid the night before. Debbie was having trouble in school. Annalisa, on the verge of graduation from the university, was enmeshed in an unhappy affair. Of the four children, only Tom was up to the occasion. With his new master's degree, he was off to Harvard for his doctorate.

Snapshots of the family were taken near the few dying trees that distinguished the landscape. Dr. Layton never built his manor house on the site; his wife and children did not share his interest in a rural dynasty, and besides, it would have been impractical to live there. The land was sold several years later.

In the fall of 1966, Larry moved out of the Davis dorm and into the apartment Tom had vacated when he left for graduate school at Harvard. Annalisa had vacated the apartment next door on her graduation, and was now on a six-month tour of Europe before facing the "real world" of job hunting. Here Larry was provided with the luxury of solitude in which to indulge his natural inclination toward introversion and self-reflection. Whereas the atmosphere of the dorms had been straight, his roommates here didn't judge his need to smoke marijuana or to augment the journey inward with a more intense drug. Acid was a way to melt through the barriers to self-awareness. It speeded up the process, and at the age of twenty-one Larry had an entire childhood to catch up with.

The managers of the Garden Court Apartments, a middle-aged couple who had been impressed by the well-bred demeanor of both Tom and Annalisa during their stays in the building, gave Tom a worried call at Harvard. They were afraid for their latest Layton. Larry, they said, was displaying erratic, even insane behavior. Possibly he was on drugs, maybe even acid.

Tom reported this telephone call to his father, saying that Larry had been acting peculiar, but only hinting that he might be on drugs. As with Debbie a year later, Dr. Layton could not believe, refused even to consider, that one of his children had succumbed to that way of life. Then, too, Dr. Layton did not want any difficult questions asked of Larry, fearing the strain on his already shaky relationship with his son.

During Thanksgiving vacation, Larry seemed withdrawn. "[He] was with us physically," Dr. Layton wrote to Tom, "but hardly spoke. Your mother fears that he may be having some psychological troubles. I don't know. No one talks to me except to ask for money."

Tom wrote Larry a letter in which he described his first experience with drugs. It had been a bad one, and all it had taken was a few hits of a DMT-soaked joint in the company of a girl friend. He became frightened when the DMT caused him to hallucinate. He tried to ignore it and to continue his seduction of the woman. His mother's face replaced that of the woman while they lay together in bed. He panicked and fled from the woman's apartment. After that experience, Tom never again used drugs or alcohol.

Depressed over the experience, Tom wrote and asked his younger brother for advice. Larry replied:

"Tom: Trips into childhood although painful can be of great value in discovering causes of hang ups. I suspect you have not had a guide for your trip—until you have attained complete reality without hang ups, guidance is valuable. I have had a trip quite similar to yours—it had to do with masturbation and other unimportant childhood hang ups.

"We are on the quarter system now and I spend almost as much time studying as I do smoking grass. By the way, I recommend that people start out on acid, not grass.

"My social life is at an uncertain stage just now. The car is broken down and being repaired just now. . . . I really don't worry very much about school parents drugs police or anything else anymore—but my relation with all of these categories is OK and often pleasant. Good luck to you—and don't get hung up. It's all a game.

"Love, God."

Larry's social life was not as uncertain as described in his letter to Tom. He did not tell Tom about Carolyn Moore, nor did he tell his parents about her, even after they had been living together for several months.

"I was rather innocent," Dr. Layton recalls, "though I think Lisa was far less innocent than I was. We would go up to see

Larry at Davis, and I thought it was strange that this girl was always there. Larry would say that she was typing or that she had just come over to visit. I do remember that Lisa mentioned that there were two sleeping bags on the floor."

Carolyn's father, John Moore, a Methodist minister, was the campus Protestant minister at Davis. Larry's family finally learned about Carolyn when her parents called the Laytons. Barbara Moore, Carolyn's mother, startled Dr. Layton by telling him that since they were going to be in-laws, they might as well get acquainted. When Lisa got on the phone, Barbara Moore went on, "You know, Carolyn has been interested in other boys, but never to the extent as with Larry. They've been living together," she confirmed, "and she's never done that before." Dr. Layton had the impression that the Moores were happy that the two families would become related through marriage.

Carolyn was a sophisticated and attractive young woman, slim and sharp-featured, with a slight arrogance about her. Her aggressiveness, seemingly a counterbalance to Larry's passivity, soon caused friction between her and Dr. Layton, who saw her as attempting "to wean Larry away from the family." Specifically, what bothered him most was the fact that "from the first time she was in our house, she was telling us how wonderful her father was. The inference I was supposed to draw was that I couldn't measure up to anything like that. She would argue with me, try to find fault with things I would say. Once when I was speaking at the dinner table and she interrupted with a criticism I said, 'Just a minute, I'm talking.' And she broke down crying. She told Lisa that no one had ever spoken to her that way before and that her own family, in contrast, was so loving. She wouldn't let me open my mouth without having some comment or objection. I was supposed to listen to whatever she had to say.

"I think that very early on Carolyn took an intense dislike to me, although I think she got along all right with Lisa. In the early summer of 1967, Carolyn was describing to us their wedding plans. And I said, 'I'll bring my camera and take some pictures.' Carolyn blew up at that. She said, 'Look here, this is my wedding and I don't intend to have anybody taking any pictures during the ceremony.' Well, of course I wasn't planning to take pictures during the ceremony. So I said something like, 'Do you think I'm a fool?' I remember that she always spoke of it as 'my wedding.' She said, 'You're not going to take pictures at *my wedding*. This is going to be *mine*, and I'm not going to have any of that.' It annoyed me that she thought that I would be so foolish as to go jumping around during the ceremony taking pictures. The way she expressed it, she implied that I was uncouth."

The wedding took place in July of 1967, in Davis. Dr. Layton, Lisa, Debbie, Tom, and Annalisa attended. With Annalisa was Ray Valentine, whom she was dating steadily. Tom drove over from Nevada, where he was excavating caves for his doctoral dissertation.

Carolyn's father performed the marriage. Her sisters, Annie and Becky, provided the music, playing flute and guitar duets at various moments during the ceremony. It was observed that only two persons cried during the service: John Moore and Dr. Layton. As a wedding present Dr. Layton gave the couple an old yellow De Soto and a check for five hundred dollars. He also gave them a couch, a table, and a set of oak chairs. The couple enjoyed a one-night honeymoon in San Francisco, then returned to Davis, where they eventually moved into married students' housing. Dr. Layton helped them move, loading their belongings into his Volkswagen bus.

"After the marriage," Dr. Layton recalls, "Carolyn was somewhat rapacious about wanting material things from our family. She wanted anything she could get her hands on. And she would always do it in such a way that you ended up feeling as if you had not done them a favor. If I had something that I thought was very nice and I asked them if they would like to have it, she would say 'Only if you don't want it.' Whenever I offered them something, she would say that. And that was exactly the opposite of the basis on which I was offering it. I would only offer things to Larry and Carolyn that I really liked."

All through college, Carolyn's paternal grandfather had given her an allowance. When she married Larry, the allowance stopped, the grandfather feeling that now that she was married and on her own, it was up to her husband to support her. The Laytons began giving Larry an allowance to take up the slack.

Later in the summer of 1967, they drove up to Davis to see Larry and Carolyn. It was a surprise visit. Carolyn answered the door and told them, "Larry's not able to see anybody right now." She added that he was "napping or something." Dr.

Layton did not consider that "an adequate explanation, so I insisted that I wanted to see Larry. Finally he came out of the bedroom. Apparently he was drugged, and he was very unfriendly." Larry's parents decided to walk over to the Moores' house, which was nearby, and left their car outside Larry's apartment. Soon Larry and Carolyn drove past in their De Soto. Larry stopped only because his father flagged him down, and then he said hardly a word to them, simply dropping them off at the Moores. Lisa and Laurence returned to Berkeley that same afternoon, without seeing their son again.

That fall, on September 16, 1967, Annalisa and Ray Valentine were married at the Laytons' home in Berkeley. Both had been working in the biochemistry department at U.C. Berkeley. With her bachelor's degree in microbiology, Annalisa now had a job as a lab technician. Ray, a young professor with a Ph.D. in biochemistry, worked on the same floor. The couple had dated for about six months. The entire family attended the wedding, and John Moore performed the ceremony. Larry remained quiet and detached.

The elder Moores and the Laytons had become friends, and when Lisa confided to Barbara Moore how worried she was about Debbie's involvement in the Berkeley drug scene, the Moores invited Debbie to come and live with them in Davis. Debbie had become very close to the Moores' daughter Annie, and she was eager to get away from home. But her troubles continued, and she soon found a drug connection in Davis. The high school contacted the Moores; if Debbie was to stay in school, she would have to have psychological counseling. Barbara Moore called Lisa to get her permission, and of course Lisa and Laurence had some questions they wanted answered. After that, Debbie never trusted the Moores; she felt that they had betrayed her to her parents.

As time passed, Dr. Layton began to wonder when Larry was going to graduate. Both he and Lisa wanted to attend, just as they had attended Tom's and Annalisa's graduations, but Larry had said nothing about it. In fact, Larry graduated in the spring

Lisa Philip at Penn State University, 1941

Laurence L. Layton working on his M.S. thesis at West Virginia University, 1939

Laurence upon receiving his Ph.D., in 1942

Lisa Layton in Rochester

Laurence, Lisa, and "Tom" in 1942

Laurence Layton in Baltimore, 1950

With (left to right) Laurence John, Annalisa, and Tom, outside the Baltimore Homewood Friends meeting house, 1951.

Tom, Annalisa, and Laurence John
at the family's Baltimore home

Laurence John with
Goldie, the dog he was
so devoted to, in Utah,
1953

Tooele, Utah, in 1953: Lisa
brings home Debbie

Lisa Layton washing diapers—Indian Head, Maryland, 1954

Laurence L. Layton after arriving in Utah as the new chief of chemical warfare at the U.S. Army Dugway Proving Grounds, late 1954

The Layton children: Christmas, 1954

Debbie, Tom, Lisa, Larry, Dr. Layton, and Annalisa at 670
San Luis Road, Berkeley, in 1960

Tom and Larry (far right) with Tom's friends and one of his Model A Fords in the process of being rebuilt, 1961

Dr. Layton in his laboratory at Berkeley, 1963

Dr. Layton receives the Distinguished Service Award from Secretary of Agriculture Orville Freeman, May 1963

The Layton family in Berkeley, 1963

Tom and Debbie in 1965, "in our private park"

The family's visit to Vacaville property in 1966 (page 90), with Grandmother Layton on the far left.

of 1968, but he didn't let his parents know until after the event. He had not wanted them to attend.

After graduation, Larry and Carolyn moved north to the small farming community of Ukiah. It was the summer of 1968, when the war in Vietnam was at its height. The Tet offensive in January of that year had made a mockery of official U.S. claims to military control of the war. The Chicago Democratic Convention, with its street protests and violence, merely underscored Lyndon Johnson's description of the "division in the American house." Ten thousand draft dodgers had fled to Canada. For Larry, it was a time for radical answers to radical problems, and a new if somewhat uncertain sense of direction.

"As a child," Larry was to recall from a prison cell in Guyana, "I had great fear that people would discover I was insane and put me in an insane asylum. This fear reappeared when I got to Davis. With college came alcohol, an interest in psychology, sociology, and unfortunate experimentation with pharmacology. That caused me to see pot and LSD as the answers to my problems. Straight society—with its race for money, power, and lack of brotherhood—and I became further separated. The draft was on my heels, so I really was looking for a happy existence and this, after graduation, led me and Carolyn, whom I loved very deeply, to head to Ukiah in search of utopia."

PART TWO

Fanatics have their dreams, wherewith they weave
A paradise for a sect . . .
—*John Keats, "The Fall*
of Hyperion"

6

The Promised Land–I

The farming hamlet of Redwood Valley is located about 115 miles north of San Francisco. Small herds of grazing cattle roam the rolling hillsides. Espaliered grape vines form neat, orderly rows along the flatlands. It is a quiet community— unhurried, unpretentious, and unbothered by its proximity to the cosmopolitan Bay Area to the south.

It was to this calm valley that the Reverend Jim Jones and his flock of sixty-five followers emigrated from Indianapolis, Indiana, between May and October 1965. They came because their leader, a charismatic preacher they devotedly called "The Prophet," told them that he knew by divine inspiration that the rich green valley would be safe from the nuclear holocaust he foresaw. He had read about this refuge three years earlier in an *Esquire* magazine article entitled "Nine Places to Hide."

The main criterion for a "place to hide" was its distance from a strategic target of interest to an enemy nuclear power; other factors included wind direction from such a target, latitude, rainfall, and sources of food and water.

The safest place in the United States, the article said, was Eureka, California, the principal city along California's lightly populated northern coast. Eureka lies on a stretch of that coast well north of the vulnerable urban and military targets of the San Francisco area, and south of the heavy rainfall areas of Washington and Oregon, where the prevailing winds would be laden with radioactive fallout.

Before settling on California as his destination, Jones had done some reconnoitering. Another of *Esquire*'s "safest places" was Belo Horizonte, Brazil, the South American city most likely to "blaze a new economic trail." In the summer of 1963 Jones and his wife, Marceline, and their four children traveled to Belo Horizonte for six months of missionary work and to set up an orphanage. Jones and his family returned to his Indianapolis church in December of that year. On the way back, they made a brief stop in Guyana, which in 1963 was called British Guiana. They also visited Hawaii and the San Francisco Bay Area.

Jones returned to Indianapolis with an anti-American message more extreme than ever. His sermons focused not so much on the dream of a socialist utopia as on a repeated litany of evil U.S. coercions, controls, manipulations, and interventions in the affairs of the people of Latin America. Punctuating his message with carefully calculated profanity—which had become the trademark that distinguished him from other Indianapolis Bible-thumpers, and which would become even more characteristic in appealing to the unpious and alienated young people he would court in California—Jones railed from the pulpit: "This fucking country has fucked those people over good, and those poor people are justified in hating us. We've bent them over and done it to them."

Jones' fear of nuclear destruction amounted to an obsession. He predicted, for example, that nuclear war would begin on January 16, 1964, at 3:09 A.M. Central Standard Time. Somehow the world survived. But Jones' preoccupation with nuclear war continued, until finally he decided to move his flock to the safer locale of the California coast.

Where they actually ended up was in Redwood Valley, 170 miles south of Eureka and dangerously close to San Francisco and to Hamilton and Travis Air Force bases. Jones justified this mislocation on two counts. First, the *Esquire* article did say that "the safest places from fallout in the United States are west of the Sierras"; he was west of the Sierras. And second, an old friend from Indianapolis lived in Redwood Valley and taught high school in nearby Ukiah. The man had promised to assist with the relocation and to help Jones secure a job as a teacher. Once established in Redwood Valley, Jones taught sixth grade full-time at the Anderson Valley Elementary School, and taught part-time at the Ukiah Evening Adult School. Church services were held in the garage of the Jones home.

What Jones had promised his flock of devoted followers was a safe refuge. Most of his congregation was poor and elderly, vulnerable to the pressures and hazards of urban existence; many were also black, and in Redwood Valley they hoped to find safety from the racial strife they had experienced in Indianapolis. As for Redwood Valley as a refuge from the nuclear holocaust they expected at any moment, it didn't matter that it was 170 miles south of Eureka: that was safe enough. And after the bombs had destroyed this racist, capitalist society, Jones' multiracial band would rise up from the radioactive ashes and build the New Jerusalem, a socialist society of brotherly and sisterly love led by their beloved Prophet of God.

On November 26, 1965, the Peoples Temple of the Disciples of Christ of Redwood Valley incorporated as a California corporation. "The specific and primary purpose," the articles of incorporation declared, "is to further the kingdom of God by spreading the Word." Eleven clauses enumerated the corporation's "purposes and powers," which included "to receive property by devise or bequest . . . ; to sell, convey, exchange, lease, mortgage, encumber, transfer on trust, or otherwise dispose of any such property . . . ; to make and perform contracts . . . ; to act as trustee . . . ; to borrow money, contract debts, and, from time to time, issue bonds, notes, and debentures, . . . ; and to sue and be sued."

Article 10 stated, "No substantial part of the activities of this corporation shall consist of carrying on propaganda, or otherwise attempting to influence legislation, and the corporation shall not participate or intervene in any political campaign on behalf of any candidate for public office."

Article 10 quickly became a mockery as the Temple made its presence felt in Redwood Valley. By 1967, less than two years after his arrival, Jones had been appointed foreman of the Mendocino County Grand Jury and had become a director of the Mendocino and Lake Counties Legal Services Foundation. His wife, Marceline, was a state nursing-home inspector. Tim Stoen, an idealistic young lawyer who was the county's assistant district attorney, had visited the Temple, been attracted to Jones' reform socialism, and upon joining the Temple volunteered his legal services to help the group. He was soon promoted to the rank of "assistant pastor," thus becoming one of Jones' top advisors. Legally, it was a potent combination. Jones, as grand jury foreman, headed the lay panel over which his own "assistant pastor," Assistant District Attorney Stoen, had jurisdiction in the handling of criminal prosecutions.

The Temple soon opened a pet shelter, three convalescent centers, and a forty-acre home for boys. Many in the congregation had taken foster children into their care. All of these activities reflected well on the church in the eyes of the community. In Ukiah's population of ten thousand, the four hundred Temple members made up a formidable voting block—Jones could easily account for 16 percent of the turnout in an off-year election. In a remarkably short period of time he managed to impress local conservatives with his efficient good works and to attract a loyal liberal following through his combination of social consciousness and ostentatious faith healing. The few who spoke out against him were ignored or considered cranks, red-necks, or racists.

From this small but solid base of power, Jim Jones could develop a plan of attack on what he called the "Big Time"— first San Francisco, then California, and in the end, the entire nation.

Jones' first forays into the Bay Area were concentrated in Oakland. In May 1966, Temple organizers rented the Jenny Lind Hall in a mostly black section of North Oakland. For weeks before that first meeting, Jones' aides blanketed the East Bay with leaflets proclaiming their leader's powers.

PASTOR JIM JONES

Incredible! . . . Miraculous! . . . Amazing! . . .
The Most Unique Prophetic Healing Service
You've Ever Witnessed!
Behold the Word Made Incarnate in Your Midst!

God works as tumorous masses are passed in every service. Before your eyes, the crippled walk, the blind see!
Scores are called out of the audience in each service and

told the intimate (but never embarrassing) details of their lives that only God could reveal!

Christ is made real through the most precise revelations and the miraculous healings in this ministry of His servant, Jim Jones!

The sane spiritual healing ministry does not oppose medical science in any way. In fact, it is insisted that all regular members have yearly medical examinations and cooperate fully with their physicians.

See God's Supra-Natural Works Now!

And Jones did provide "wonders" for all to witness, miracles that were in fact spectacular, stupefying, stupendous. An elderly black woman hobbled down the church aisle on crutches. Jones hugged her. "God loves you. I love you," he said quietly to her. Then he gently touched her leg. Almost instantly she threw away her crutches, straightened her twisted frame, and ran and leaped back up the aisle.

An elderly black man, bent over with pain, approached Jones and asked to be cured of his stomach cancer. Holding his left hand on the man's stomach, his right hand in the air, Jones prayed with the supplicant and then led him behind a screen where an assistant, usually Jones' wife, Marceline, helped the man "pass" his cancer. The tense silence of the auditorium was broken by a joyous whoop, and the man emerged smiling with several of Jones' assistants, one of whom was holding up a plastic bag containing what appeared to be pinkish-gray fleshy entrails. "The cancer has passed," Jones told the cheering audience.

Such "spiritual" theatrics won the devotion of many poor blacks, but they also raised the eyebrows of the liberal middle-class whites committed to the church's humanitarian works. This conflict was easily resolved once Jones let some of the congregation's white leadership in on a little secret. The poor were overly religious and susceptible to such hokum. The performances were merely a means to an end, a vehicle to get their attention and secure their faith in Jim Jones. Once that was accomplished, he would guide them toward a belief in socialism and ultimately help them to a better life. When he told the poor, uneducated masses that he was the reincarnation of Jesus Christ, and when they believed that he was God, it was for their own good.

Of course Jones seldom went so far as to admit that the

elderly and crippled petitioners he cured were actually young, healthy, and trusted aides in disguise; or that the cancerous masses they passed were chicken entrails that had ripened for several days in a warm room.

Collections were a major part of all meetings. Sometimes the collection plates would be passed only once: sometimes they'd be passed several times. After each offering, aides would quickly count the money, whisper the total in Jones' ear, and then he would decide whether or not to pass the plates yet another time. By 1972, a weekend take for the Temple road show in San Francisco usually totaled about fifteen thousand dollars; in Los Angeles, the total would reach about twenty-five thousand dollars.

In good fundamentalist tradition, these meetings would also be filled with gospel singing, bands, group dancing, and a lengthy discourse by Jones on the evils of racism, the promise of socialism, and the rainbow of brotherly and sisterly love. After the meeting ended, Jones' aides scurried around the hall, reminding newcomers of the next meeting, taking down their names and addresses, and asking for the names and addresses of friends who might also be receptive to the Temple's healing ministry.

Finally, in the small hours of the morning, the weary regulars would board their buses and return to Redwood Valley.

Carolyn Moore Layton was the first of the Layton family to visit the Peoples Temple. It was the summer of 1968 and the war in Vietnam was at its height. She was impressed with the darkly handsome preacher in sunglasses, white turtleneck, and sports jacket. She listened attentively to his diatribes against social injustice, the war, and racism. Both she and Larry were ready for Jones' message, and the opportunity for service that the Temple offered.

It had been nearly two years since Larry had begun applying for C.O. status. The draft board was choosing to ignore his claim of a lifelong commitment to the pacifist Quaker faith. He contemplated going to jail if they tried to draft him. Carolyn found a job teaching at Potter Valley High School; Larry began his alternate service as an aide at Mendocino State Mental Hospital while awaiting the draft board's approval of his status as a conscientious objector.

Larry's work with drug addicts at the same hospital attracted him to the Temple's rehabilitation program. As a Quaker, the most seriously committed of all the Laytons, he was drawn by the group's dedication to the service of humanity. By the time Larry and Carolyn began attending Peoples Temple regularly, Larry had lost several appeals to his draft board. One Saturday, he mailed in his final appeal. At Temple services the next day, Jones told him that he would dictate a letter for Larry that would be guaranteed to result in C.O. status. Larry replied that he had already mailed in his appeal. Jones told him to retrieve the letter at once.

On Monday morning Larry went down to the post office and convinced the postmaster that his cause was important enough to justify searching through the full mail sacks. As the first sack was emptied onto the floor, three envelopes fluttered to one side, separating themselves from the hundreds of others. One of them was Larry's. A small sign, soon to be followed by a larger one. Through his political connections, Jones did get Larry classified as a conscientious objector. To Larry, who had been working toward that objective so hard and for so long, a miracle had been performed on his behalf. He and Carolyn officially joined the Temple.

Late in the fall of 1968, Larry wrote to Tom, at Harvard:

"I hope you are well and as happy as one can be in this insane system. Carolyn and I are fine as is our [Temple] family.

"Teacher-student strikes are all over the state now and Cecil Pool US D.A. has 1 million warrants to be served if a state of emergency is declared [under the McCarran Act].

"Meanwhile back at the farm our church group has grown and our building is almost completed. We have many friends now who are dedicated social revolutionaries. I hope things get better but I am ready for the worst. . . .

"Love Larry and Carolyn

"P.S. Don't become engulfed by the status quo—you should apply your brain to help reform or destroy this stupid system. As I see it we will have a nuclear war or socialistic reforms but of course I'm just a dumb sociologist-mystic nut.

"Peace. LJL

"P.S. Did I tell you I've given up pot smoking? I want to have a cool head when things start to happen—and they have already started."

Larry divided his time between hospital duty, church services, and helping to erect the new temple building mentioned in his letter, complete with a forty-foot indoor baptismal swimming pool. Like others in the church, both Larry and Carolyn made the commitment of contributing 25 percent of their income to the Temple. In Larry's case, part of this income was unwittingly supplied by his parents.

Although Larry was still cashing his monthly allowance checks, his estrangement from his father continued. In December 1968, just before Christmas, Lisa, Laurence, and Debbie drove up to Ukiah to visit Larry and Carolyn. The young couple were friendlier than before, in a distant sort of way, but there was so much activity in the house, such a constant stream of Temple members coming and going, that the Laytons didn't have a chance to do much visiting. Larry did take them over to see the new church building, and they were duly impressed.

That visit was the last time Dr. and Mrs. Layton saw their younger son until the spring of 1971, three years later. "After that," Dr. Layton recalls, "I would telephone occasionally and have what I thought were friendly conversations with both Larry and Carolyn. Then, suddenly, I could never reach Larry. Carolyn would say that he was at work or over at the Temple and that she would have him call me back. I would get a call and some cool greeting. Finally, I couldn't even get a return call. I called Carolyn's father, Dr. Moore, and received vague statements. Finally, after several weeks, he told me that Larry and Carolyn were separating."

This was early in 1969. Dr. Layton, concerned as always by his younger son's mental state, and especially now with the breakup of his marriage, continued to call, but Larry refused to speak to him. Sometime later Larry wrote a three-sentence note to his parents, stating that he and Carolyn had gotten divorced; that he had remarried; that his new wife, Karen, was beautiful; and that he would send a picture later. The phrase "black is beautiful" was current at that time, and knowing the devotedly interracial nature of the Temple, the Laytons were relieved when the promised snapshot showed Karen to be an attractive, feminine, blue-eyed blonde.

The Laytons and the Moores agreed that the breakup of Larry's and Carolyn's marriage and Larry's subsequent remarriage to

Karen Tow were awfully sudden. What they didn't know then was that Jim Jones had become interested in Carolyn for himself and had simply taken her as his mistress. Carolyn was the most attractive woman to have joined the church in a long time. She was intelligent, articulate, and extremely frank. In fact, many people thought that with her sharp angular features Carolyn bore a strong resemblance to Marceline Jones.

Jim Jones had confided to John Collins—his son-in-law and trusted aide—that his sexual attraction to Carolyn was so strong that he didn't know if he was going to be able to hold it in check. Because of his psychic ability, he said, he knew what she looked like in the nude, and that made things even harder for him. He realized intuitively that she was as attracted to him as he was to her. He had never been unfaithful to Marceline, he explained, "except when the cause demanded it"; but this was different. Jones claimed to be the reincarnation of V. I. Lenin; and Carolyn, he said, was the reincarnation of Inessa Armand, one of Lenin's favorite lovers.

Jones used his pulpit to set the scene for taking Carolyn away from Larry. He informed his congregation of three or four hundred that his wife was no longer able to fill his sexual needs. Marceline had just had an operation to fuse several vertebrae because of degenerating discs. Jones claimed that the doctor had told him that she would never be able to have sex again, and that a man with his phenomenal sex drive could not live without sexual gratification. Or, as he told his flock, he had to "fuck somebody or die."

After that sermon, Carolyn seemed unusually upset, and she was stiff and tense with Larry, backing away when he tried to put his arms around her.

Later that evening, Jones told John Collins and his wife, Sue, that he was having an affair with Carolyn Layton, and that she was going to tell Larry that she wanted a divorce. He felt very sad about that, because of course he didn't want to be a home-wrecker, but he claimed it was "sufficiently important to the work I have to do, because I would die without this sexual release."

The next evening, a select committee of the Board of Trustees met. Larry and Carolyn were both asked to attend, Larry unaware that the purpose of the meeting was to arrange his own divorce.

Carolyn broached the subject without preamble. She turned to Larry and said, "I'm not happy with you. I want a divorce. I want to be free to work for the cause and I don't feel I have that freedom with you."

Larry appeared to take the news calmly; he was too stunned to react. Jones supervised the property settlement right there, and then informed Larry that he was to leave for Reno the next morning to begin six weeks of residency for as quick a divorce as possible.

With those details out of the way, Jones let the entire committee in on what was going on. "Now that you two are splitting up," he told Larry and Carolyn, "I want you to know—I want this whole committee to know—that I am going to pursue this woman, because I am attracted to her and I see certain things in our psychic makeup that are going to compel me to pursue her."

Then Jones turned to Larry and asked him what other woman in the group he was attracted to. Even though everyone present was used to Jones and his ways, this still seemed a remarkable question to ask someone who had just found out that he was getting a divorce. With Jones' coaching, Larry said he guessed he found Karen Tow, a new member of the church, attractive. Karen was brought into the room and Jones told her what her assignment was. "That's fine with me," she said, "I guess I'll see you later, Larry." It is possible, but by no means certain, that Jones had set the situation up beforehand with Karen.

Pretty, blue-eyed, blonde Karen, once a high school beauty queen and the daughter of a northern California plumbing contractor, was typical of the disaffected youth of the late sixties, those commonly described as hippies. Before joining the Temple, Karen had run off to Hawaii with an older man and together they had lived on a borrowed boat, working on their suntans and experimenting with various combinations of drugs. One day they came back from town to see the boat in flames, all their belongings destroyed. Their next move was to Ukiah, where the boyfriend was arrested on a drug charge. With no one to turn to, Karen sought out the Good Samaritan everyone had been talking about.

Marceline Jones answered the door of their home that day in 1968. "Jim's dead tired, he's gone without sleep for days helping people," she told Karen.

Jones overheard the conversation and insisted that they couldn't turn the girl away. Instead he invited her in, arranged for bail for her boyfriend, and put her through the Temple's drug rehabilitation program.

If Marceline Jones knew about her husband's affair with Carolyn Layton, she didn't let on. At first, it was conducted for the most part outside Ukiah. Whenever Jones went down to San Francisco on Temple business, he and Carolyn would rendezvous at the Hilton Hotel for the weekend.

Before long, Carolyn introduced Jones to her parents, John and Barbara Moore, and they all became quite friendly. The Moores moved from Davis to Berkeley, and Jones began spending much of his time at their house. He flattered them by sharing inside information about the true socialist goals of his church, and soon they regarded him as a virtual son-in-law.

The affair was not to be known beyond the Moores and a few trusted aides. In 1973, when Carolyn became pregnant, she dropped out of sight at the Temple. Jones maintained that she had been arrested in South America while on a revolutionary mission for the cause, and was in jail. Actually, she was quite comfortably settled in her parents' Berkeley home. Temple members didn't see much of Jones either during that period. They thought he was out working on some revolutionary venture, while he was actually at the Moore home with Carolyn. Even after Jones' sons, Jimmie Stephen and Lou, and a few other Temple members started dropping by to see him at the Moores', it was still supposed to be a big secret. The charade became particularly vulnerable when Jones began to have Tim and Grace Stoen's son, John, brought down to visit him. Three-year-old John couldn't keep a secret—he would say the wrong thing to the wrong people in the church. So Jones took to calling Carolyn "Ruth" when John was around. If he couldn't shut the boy up, he could at least confuse him.

A couple of months before their baby was born, Jones took Carolyn, his two sons, and John Stoen to Hawaii for a vacation. Marceline, then working for the state as an inspector of nursing homes, couldn't get much time off, but she did manage to join her husband and the boys during the middle of the trip. Carolyn made herself scarce during those three or four days.

Just before the baby was born, Jones had Carolyn marry Temple member Mike Prokes so that the baby would have a legal father. Carolyn and Prokes never had any sort of marital relationship; she continued her affair with Jones. They named the baby Kimo—Hawaiian for Jim.

By early 1970, Dr. Layton was extremely curious about Peoples Temple. He wanted to know more about the group, and he also wanted to find out why Larry was not communicating with him. He discussed the matter with Tom, who was also curious. At that point in Tom's career, he was considering moving from archaeology to cultural anthropology. One way to establish himself as a cultural anthropologist would be to write an ethnography. "And what better candidate for the ethnography," as Tom recalls the idea, "than the strange, utopian, interracial, and apparently vital Peoples Temple."

One Sunday morning in February, Tom drove to the church in Redwood Valley. He arrived just after services, unannounced. "I particularly remember the large number of children running about excitedly. Many women were carrying covered dishes in preparation for a potluck lunch. I asked for Larry and someone pointed him out. He was very busy talking to people and getting things organized for the potluck. We chatted for a few minutes, and he introduced me to Karen.

"I remember feeling rather conspicuous, and not knowing anybody. I wondered how I could approach a description of such a large and apparently complex group. I chatted with several people and found that all the conversations reduced me to general small talk and talking about myself. I served myself from the potluck table and ate my food from a paper plate, standing up. I didn't get to see Larry because he was busy; so in my discomfort, I thought up an excuse, and left shortly."

Tom went to find his brother to say good-bye. The young woman who helped him find Larry then walked him toward a side door. As he was about to leave, Jim Jones approached, and the woman introduced Tom to Jones.

"I was struck," says Tom, "by several quick impressions. First, he had a vaguely American Indian look about his face. In fact, he looked a little bit like the photographs I had seen of my Dad's father [John Wister Layton] who had died in 1922.

Next, Jones seemed shorter than I had expected. Third, there was something about his thick, overly groomed hair that shouted 'custom razor-cut.' There was that slick look about his hair and stylish glasses that oozed the Oral Roberts-Billy Graham-Southern fundamentalist-television preacher look. Our conversation was short. I complimented Jones on the beautiful church building and the happy vitality of the busy and friendly members. He said something perfunctory but friendly like 'It's good to meet you.'"

Tom made his excuses, shook Jones' hand, and headed for his car.

"I felt a sense of relief as I drove away. I had not felt comfortable during my short visit. Perhaps it was the vapid nature of the small talk. Perhaps it was because Larry was so obviously busy with 'duties.' I was not taken on a tour of the building. I was not invited to visit Larry's house. None of the people my age who engaged me in conversation would say anything about the church.

"In retrospect, I suspect that following my unannounced arrival, a series of people were assigned to talk to me. One member of the Temple who defected later told me that someone pointed me out to him, and the tenor of the situation was 'Hey, that's Larry's brother from Harvard. Be cool.'

"In any event, I left Redwood Valley knowing not a bit more about the real structure of the church than when I arrived. I had acquired only some mental pictures of happy people in a pretty building. As I drove back to Berkeley, I still thought I would like to do an ethnography of the group. I would try to be unthreatening, keep my eyes open and my mouth shut, and see what might develop.

"Another unfamiliar feeling I experienced from the visit was that on this turf I was not in control. Larry and his friends were in control here. In the past I had always been in control whenever I was around Larry, perhaps because he had never had a support structure of his own friends before. Here, Larry seemed to be functioning independently of me and of the family. That was a strange feeling. There is a line from a Jefferson Airplane/Grace Slick song: 'And your friends they treat you like a guest.' Well, I felt that I had been treated with all the polite distance of a guest. I surely was not treated as a member of the family would expect to be treated."

Tom's final impression of his visit to Redwood Valley was that it had occurred during a time of great personal stress. His focus was on his own career, and his own directions. "The thought occurred to me that it would be so easy to throw out my career and join a commune and settle into a life where I didn't have to continually market myself. For years, I had had a fantasy of setting up my own school, with friends from graduate school, somewhere in the country, where we would enjoy a communal life. In Redwood Valley, Larry seemed to have found such a situation. I was happy for him, but at the same time I knew that this commune was not for me. I would have to be the leader, head honcho, owner, and in total control of any such group in which I would become involved. In my archaeological projects, I enjoyed the communal life of a small group off in the desert, but only so long as I was in total control. Larry was capable of annihilation of the 'self,' but my ego would never allow such a submissive posture."

A few weeks after the visit, on March 5, 1970, Larry wrote Tom a short note:

"Thank you for coming to visit me. We enjoyed your being here. Jim knows much about you metaphysically* and feels very kindly towards you. . . . I hope that all goes well in your PHD business. We need people with your brains in the world.

"Peace, Larry

"*I know this because he has told me things no one could know about myself, you, Debbie, and many other people and situations."

At seventeen, Debbie Layton was still emotionally troubled and an underachiever scholastically. After her calamitous freshman year at Berkeley High School's West Campus and her unhappy stay with the Moores, schooling had been forgotten for one semester. In the spring of 1968, Annalisa took in her problem sister, and Debbie completed the school year at El Cerrito High. But a more stable and permanent solution was needed. The Laytons wrote to Quaker friends in the East, and got recommendations for several Friends boarding schools. One of these leads took them to the American Culture Commission in London, and from that they heard about Ackworth, a spartan Quaker school that was inexpensive and known for its rigid discipline. It sounded just right, and after some quick arrangements Debbie was packed off to England.

Ackworth failed to "straighten her out." Debbie missed her family and friends in California. To please her parents, she tried desperately to conform to the school's severe regimen, but failed miserably.

"I wanted to be good," she remembers. "I would cry over my parents' letters because I knew I wasn't living up to their expectations." She wrote a poem titled "Can't Be Judged," which she sent to a friend in America:

> My life is made up of troubles
> No one knows the hurt
> I've hurt so many already
> With my forbidding ugly nature
> No one wants to get real close
> I am untrue to life and myself
> I am a wanted convict who
> Cannot be convicted

Debbie became the school daredevil, actively seeking attention, cutting classes, drinking, taking drugs; she was generally considered a bad influence on her schoolmates. Along with this inner confusion, she felt despair over the state of the world. In April 1970 she wrote to her father, "Pray for Apollo 13. Boy, what next: Our world is turning into a vicious cycle of chaos and continuous risks. I am frightened to bring my children up in a world like ours today. Nothing cannot happen today in the '70s. Man would be a great deal happier if he was a little less intelligent and aware."

There was one good thing in Debbie's life at Ackworth. She met and fell in love with Phil Blakey. One afternoon she came into the school common room and was immediately drawn to this tall, awkward boy, homely but not unattractive. As they struck up an acquaintance, she found the quiet and ingenuous Northumbrian farm boy a nice contrast to her old racy crowd in California.

But even her friendship with Phil was not enough to pull her out of her slump. When she smashed her fist through a window at the school, both her parents and teachers thought that it was a suicide attempt. She insisted, however, that she was merely showing off for her friends. Two tendons in her wrist were severed and the main artery was cut; an operation was required, after which she had to spend some time in the hospital to recuperate. She was extremely depressed when she was released, and it was then that she received a letter from her brother Larry.

"He said that there was a man who knew all about me and cared for me. I thought, 'Wow, Larry's on drugs again!'"

During summer vacation of 1970 Debbie returned to California to spend several weeks with her parents in Berkeley. At first they were reluctant to allow her to visit Larry in Ukiah, but she insisted, and finally she got her way, only a couple of weeks before she was to return to England for her final year of school. She was eager to meet her new sister-in-law, Karen, and to find out more about this preacher Larry had written about.

Unlike Tom, Debbie felt immediately welcome in Ukiah, and she was impressed by the warmth of the relationship between Larry and Karen. "Karen was always affectionate to Larry," Debbie recalls. "She was very different from Carolyn. Karen would walk up and hug Larry, or laugh at something he said, and he would blush. They were a very loving couple."

Larry and Karen wanted to show Debbie the beautiful Mendocino coast. They loaded their old car with camping gear and drove to the beach at Fort Bragg. They cooked dinner on the beach, toasted marshmallows over the campfire, and ate breakfast in a beachfront restaurant. Debbie felt like she had come home.

That Sunday morning they all went to church. From the moment Debbie walked through the Temple doors, Jones began to work on her poor self-image. He made her feel special.

The service, she recalls, was "not religious at all. He was going on about the war in Vietnam, current events, talking about equality for all and social commitment." After the service all the children in the congregation clustered around the preacher and he kissed each one on the forehead. "I thought it was so warm to see this man kissing each child, and they were so happy and glorified that he had paid them the attention. Then he asked everyone who was new to the Temple to come forward. I was new, so I went up. He took my hand, and he acted as though he was getting something from what he called the 'ether' plane, another consciousness where spirits of the dead would communicate with him. I started to walk away but he kept hold of my hand and pulled me back. 'You're Larry Layton's sister,' he said, and I thought, 'Ooowee, Larry was right—this guy knows things!' So I said, 'Yes I am.' He said, 'I could tell from the warmth of your hand.' "

During her brief visit to Ukiah, Debbie was buoyed by Jones' continuing attention and intrigued by the close-knit atmosphere and sense of purpose of the group. Her indoctrination began in earnest under the spell of her brother's and sister-in-law's enthusiasm. She was made to feel welcome by the "love-bombing" of Temple members. A number of these proselytizers were students around Debbie's age, and the idea of attending Sonoma State College or Santa Rosa Junior College, where the Temple had "colonies," was very attractive to her.

They began to play with her perceptions of reality. Karen told her that all men were homosexuals. Jim Jones preached it and that made it true. For an impressionable seventeen-year-old, it was an earthshaking revelation. "I thought, 'Wow, Phil has been leading me on all the time.' " She dashed off a letter to Phil in England:

"I feel this is a very important letter. I have found a very beautiful environment at Larry's house in Ukiah. The atmosphere is that of truth and love. I feel I must live there with the Peoples Temple family, the group Larry is with. I am going to try and convince Dad to let me live there. I shall break all my contacts with the 'rat race' society and join the family of all colors.

"I still think a great deal of you, but I do not think you are the right person for me. Don't get any wrong ideas. I have been faithful to you and I have not found anyone quite like you. I just know my home lies in the mts. with Rev. Jim Brown [*sic*] and his 'family' of followers.

"I need in all honesty in front of God to know if you are willing to sacrifice. Are you really the guy for me? Do you care?

"Does homosexuality bother you and make you feel incapable? I love you Phil. I am sorry if I sound crazy, but I must know for the sake of our relationship.

"My life depends on your honesty with me.

"God forgive me if I am a bitch.

"Sincerely, Debbie."

Once the fervor of the moment had passed, Debbie decided not to mail the letter.

By the end of her stay in Ukiah, the Temple had captured Debbie's mind and heart. Jones told her that she should not return to England to finish school. Her new friends claimed that if she went back to England she would never see them again because the nuclear holocaust would wipe the Ackworth School off the map. All would be lost unless she joined them right then and there.

The Layton children had grown up with such apocalyptic threats. Dr. Layton had infused their childhood with a terrible fear of nuclear destruction. During the Cuban missile crisis, he had briefed the family on where to meet and what to do should the Bay Area suffer nuclear devastation. On October 24, 1962, at the height of the crisis, Dr. Layton had written to Tom and Annalisa, at school in Davis, "With the world situation in such a critical (explosive) phase, I am most uneasy about my children. I think you and Tom are probably safer from direct blast effects than are Laurence and Debbie, however the fallout effects should certainly affect Davis and points East and up the main valleys of the rivers. I prefer that you both stay out of the cities until the crisis has passed. Do not come to Berkeley until we all agree that you should. I suppose the only relatively safe area of California is north and west." Years earlier Dr. Layton had spoken about the possibility of moving to New Zealand to escape the nuclear holocaust. Christchurch, New Zealand, was also one of *Esquire*'s "Nine Places to Hide."

Debbie returned to her parents' house in Berkeley inspired by her experience in Ukiah but terrified by Jones' reiteration of the threat of a nuclear holocaust. When Karen called to invite her to a Temple meeting in San Francisco, her father absolutely refused to let her go. Debbie was furious; she was being cut off from this marvelous new force in her life. Suddenly her father changed his mind—she could go to the services. To Debbie that was a miracle.

Some of the San Francisco group picked Debbie up on the night of the meeting. When they arrived at the Temple building, in the heart of San Francisco's black ghetto, at about eight-thirty at night, the sermon had already begun. "When we walked in Jim couldn't see me because I was in the very back. After the sermon I was talking to Karen and Larry, and Jim walked up and said, 'I knew when you came in, I felt a warmth in the room.' He told me that my aura was really special. That filled me with pride—here I was, this little fat overweight thing, and this man was telling me there was a special warmth when I walked into a room.

"He talked to me for about half an hour. He told me that my father was a manipulator. I didn't know what manipulator meant, but I stood there and said, 'Yes, yes.' He told me that I was very strong, that I knew my strength, deep down, and that if I didn't want to go back to England I didn't have to—that I was strong enough to stand up to my parents and stay here, with the Temple.

"After he finished with me, Karen told me that I should really appreciate all the attention, because he didn't give it to just anybody.

"When it came time for me to go back to England, I put up a big fuss. I refused to go and thought of all kinds of things to do. I was ready to jump out of the car on the way to the airport."

Debbie ended up obeying her parents and returned to England to finish her last year of school. Actually, she wanted to go back; she wanted to be with Phil. She wrote a letter to Jones expressing guilt for not having stood more firmly against her parents, and assuring him that she was devoted to the church's "cause" against social injustice. She did, however, question his claim to be the reincarnation of Jesus Christ.

Jones replied on September 18, 1970:

"I will be around for as long as you need to convince yourself of who I am and the character of what I stand for. Don't feel guilty about what you've done. Your actions were no surprise to me; contrarywise, you were quite capable of standing up to your parents but you lacked the necessary background experience and the deep, heartfelt conviction about our principles and me as the principle bearer. Thus I can well empathize with your vacillation. Please don't be so hard on yourself. Everyone I minister to at one point or another has the same ambivalences and also the same awareness of their own ego that is involved in the service of giving to others. You must remember, although it is a trite phrase, that one must crawl before one can learn to walk, and mankind generally is in the crawling stage.

"We all love you and are looking forward to seeing you when the time is right. We speak from the highest plain of truth, and when you have time to test this affirmation thoroughly <u>you will not be disappointed.</u> Sincerely, Rev. James W. Jones."

Jones' secretary, Jim Pugh, added his testimony in a postscript. "The foregoing was dictated to me by our beloved Pastor, Jim Jones, who is greatly concerned about you, what a friend to have, many who have been touched by his life and ministry rise up to call him blessed and to declare most emphatically that Jim is the most wonderful person alive today. . . . I would not be alive today were it not for Jim who healed me of cancer, heart trouble and diabetes. Cancer, which is the number one killer in the world today, is Jim's specialty. I can't tell you how many I have seen that come from pain wracked bodies at his simple word of command."

Things would never be quite the same for Debbie in England. When Phil asked what she had done on her summer vacation, she told him she had met a man who claimed to be the reincarnation of Jesus Christ and to have the power to heal people.

"He believed me. At that moment, he looked up and saw some funny cloud formation in the sky, and he took that to be a sign that what I said was true. Over the months, I told him all the positive things about Peoples Temple, but also that I questioned Jim Jones' ability to heal and that he was the reincarnation of Jesus Christ. I had real doubts, but then Phil was becoming a believer. Phil wrote me a note just before my exams saying, 'Read the examination over first, then go back and answer the questions—and remember, Jim loves you.'" This mandatory Temple phrase of greeting, departure, and encouragement—"Jim loves you"—instilled in members the belief that *only* Jim could love with purity and unselfishness. Somehow Phil Blakey had picked it up from halfway around the world, and without ever having met Jones. Debbie was impressed.

Larry and Karen continued to show an active concern for Debbie's future. A steady stream of transatlantic letters, peppered with colorful anecdotes of Jones' good works, urged her to come live with them after graduation and to enroll in one of the two colonized colleges near the Temple. After staying up all night with a twenty-six-year-old heroin addict in the throes of detoxification, Karen wrote, "It could so easily be me, as caught up in the drug world as I was before meeting Jim. I am so blessed to have met him, as he has spared my life in every way so that I now have the opportunity to be the server of truth. Every day is an exciting experience, and every day I find myself growing and becoming a better person."

During this period Karen and Larry took guardianship of Bruce, an eleven-year-old black boy. Larry wrote to Debbie, "Bruce is out of sight, smart and neater than I am. And would you believe, he doesn't cuss at all!" Temple families were encouraged to take in foster children, and the Temple's reputation as a haven not only for children but also for unwanted animals was growing in both Ukiah and San Francisco.

In their letters, Karen and Larry often described the miracles they had witnessed. Larry wrote,

"Did I tell you about the week we had warning to check our wheels and brakes? I didn't heed this and lost my brakes coming off the Golden Gate Bridge. When I got to a gas station the wheel was 2½ inches away from where it should have been. The repair man said not to shake the car while he jacked it up—and when he did jack it up the wheel fell off. The bearings had burned out and the brake drum expanded and the cylinder broke and by all logic I and my passengers should have been dead. These things happen so often I lose track of them.

"Peace, Larry."

And from Karen: "Jim healed three women of cancer yesterday. They were dying but they spit the growth up right in front of us and now they are made whole! There were also several cured of disease."

Almost every letter stressed how busy they were, how little time they had for anything but Temple business.

"Sorry I have not written sooner. You will never believe how busy I am, and with a son, even more so.... Jim has two radio broadcasts now in San Francisco & has to spend many hours each week making tapes. Our choir is in the tapes too, singing at the start. (We are cutting our own records too. Did Larry tell you?) Our group is actively engaged in so many projects you wouldn't believe it. The fair is coming up so the youth group is busy making candles, pottery, clothes, jewelry, etc. We're going to San Francisco this weekend for a meeting where there are so many people who need to hear the truth. We are also making plans for our annual vacation in beautiful Oregon right on a clean sparkling river only 5 miles from the ocean. We are going toward the end of July. Jim goes & like last year when we took 200 kids we are again opening the trip to any children, even outside our group who want to go (& free of charge too). Who else would take on the responsibility of 200 children (many from ghettos), but Jim Jones our loving Prophet. Love, Karen."

The prospect of life with Peoples Temple glowed like a beacon. Lisa Layton's suggestions that Debbie attend Diablo Junior College and live at home with the old folks paled in comparison.

With Debbie, her baby, gone from the nest, Lisa was faced with a hard reality. Raising her children had kept at bay the coldness she felt for her husband. They had stayed together all those years for the sake of the children. Now that they were alone, truly alone, the relationship became an endurance test. In the spring of 1971, Laurence suffered his first heart attack. At Lisa's urging, it was decided to sell their huge, rambling house in favor of a smaller home in the same general area of the Berkeley hills. Under the stress of selling the family home and of hunting for a new house, Laurence had a second heart attack, this one much worse. He always felt that Lisa was to blame for his second attack because she dragged him along house-hunting while he was still under doctor's orders not to exert himself.

From his hospital bed, he wrote a letter to his family in West Virginia, evaluating both his health and the state of the family.

"Well, I suppose that I have 'had it,' since I do not feel that I am improving. There is no great pain in the physical sense, but very great mental suffering unfortunately, so much so that I have given up wanting to recover. I do have a cramped feeling around the heart.

"I still have Laurence John and Debbie to 'look-out' for. They will get a small amount of insurance and Lisa will handle it according to her knowledge and my wishes. Tom we have given all that we can give save some insurance to start him off with a down payment on a home.

"Annalisa is a lovely daughter—warm, intelligent, loyal. I only wish that I could have done more for her and for Laurence J., who is just the opposite in action. Laurence once was my warmest baby, I loved to hold him close. He was almost angelic, but bad psychology and worse associates have destroyed him as a real person. His hatreds and resentments are probably the result of childhood experiences and jealousy, but I still say that I am not only innocent but also ignorant of any part that he seems to 'think' that I had. There is no way to penetrate his 'prison walls' of what he thinks are 'memories' of 'experiences.' When I learned that he was on drugs I nearly died of ulcers. I then read some articles on LSD and 'pot' only to learn that people on these drugs have 'memories' of things that never occurred!! But they remain convinced that this was/is the real 'memory.' There seems to be no way around this 'false' memory or reaction to fantasy save through extensive or intensive therapy.

"So there he is in his fantasy of bad 'memories'—a prison as it were—and here are we—the rest of his family suffering for 'sins' never committed, but 'real' to him."

From his hospital bed Laurence also wrote to Debbie, informing her of his condition but asking her not to let Larry know. He didn't want his son to visit him out of a sense of duty, rather than love. Debbie, however, did write to Larry, who in turn surprised his father by writing that he would like to see him. The Sunday after Dr. Layton was released from the hospital, Larry, Karen, and Bruce drove down to Berkeley. It was the first time father and son had seen each other since Christmas of 1968, and the Laytons had never met Karen or Bruce. They got along much better with her than they had with Carolyn; Lisa especially felt close to her new daughter-in-law. Bruce, on the other hand, proved something of an embarrassment.

Dr. Layton recalls, "My mother, Eva Chandler, was visiting

us at this time. She became quite upset that Larry and Karen referred to this little Negro boy as their son. She kept saying, 'Why don't you have your own?' or something to that effect. She was turned off to the situation, and as a consequence Larry became turned off to her. The relationship got worse several weeks later, when we were preparing to move out of our big house into the smaller one on Vistamont Avenue. We offered our old stove to Larry, and a few days later he arrived in a pickup truck accompanied by a young white man and an older Negro man. My mother, thinking the Negro had been hired to help move the stove, made some comment. Actually, the Negro was a well-dressed professional person who had loaned Larry his truck to haul the stove. Well, my mother made this racial comment to Larry, and I think again referred to Bruce. As far as I know, Larry never had anything to do with my mother again." (Tom had his own memory of his grandmother on this point; "I remember she once said to me, 'I've got nothing against niggers. Lord, I've worked with them all my life.'")

About that first visit, Karen wrote Debbie a letter with no mention of Grandmother Chandler. "Met your Mom who is very sweet, your Dad who was kind to me, Annalisa who is a sweetheart. I enjoyed my visit very much and we are going down again as soon as we have time."

After a couple of such visits, Dr. Layton told his son that if he wanted to go back to school he should do it while his father was still alive and able to help him. Larry decided it was a good idea, though not, as his father urged, with medical school in mind. Larry enrolled in a community college program to become an X-ray technician.

In the summer of 1971, Debbie Layton and Phil Blakey arrived in California. Debbie was to begin school in the fall at Santa Rosa Junior College, one of the two colleges attended by Temple members, and Phil had accepted her invitation to see America and to experience Jim Jones and Peoples Temple. The two teenagers stayed with Larry and Karen in Ukiah, and attended Temple services in Redwood Valley a few miles away. Jones was impressed with Blakey's practical intelligence and knowledge of farming, both resources needed for the agricultural activities he envisioned. Then, too, Phil's attractive Northumberland accent lent an air of international class to their "family of colors."

Unlike Phil, Debbie was still not convinced that Jones was what he claimed to be, a healer and miracle worker, the reincarnation of Jesus Christ. At the first service Debbie attended on her return to Ukiah, Jones announced, "I am going to turn water into wine."

"He had us all stand up, holding hands," Debbie recalls. "Everybody was very emotional. He told us all to close our eyes. Then someone screamed, and when we looked the pitcher of water he always had at the pulpit had turned into red wine. He had it poured out into little paper cups so people could taste it, and in fact it really was wine. There wasn't enough to go around, so Jim called for more water and said he would do it again. I decided that this time I wouldn't close my eyes. Obviously he couldn't do whatever he planned to do, with me watching. He looked right at me and said, 'For your disbelieving eyes, it will be white wine.' Everybody knew he was talking about me because Phil and I were the only newcomers there, and it was already obvious that Phil believed in Jim's miracles."

Lisa Layton took an active part in helping Debbie prepare for her first term in college. Lisa had hoped to reestablish her bond with her youngest daughter while helping her adjust to the new campus and community, and it saddened her that Debbie wasn't just going off to college, she was going off to join the Peoples Temple. From what she had seen of the effect on Larry, Lisa feared that the connection would taint all of Debbie's relationships with anyone outside the church, including her family.

Debbie, Phil, and Lisa drove the family Volkswagen camper to Santa Rosa on class-registration day. They lunched on the sandwiches and iced tea Lisa had packed and spent a pleasant afternoon inspecting the campus. Phil was impressed, and thought aloud about staying in America to study there. Both Dr. and Mrs. Layton liked the cultivated English boy, and Lisa agreed to do what she could to help him stay in the United States. She realized that Phil and Debbie were very close, and it pleased her to see her daughter happy at last.

After their picnic lunch, they drove over to examine the

Temple-owned dormitory where Debbie would be living, a crowded three-bedroom duplex in a run-down tract on the outskirts of Santa Rosa. The bedrooms had been divided with cardboard partitions into study cubicles for the nineteen female residents, with the garage converted into a sleeping ward with bunk beds lining the walls. Without benefit of heating or insulation, it remained a cold, drafty place despite the posters tacked to the walls and the secondhand rugs on the cement floor.

Lisa was offended by the drab surroundings. She and her husband had paid a semester's boarding fee of seven hundred fifty dollars for this? But Debbie was enthusiastic. For her, this was what the church was all about: an interracial, egalitarian group learning to live in communal harmony. Waiting in line to use one of the two bathrooms could be considered a revolutionary sacrifice.

Phil tried to convince his mother to let him stay in America. He wrote her that Dr. and Mrs. Layton would help him find work, and that he wanted to go to college in California, and to join the Peoples Temple. But Mrs. Blakey refused. And until he reached the British age of majority, eighteen, in two months, he would have to obey her order to return.

On September 11, Debbie and Lisa drove Phil to the Oakland airport to catch his scheduled charter flight home. They dropped him off at the curbside check-in; he promised he'd be back as soon as he could.

The following day, Mrs. Blakey called from the airport in England. Phil had not arrived. On a hunch, Lisa telephoned Larry. Yes, Phil had taken the bus to Ukiah and was staying with them. He was going to register for classes at Santa Rosa Junior College, and the church had a well-placed attorney in its ranks to help with a permanent visa. Lisa couldn't get angry; Phil's determination and resourcefulness appealed to her sense of youthful rebellion. "I guess I just never grew up," she admitted to a friend.

Mrs. Blakey did not share those feelings. Furious, she contacted the British consul general in San Francisco and demanded that her son be returned. Jim Jones called her in England to assure her that Phil would be safe in his care. Mrs. Blakey flew over, and after a visit to Ukiah, where she spent three weeks as the guest of Timothy and Grace Stoen, Phil's mother was forced to resign herself to the fact that her son had been captured by Peoples Temple and the Americans.

As it turned out, the Laytons saw more of Phil than they did of Debbie. He went to work for them, clearing brush and helping to prepare the backyard of their new home for a swimming pool. The number of weekends when the church would allow Debbie to visit her parents was limited; she spent most of them with Karen and Larry at their home in Ukiah.

Holidays, traditional gatherings for the Layton family, were also taken over by the church. Debbie spent that first Thanksgiving back in California on a Peoples Temple bus to Los Angeles, and Larry, Karen, Debbie, and Phil celebrated Christmas with the church in Ukiah.

The family did have to admit that, as far as they could tell, Debbie's behavior had improved immensely. She no longer took drugs or drank alcohol, and she seemed much happier. This pleased her parents and led them to believe that, despite the church's mysterious hold on their children, the Temple might be good for them. Debbie's grades came closer to family expectations, and this gave her father something to be proud of. She earned a B average, with an A in anthropology, that first semester—the best grades she had received in years. "Debbie seems much more sensible, but still not terribly wise," Dr. Layton wrote to Tom in November 1971. "The Church group is probably right for her and for Phil until they grow up."

Mom and Dad had little idea of what actually went on in the church itself, although the children would occasionally talk about certain of the church's views. On one such occasion, "Larry spent the night and discussed 'religious concerns,'" Dr. Layton wrote to Tom. "On these he is in transition. I believe that he hears lots of ideas, but that he is not reading enough himself." Dr. Layton gave his son a few "searching books," not realizing that the Temple wasn't searching for anything. It had been founded upon the gospel according to Jim Jones, and of that there was no searching or disputing.

The Temple group attending college soon assumed the smug airs of Hitler youth. They were to be on their best behavior at all times, setting an example the other students could look up to. They were expected to be well-disciplined academic over-achievers, for as the Reverend Jim Jones told them, they were the leaders of tomorrow. This wasn't any ideological message such as one might hear at a Harvard commencement; this was prudent preparation for the holocaust to come.

One night a week would be spent in socialism classes. At the end of each session, the students were tested on how well they had learned their lessons. After socialist ideology came survival and guerrilla warfare training. They'd be led to the open fields surrounding the housing tract and drilled on the use of compasses and maps, learning to chart their way through strange territory. They were taught military tactics and the meanings of words like *flank* and *guard*. Finally, they would run laps on the streets of Santa Rosa so they would be in top physical condition when the nuclear holocaust came.

Tuesday night at the dorms was catharsis night. Blacks and other minority members of the integrated group berated the whites as honkies and racists. The whites accepted these judgments as their due. It was a time for the privileged whites to wallow in their liberal guilt.

Debbie came to know intimately what it was like to be a member of an oppressed minority. Encouraged by one of the black girls in the dorm who thought that Debbie, with her dark exotic features, didn't look Caucasian, she frizzed her hair into an Afro and adopted the name of Solano. As far as the professor of her ethnic studies class was concerned, Ms. Solano was a militant Chicana. He was impressed with her extemporaneous speeches on the pain of minorities in a racist society and her strident justification for hating honkies. Debbie had always been a good enough actress to turn a game to her own advantage; Solano became the teacher's assistant and received an A in the course.

Temple youth were discouraged from dating; Debbie and Phil saw very little of each other in those days. Dr. Layton had always thought well of Phil. "He's a fine country boy with a good head and a good disposition. Debbie could do worse," he said. Still, it came as a surprise when Debbie called on March 20, 1972, to say that she and Phil were married. The Laytons would have preferred to celebrate with a proper wedding, but they made do with engraved announcements, a simple reception, five hundred dollars and a Ford station wagon.

The marriage was actually Jones' idea. There was little concern for love or holy matrimony when he signed the marriage certificate at the irreverent hour of three A.M. Phil needed an American wife to obtain an immigration permit. The two did care for each other—Debbie was in fact very much in love with Phil—but Jones' control of Phil's mind prevented him from consummating the marriage. Jones preached against sex, at least for others—it was egocentric, counterrevolutionary, and antisocialistic. And Phil believed in Jones totally.

Debbie would drive to Redwood Valley on weekends, hoping to be with her husband, but Phil refused to touch her. Instead of husband and wife, their relationship became that of holy man and temptress. Debbie promised to keep their indulgences a secret, but Phil refused to be defiled. Despite a mutual desire for a close relationship, the two drifted apart.

In the late spring of 1973, Phil and Larry were given positions of responsibility in the church when Jones appointed them to the newly created Planning Commission, which was to be the Temple's governing body, and to the counseling staff for the Wednesday night, members-only services. Although the membership of the Temple was largely elderly and black, the P.C. was mostly white, and the average age was about twenty-five. This group was the elite of the Temple. Most had donated all their worldly possessions to the church, even going so far as to sell their homes, cash in their stocks and bonds, and turn all their goods over to the Temple. Every member had sworn complete fealty to Jones.

P.C. meetings were cathartic marathon encounter sessions, with members taking turns "on the floor." Most ran four to eight hours, some as long as twenty. They were grueling experiences for everyone except Jones. Wearing his dark glasses, Jones reclined full length on a couch during the sessions. Sometimes he napped. Near his pillowed head was an ever-present white medicine bag. On the table next to the couch a bowl of fruit was handy. Occasionally during the meetings Jones would be served steak. He would apologize during those all-night sessions for taking drugs to stay awake and for eating fruit and meat in front of the group while they made do with sunflower seeds. His unbalanced blood sugar was to blame, he said. If his insulin were thrown out of whack, his temper would flare dangerously and he might end up killing someone. Jones was also on speed, in fact had been addicted to the drug for some time. Such were the secrets of the P.C. In return for the intimate knowledge, each P.C. member was sworn to silence and made a counselor for life. It was assumed that extreme punishment, even death, would be meted to anyone who tried to leave.

When a member was "on the floor," it was his or her turn to bear the brunt of the group's criticism. Many of these attacks were over relatively minor lapses in a member's character or deeds. Jones claimed to be extremely concerned about such minor matters because he believed that small things pointed most clearly to a person's fundamental moral strength. And if a member couldn't see how that was true, that in itself was an even greater defect. A crucial consequence of such exercises was to make each member appear weak and untrustworthy in the eyes of the others.

"On the floor" meant that the offender would come forward to face questions from Jones, the Planning Commission, and the congregation. Everyone would take turns directing accusations and personal attacks at the offender, building to a climactic session of browbeating until a satisfying catharsis had been achieved. A member might be on the floor through a succession of dozens of attackers. During an attack, the offender had to stand ramrod straight in a manner that conveyed the utmost respect for Jones and other members of the group. The husband or wife or closest friend of the person on the floor was expected to lead the attack.

The closer their relationship to you the quicker you were supposed to be in confronting them, one member recalls. "It was an established rule. If you were on the floor, and your wife didn't attack you right off the bat, once they finished the catharsis with you, they'd turn right on your wife and say, 'Hey, you know the rules. You're supposed to be on his ass first thing.'"

In the beginning, the browbeating was administered in an atmosphere of love and caring. Later, in congregational meetings, physical punishment became part of the catharsis. A large wooden paddle, labeled "The Board of Education," was brought in. Spankings were fairly ritualistic at first, five or ten whacks followed by a hug from Jones. Then it was fifty or a hundred blows, with nurses standing by to treat the wounds. After a session, Jones would comfort those who had been attacked, assuring them that they would be stronger for having suffered. He was their emotional coach, he explained, and they had to get tough to win the game against the outside world.

Defending against a criticism from the group was one sure way to make more trouble for yourself, but many members soon learned formula responses to attacking statements. "You had to say what they wanted to hear without letting them know it. So, with a straight face a person would say, 'Well, the reason I don't like doing this is I don't like facing my homosexuality.' That was a great response. You could sit your ass down with a response like that. Get right off the floor."

One member of the commission was John Collins, who, as Jones' son-in-law—husband of one of his adopted daughters, a Korean girl named Sue—enjoyed Jones' private confidences. John was called on the floor because of an innocent affectionate hug he had given a woman other than his wife. When word got back to Jones that "John hugged Julie," Jones called him into a private session. "Don't worry," he told John, "we can handle it here. We won't let anybody know." And then Jones went on about his own sexual prowess, and how he had to have sex with other men's wives to help them out, all the time telling his son-in-law how attracted he himself was to Sue. John thanked Jones, thinking that the incident was closed.

Then came the next P.C. meeting. "There I was, sitting in the meeting with my wife," John recalls, "and Jim said, 'John, why were you sitting next to Julie on the bus yesterday? What are you up to with Julie?' Now, here's Sue sitting there. I told him, 'Nothing.' Then Larry Layton jumped in. 'You know,' said Larry, 'you never talk about your homosexuality and your homosexual fears. Why don't you tell us what they are.' Larry had this way of trying to be overbearing. Now, I don't blame Larry. Jim had so emasculated the poor guy, taking his wife Carolyn, handing him Karen, and making fun of him all the time. I had this underlying sympathy for Larry because of the things he'd been through. I thought, I could never take that.

"Well, Larry was considered kind of a joke in Planning Commission meetings because he would make these comments and everybody would just say, 'Oh, shut up, Larry.' Or Larry would scream and holler and it would be Larry Layton doing his thing and it was a big joke. It was hard not to laugh at him. Especially when Jim would laugh at him.

"So Larry jumps up and says something about my not admitting my homosexual feelings. I came back, 'Well, the one thing I'm really afraid of is that Jim is going to have to screw my wife.' That brought down the house. 'Oh God,' Jim says, 'how can you say something like that? I've loved you and done all this stuff for you. Why, you dumb bastard, you wouldn't even have had her if I hadn't brought her around to you. How can you have these evil thoughts about me?'

"But I'm glad I said it. Because I think that was the one thing that kept Jim from Sue."

Jones himself was never on the floor. (Nor was his wife, Marceline, a strong assistant minister whose presence held people in place when Jim was absent. Marceline seldom attended Planning Commission meetings.) "I would love to have the opportunity of being on the floor," Jones would say, "and I would love to be able to accept your criticisms. Believe me, everything you say about everyone else, I do look to in myself. But brothers and sisters, we need a strong leader here, and it would not be wise." Rarely did Jones have to make such an explanation. Someone else would usually jump up and interrupt him in midsentence to offer it for him.

The last statement required of each Temple member who was on the floor was, "Thank you, Father." Even when Jones attacked a miserable spouse and complained mightily that he, Jones, was forced to have sex with the miscreant's wife or husband, the required dutiful response was, "Thank you, Father. I really appreciate your having done this. It has made me a better socialist and I am more selfless now."

Jones had originally composed the Planning Commission almost entirely of men, but now he began to see that the exclusion of wives posed a security risk. The P.C. shared certain clandestine knowledge that Jones didn't want leaked to non-P.C. members. To forestall such leakage, Jones decided that the Planning Commission would be more secure if the wives joined in and shared in its secrets.

Therefore, one day several months after he became a P.C. member, Phil approached Debbie with a big smile on his face.

"Something good is going to happen to you tonight," he said cryptically. "I'm really proud of you." Debbie hoped that Phil was hinting that Jones had finally given them permission to consummate their marriage.

During the counseling meeting that night, Jones read out the names of the women he wanted to meet with after the service, so that they could assume extra responsibilities. Debbie was on the list. Later, as the chosen women stood around the large baptismal swimming pool, Jones told them that the men of the Planning Commission were not doing their job well because they were taking advantage of their position to indulge personal relationships. The cause would be better served, he said, if wives were also on the P.C. Then the men would have to be more disciplined.

Jones divulged some of his secrets to the new P.C. members. Certain women, he said, had been coming to him "begging for it." He had been forced, for the sake of the cause, to have frequent sexual relations with at least one of the nurses who assisted at the healings. He claimed to be the father of Grace and Tim Stoen's three-year-old son, John. He then spoke about his health. The Planning Commission was never to let on to the rest of the congregation that Jones had cancer and a heart condition, though they would know that if he clutched his chest during a heated confrontation, he might be about to give his life for the good of the cause.

The new women members of the Planning Commission were impressed. "Because he trusted us enough to make these revelations," says Debbie, "we felt powerfully obliged to pledge our loyalty in return."

This was Debbie's first position of responsibility in the church—or, for that matter, in any group—and initially she thought it was a glorious thing. Later, however, she came to dread it. The P.C. sessions often lasted most of the night, cutting into her study and sleep hours. Counselors were spared confrontation before the congregation only to be ripped apart by each other in the private P.C. meetings. Sometimes Debbie and the other college students barely had time to drive up to Santa Rosa for their classes on the morning following a P.C. meeting.

Larry's tenure on the Planning Commission was not going as well as Phil's and Debbie's—he started getting into trouble with Jim Jones. Several months after Larry's and Karen's marriage, Jones became concerned that his matchmaking had been too successful. The attractive, affectionate couple were an open threat to the doctrine that no one but Jones could satisfy a woman. So he increased Karen's load of work for the church until she had almost no time to be with Larry. And then he seduced her. He told her that he had fantasized about her for a long time, that he had to have her "so that I can continue my work." Probably he slept with her only two or three times— just enough to weaken the marriage, and to cause Larry to dwell on his inadequacy as a husband.

When Larry's anger and frustration became evident, Jones took him aside for a private conversation. Jones asked, "How do you feel about me, Larry?" Larry opened up and told him his honest feelings. "I hate you," he said.

At the next meeting of the Planning Commission, Jones addressed Larry publicly. "Something bothers me about you," he said. "You have told me you hate me." He did not mention any reasons that Larry might have had for this feeling. The members of the P.C. at least pretended to be aghast at the revelation; Larry had no right to such negative feelings, after all that Jim had done for him.

The next night Larry was again put on the floor, this time in front of the entire congregation. Jones announced that he was going to make an example of a Planning Commission member, to show that they were not immune to error and correction. Larry's punishment was to be a boxing match. Peoples Temple boxing matches had an unusual rule—offenders were supposed to take the blows of their opponents without defending themselves or hitting back. The point was to feel the pain and be remorseful for the offense. Each round lasted three minutes; for each round a new opponent would step up to beat the offender.

Larry's opponents did not pull their punches; he was struck hard in the face and stomach. By the end of the third round his eyes were swollen and his face and nose were bleeding. In the fourth round he suddenly gave way to anger and began to fight back. Jones screamed at him that he was a coward for returning the blows.

Larry was still dedicated to the goals of the Temple, and he remained a nominal member of the Planning Commission;

but he never again held any real power in the church. In fact, more and more, most of the people to whom Jones allowed any meaningful power were women. It was easier for him to control them sexually.

Temple members were always hearing from Jones about his enormous sexual prowess. One person who was particularly favored with such tales was John Collins. "It got to the point where I thought that women had a socialist nerve that went from the vagina to the base of the brain," John says, "and once it was stimulated, they'd be a socialist for life. I half-jokingly believed it. I mentioned it to Jim because he was always talking about how this socialist thing did the trick. I said, 'It seems to me like there's this socialistic nerve down there.' He laughed at that."

John and his father-in-law had enjoyed a close relationship for years, ever since he and his parents had joined the church when he was twelve. When he was seventeen, they had followed Jones west from Indiana. Now John was twenty-six, and the two men enjoyed sitting up and talking late into the night.

"I felt free to ask him most questions, but he'd always get into the sex thing. He'd say, 'First of all, women come up to you because they've never had a good sex life. No one really has. I'm the only one in the world that can do this kind of stuff.' Jim would be lying on the couch. He would say, 'Now the first thing is, a woman likes to be fucked for about forty-five minutes. Generally, they don't like to be fucked for more than that. So I do that at first. But then, the next time, I fuck them for four or five hours.' He spoke very bluntly like that. 'And that totally devastates them.' He wasn't being cocky, in fact he said it as if he had some concern for them, a feeling for them. 'They get "on the clock,"' he would say, '"and that seems to keep most of them in line."'

Sometimes with John, Jones would reveal his own anxieties and fears. Jones worried about growing old, showing weakness. "He was rather defensive about dyeing his hair or not wanting to move around when his leg hurt and have people see him limp. He'd say, 'Now, people out there, show them any sign you're growing older and they'll desert you. They'll leave. You always have to be aware of that. There's an old saying:

'He who rides the tiger dare not dismount.'"

"Having put the pressure on," John explains, "Jim could never take it off. Everybody in the Temple was in that same position."

A few visitors to the Temple were not taken in by Jones' rhetoric. On a late summer day in 1972 Lester Kinsolving, an ordained minister and religious reporter for the San Francisco *Examiner*, journeyed the 115 miles north to Redwood Valley. He wanted to check out for himself the wild and dazzling claims that were going around the religious circles that were part of his beat as a reporter. His visit was unannounced; he didn't want any special preparations on his behalf.

Jones' San Francisco flock arrived in Redwood Valley that Sunday in the Temple's fleet of ex-Greyhound buses. The services began at eleven in the morning and ran until eleven at night, with breaks for communal meals prepared by the Temple's cooks.

During the service Kinsolving met Timothy Stoen, one of Jones' five assistant pastors and the prosecuting attorney of Mendocino County. Five days before Kinsolving's article about his visit was to appear in the *Examiner*, the reporter received a letter from Stoen. The following excerpt from that letter was printed in Kinsolving's column: "Jim has been the means by which more than 40 persons have literally been brought from the dead this year. When I first came into the church I was the conventional skeptic about such things. But I must be honest.

"I have seen Jim revive people stiff as a board, tongues hanging out, eyes set, skin graying, and all vital signs absent. Don't ask me how it happens. It just does.

"Jim will go up to such a person and say something like 'I love you' or 'I need you' and immediately the vital signs reappear. He feels such a person can feel love in his subconscious even after dying.

"Jim is very humble about his gift and does not preach it." As a matter of fact, Stoen added, "the Prophet eschews publicity."

That shyness sounded commendable, but Kinsolving had problems reconciling it with the three tables he had seen set up just outside the main entrance to the Redwood Valley Temple. They were loaded with photographs, necklaces, and lockets, all bearing the image of Jones, with price tags ranging from $1.50 to $6.00.

Kinsolving was also bothered by the fact that some attendants at the services wore pistols in their belts. An *Examiner* photographer counted three side arms, including a .357 Magnum, and a shotgun. Kinsolving had inquired about this and been told that these guardians were necessary because Jones and the Temple had suffered threats and acts of vandalism. "Our local law enforcement agency," a Temple attorney had explained, "has requested that we have trained persons carry firearms, and we have reluctantly acquiesced to the sheriff's instructions on this matter."

After Kinsolving returned to San Francisco he was bombarded with letters, phone calls, and a visit from a member of the Mendocino County Probation Department, all of them intent on pointing the reporter toward the true light. In spite of such pressures, Kinsolving ended his column with a paragraph that would turn Jones against reporters from that day onward. "Meanwhile," Kinsolving concluded, "his sturdy sentries lend the temporal assurance that the Temple of the Prophet is the best-armed house of God in the land."

Kinsolving was eager to attend the next religious extravaganza, a weekend festival at the Benjamin Franklin Junior High School auditorium in San Francisco on September 16 and 17, 1972. The services began in high gear.

"I know that Pastor Jim Jones is God Almighty himself," screamed a woman from the audience of more than a thousand who overflowed the high school auditorium.

Jones, smiling behind dark glasses, wore a white turtleneck sweater under his ministerial robes. He sat on a cushion-covered stool behind the podium.

"You say I am God Almighty?" Jones shot back.

"Yes you are!" the woman shrieked. The audience, completely with her, clapped, waved their arms, stamped their feet, roared their approval.

Jones held up his hand for silence. "What do you mean by that? If you believe I am a son of God in that I am filled with love, I can accept that. I won't knock what works for you— but I don't want to be interpreted as the creator of the universe." His tone became softer. "If you say, 'He is God,' some people will think you are nuts. They can't relate. I'm glad you were healed, but I'm really only a messenger of God. I have a paranormal ability in healing."

During that service Jones performed two "resuscitations" of parishioners who had fainted or gone into a catatonic stiffening during the general hullabaloo. In each instance, Jones stopped dead in the middle of a sentence, leaped from the stage into the audience, and laid his hands on the afflicted congregant. After a hushed thirty seconds, the tension of the multitudes broke as Jones lifted the prostrate worshiper up in his arms to thunderous applause.

Later, when an elderly woman began hopping up and down in a frenzy in front of the stage, Jones picked up the microphone and explained, "You'll have to understand—she was given up to die. They said she'd never be able to move again. Such experiences are not at all uncommon to us. That's the forty-third time this has happened. I just said, 'I love you. God loves you. Come back to us.' The registered nurses around her said it was so."

Kinsolving observed in his next article that none of the nurses were introduced or even identified, and added that they were hardly even apparent "given the number of large men who surrounded the reported resurrection." He did note, however, that none of the ushers wore guns to this service, something that Jones himself pointed out. "You all complied with my wishes," Jones congratulated the congregation, "and didn't bring guns, even though you are so afraid for me."

The day after Kinsolving's second report, 150 pickets from the Peoples Temple surrounded the *Examiner* building in a demonstration that lasted a week. "Invasion of privacy," read one placard. "This paper has lied," said another.

Those columns were the first published criticism of Jones and the Peoples Temple. Their skepticism infuriated Jones and reinforced his mounting paranoia about the enemy without. As for that outside world, while a number of pieces of information were becoming available about the Reverend Jim Jones' operation, there was no one yet to fit the puzzle together.

Lisa Layton attended her first Peoples Temple meeting early in 1973. Her decision to visit the evening services at the Temple in San Francisco came not at the urging of her children but at the invitation of Elizabeth and Ted Cunningham, a black couple she had met at the Quaker meeting in Berkeley, and with whom she had been friendly for fourteen years. The Cunninghams were seeking a cure for Ted's terminal cancer, and out of desperation were willing to take a chance on Jones' well-publicized healing powers. Lisa, who had always harbored a terrible fear of cancer, accompanied them, partly out of curiosity. An even stronger incentive, though, was to see for herself the powers this faith healer had over her children.

The emphasis that evening was on politics, with a few cures thrown in for the benefit of visitors. Jones had originally intended it to be a cathartic "beat-up-on-people" meeting, but he took a different tack when surprised by the arrival of Mrs. Layton and her friends. The visitors watched a man "bring up" a cancer, and they listened to Jones preach against social injustice. The Cunninghams never went back, but Lisa Layton was a changed woman from that day on. As she wrote to Tom, then teaching at Louisiana State University, Baton Rouge:

"Friday night I went to Peoples Temple for the first time. Do you remember the Cunninghams from Friends Meeting? Well Elizabeth C. called me and asked if I would like to go with her and Ted C. to the Peoples Temple meeting in San Francisco.

"Well, I went and enjoyed it very much. Phil, Debbie and Karen were there and also Annie Moore. The service or meeting or whatever you want to call it lasted until about 1 A.M. I enjoyed every bit of it. There was a lot of singing—loud and with lots of rhythm. Jim Jones talked, the Deputy Mayor of San Francisco talked, and there was some healing done. It was an experience, and I was impressed!

"Dad would have gone too but he didn't feel well enough. I am not so sure that he would have liked it."

Lisa began to attend the Temple three nights a week, frequently staying until the early hours of the morning. Then she started taking trips every other week to the Los Angeles branch for three days at a time. Lisa found the meetings stimulating. She assured everyone that she asked questions, that she wasn't blind, but to her, Jones seemed to have all the right answers to her lifelong search for meaning.

Jones captivated such relatively sophisticated upper-middle-class white people as Lisa Layton, and John and Barbara Moore, by sharing with them his professional secrets and soliciting their opinions. He took the time to explain to Lisa why he was doing certain things that might seem unacceptable to her. He made her feel a special part of the organization, in the know. Jones would tell her privately, "Of course I'm not God, of course I'm not Jesus. But these people are so religious that in order to bring them around to socialism I have to tell them these things." Lisa was willing to put up with a lot of things that violated her common sense once they were explained to her as the necessary means to the glorious objective of a socialist world of equality and brotherhood—a world without war.

Lisa soon believed in Jones to the point of fanaticism. To her children she claimed that she questioned everything that Jones said, but what Annalisa and Debbie noticed was that she never questioned his answers to those questions. She loved going to Temple meetings because she always learned something new and meaningful. She thoroughly enjoyed hearing the concepts of socialism as they were continually phrased and rephrased. She believed in all of Jones' powers. She claimed that it took so much of his energy to heal people that should she herself become sick she would not ask him to heal her. She loved and cared for him so much that she would not dare use him up.

She worried for him. She was afraid that he was overdoing it, that he wasn't taking good care of himself. She asked Annalisa for advice on purchasing a lamp for Jones' bedroom; she was afraid he was hurting his eyesight by reading in poor overhead light.

During Lisa's early involvement with Peoples Temple, she became preoccupied with fears of a nuclear holocaust, and with internment in a concentration camp. She believed Jones when he said that blacks would be put in camps and that sympathetic whites would join them. Yet her fear of such an internment was mitigated by her involvement with blacks in the Temple. As a young girl in Germany she had found herself helpless when her relatives and friends had been sent off to Nazi death camps. By joining in the work of Peoples Temple, she would never have to feel that way again.

Every Temple member, including Lisa, was convinced of

government plots against the Temple. Gradually these plots became more pervasive, more complicated, and more threatening to the membership.

Both Debbie and Larry Layton knew that their mother "missed us, and wanted to be near us. The church had separated us; she would have to join it to get back her children." The Temple could also provide Lisa Layton with a connection to the world outside her family. Never having pursued a career beyond child-rearing, she had in recent years held a variety of "interesting" jobs. Throughout the late 1960s she had worked part-time in the newspaper room of the U.C. Berkeley library, handling the radical leftist and Third World newspapers popular with the students. It was fiery stuff, but until Jim Jones there hadn't been a way for her to participate in the social revolution these publications endorsed.

And she needed to commit herself to someone, something, more than ever. At the age of fifty-nine, Lisa Layton found herself without a purpose in life. Her children were grown; her husband was concerned only with his own work and his private thoughts.

Lisa had often described to Annalisa the happiest day of her life. It had been one of those times when, at the age of ten or eleven, she had played Indians with some other children at the country home of friends. "She was in love with the boy who was the 'chief,' and he chose her to be his 'squaw.' As squaw she would make arrows for him. She said that as she made the arrows she realized that she loved this boy so much that she would have been willing to die for him. Those were her words, exactly. I don't think she felt that way again until she met Jim Jones."

For years, Lisa felt painful recriminations for her premarital affairs and shame as a Jew. She believed that her husband had never forgiven her. She could never fully surrender to him. Jim Jones was the forgiving chief she had been searching for.

Jones claimed to know everything about Dr. Layton. But even though he urged Lisa to leave her husband, the couple stayed together for a little over a year after that first service. When Lisa was at home, which wasn't often, there seemed always to be a Temple member around who needed food or transportation. Finally, Dr. Layton observed to his wife that the marriage seemed to have ended. "She agreed," he recalls, "saying that she did not have any need for sex or men, or any interest in them. But she granted that this might not be fair to me. I suggested moderation. She was reluctant. She objected to having marital relations and found ways to avoid this, or to reject me before I could achieve climax. She suggested that I get a girl friend. I was shocked, but pretended to be amused. She wrote a note giving me 'permission' to fool around. I thought this was a joke, but she insisted that it was 'for real' and put the note in my briefcase after it had laid on a table for several days. I did not oblige her on this, but I did argue for our marriage. I told her that long ago I had come to love her and respect her as a wonderful wife and mother."

Laurence Layton's arguments were to no avail. Lisa planned for weeks in advance, lining up an apartment, before surprising her husband with the announcement that she was leaving him "for a while." She had secured an inexpensive studio in south Berkeley. When Dr. Layton saw the prospective apartment, he insisted on a nicer place. He helped her find an apartment at the Watergate, a posh complex on the Berkeley waterfront. She moved in on September 3, 1974.

"I tried to pretend that it was a temporary separation, that she needed to collect her thoughts. She just became more and more cold toward me." Dr. Layton also helped to select and buy new furniture for her apartment and provided a monthly allowance to be certain that she was comfortable. It was a paternal reaction. As he told his son Tom, "I raised five children, your mother being the fifth."

Two months later she asked for a divorce, letting him know that despite her newfound faith in a simpler life she had every intention of seeking her half of the communal property they had accumulated in thirty-three years of marriage. She turned over her stocks and money to the Temple on the day the divorce became final. By the time Lisa died in Guyana, she had donated more than three hundred thousand dollars in cash, stocks, and property to the Peoples Temple.

Lisa donated all her time to the cause, working on projects like the bake sales to raise funds. She also gave her mind. She took Jones' ideas as her own, readily adopting whatever rules he laid down. Sleep was overrated, according to Jones, so she stayed up working into the predawn hours. Jones knew that this permanent state of fatigue made both minds and bodies easier to control. Everyone was homosexual, she learned, so she admitted to Annalisa that she had probably been homosexual all her life. She asked Annalisa if she thought Tom was homosexual, adding, "Some of my best friends are, you know." People outside the church were not to be trusted; in an echo of her own mother's fatal fears, Lisa accused a guest of Annalisa's of being a CIA plant. Annalisa assured her that the woman was a law student from Davis, not an undercover agent. "Don't tell that plant anything about Peoples Temple," her mother begged.

Lisa developed a blatant new honesty. All her life she had denied her Jewishness. Jones encouraged her to accept her heritage, to become a "Jewish nigger," as he put it. She wrote a story about being a Jew in Nazi Germany, and read it in front of the congregation more than once. She wrote a song about the happiness she had found with the Peoples Temple and sang it *a cappella* during services.

Her friends outside the church were surprised by this drastic change in personality. To them, the once-gentle housewife had developed a hardness, a militancy, and they refused to believe her claims of having found total happiness.

Thanksgiving 1974 sounded a kind of death knell for the family dynasty that Laurence Layton had longed to build. The previous year, with Debbie, Phil, Larry, and Karen kept busy by the church, the family had been a shadow of its former self. Now, just one year later, with Lisa also gone, it was virtually destroyed. The Temple had dismantled his marriage, taken his wife, and alienated his family. On November 26, 1974, under the heading "Recent Problem," he wrote in his journal, "Our marriage was rather calm and uneventful for 30 years. I was/am not an ardent lover, but was loyal—as I believe my wife was. The marriage might have been viewed by some as loveless. Lisa may have viewed it as boring and now, of course, as repulsive." Looking back on that year, he remembered that he had been involved in researching a major project in molecular biology. "It seemed as if one day, all of a sudden, I looked up from my books and everyone was gone."

7

The Temple on
Geary Boulevard

The next step in Jim Jones' battle plan to go "Big Time"—Target San Francisco—proved not quite as instant as he had prophesied. The move of Temple headquarters from Redwood Valley to the Bay City took two and a half years, from the purchase in November 1972 of the San Francisco Way Club (originally a Jewish synagogue) until Jones himself moved down to the cosmopolitan center in the spring of 1975. The move was formalized on November 1, 1976, when the church filed a certificate of amendment of its articles of incorporation, changing its place of business from Redwood Valley to San Francisco.

Soon after Lisa Layton joined Peoples Temple, she began to use every opportunity to try to convince her older daughter to join. Repeatedly she told Annalisa of the high humanitarian and egalitarian principles the Temple stood for and of the many wondrous miracles that Jones performed.

In the summer of 1975, Annalisa and her husband, Ray Valentine, together with their two children, moved from San Diego up to Davis, about an hour's drive east of San Francisco. Soon after the move, the couple began quarreling seriously. Lisa was there to suggest that now was the perfect time to consider joining the Temple. Annalisa agreed that she needed something, so in October she attended her first Wednesday night meeting. She was not impressed. Her mother, however, insisted that this was the first boring meeting she could remember and that Annalisa would have to attend at least three or four others to get a full sense of what was going on.

Several meetings later, Annalisa was even more confused. She heard constantly how the Temple and Jones had saved people from various kinds of self-destruction, and she could see all the "good things" that were happening, but suddenly, during one meeting, she was overwhelmed with fear that if she left the group some undefined calamity would strike, that an American gestapo group would hunt her down and capture her in her own home. She felt as if she were going crazy. She decided she needed to see a psychiatrist, but doubted that any psychiatrist would understand her situation.

Annalisa talked to Jones about her misgivings, and he reassured her. She told him she was considering joining the Temple but that she had deep doubts about his healing miracles. As far as she could see, it was all a fraud. Jones told her it was just as well she felt that way, because his "healing power" was no reason for someone like her to join. She didn't need miracles on which to secure her religion, since she had no religion, but she should at least see the need for ridding her country of capitalism, and should dedicate herself to helping to build a socialist society. He confided that his healing powers were actually a burden to him because most of the members were attracted to the Temple through their belief in those powers. Without that belief they would either leave or withhold their full support. And if they left, they would be condemned to lead miserable lives. He said he really loved these fine old people and was working only for them.

It was a point that Annalisa's mother used to continue her own pressure. Lisa told her daughter that Jones wanted to help the people, especially the old and the poor, those who had no defender. He was not out to save the rich, people who were too tied to their status and money to consider socialism. The poor and the blacks were the true nobility of American society. They had been given nothing but religion, a hope in the after-life. Their actual life was so miserable, and these people were so tied up with God, Jesus, and religion that he, Jones, had to replace that dependency with something else. It was Jones' plan, Lisa explained, to transfer the object of their worship from Jesus to himself. While this transfer was taking place he would be teaching them about socialism. When his followers were intellectually strong enough in their understanding of so-cialism, Jones would then remove himself as a savior image.

In spite of her attraction to the life of service the Temple offered, Annalisa had problems with accepting the whole pack-age. The more she listened to the descriptions of the beauties of socialism and Jones' personal interpretation of world events, the more convinced she became that it was money speaking, not humanity. She was also bothered by the illogic of those Temple members who were not fooled by Jones' healing pow-ers, or his claims to be Jesus, yet who were convinced that Jones could foresee the future, that he had information that no one else was aware of. These members also believed that the Temple was the only antidote to all the ills of the world, that whatever happened in the United States of a bad or evil na-ture—the pollution of a river or the assassination of a political leader—Jim Jones automatically and always had the answer. Jones and his followers portrayed him as the good to counter all evil. And Annalisa just couldn't accept that.

Karen Layton assumed a take-it-or-leave-it attitude on the question of Annalisa's joining, and began to evidence a real dislike for her sister-in-law. Karen criticized Annalisa for plac-ing her concerns about her own family above those of "the greater community." Whenever Debbie, Larry, and Karen vis-ited the Valentines in Davis, Karen would drop disparaging remarks about the children's behavior or the fact that Annalisa's husband, Ray, enjoyed watching football games on television. Temple members did not watch football because it was a violent sport. Jones had told Karen that he thought Ray was working for the CIA; he claimed that his psychic powers had picked up the information from another plane.

Karen may have felt threatened by Annalisa's beauty and keen mind. Displeased by the fact that Annalisa took so much of Jones' time with her constant questioning, she labeled Annalisa as "super-critical." This pattern of criticism and jealousy was common among the women most closely involved with Jones.

Actually, whatever Karen's suspicions, Jones had never liked Annalisa. In the complex of her own personal troubles and viewpoints, she wasn't vulnerable enough for him to gain access to and control over her will. He confided to Debbie that Annalisa's eyes were untrustworthy—green and glassy like a cat's eyes—and that she reminded him of one of the Temple's three "traitors," a nurse who had defected about a year earlier. One evening when Annalisa and Debbie were talking after services in a room adjoining the main auditorium, Jones entered, pointed a finger at Annalisa, and shouted at her, "You doubt me. If you still have doubts why don't you get the hell out of here. Don't come anymore."

By the end of the winter Annalisa felt pulled in opposite directions: on the one hand held by her mother's involvement, and on the other repelled by Jones. She appreciated much of the Temple's work and aims—all her life she had been a Quaker and had believed in liberal humanitarian ideals—but she was definitely not an activist. In the past, close friends had urged her to join—to protest against the Vietnam War, to rally against the draft, to march with Martin Luther King. She believed in those causes, but she had not joined. Once again, the same kind of decision was facing her. She wanted to do good, but she could see that Jones had become obsessed with the Temple as a mirror of his own power. When she complained that there was no democracy in the Temple, members explained to her that if there were everyone would go his or her own way and there would be no group.

Meanwhile, Ray had become so disturbed by her visits to the Temple that he was ready to force her into a choice. "There are no such things as miracles," he told her. "The whole thing is a fraud. All of these socialist and humanitarian works are worthless because they are built on a fraudulent foundation." When she continued to resist his arguments, he told her that she could leave him if she chose, but that he would not allow their two children to join the Temple with her.

Annalisa saved herself by a gradual withdrawal from the Temple. She continued to attend meetings throughout the winter, but went as seldom as she could get away with. Jones, apparently realizing that his hold on her was not sufficiently strong to break her away from her husband and children, excused her from attending the usual five meetings a week because of her "domestic commitments."

In May 1976, she went to Jones for a last conversation. Jones by then had given up on her, whether out of frustration or unwillingness to be in the middle of a child custody battle between Annalisa and her husband. Annalisa complained about the constant intimidation that she felt from his followers and from him. She repeated her early fears, telling Jones that she was afraid of the implications of what he said in services, that if she or anyone left the group something terrible would happen. Jones replied that no such implication existed and that if she wanted to walk out and never return there would be no repercussions. He did add that if she did so he was convinced that she would lead a meaningless and unhappy life.

Annalisa never returned again. Her mother kept her informed on Temple activities and continued to maintain that the time would come when Annalisa would be ready to join wholeheartedly. Lisa's enthusiasm for her daughter's conversion never waned.

While Annalisa was struggling with the decision of commitment to the Temple, Debbie was working hard to prove her loyalty as a member of the Planning Commission. The Temple reward for hard work was always more hard work, and Debbie was so responsive that she was appointed to the Diversions Committee as well.

As a tax-exempt nonprofit charitable organization, the Temple could not legally engage in political activity. On the other hand, the church's espoused goal was to create political and social change. To resolve this conflict, the Diversions Committee was formed. Committee members would draft letters in support of whatever legislation Jones favored and would type them out on special "D" (for Diversion) typewriters purchased from thrift shops. These letters were handled and inserted into their envelopes with surgical gloves so that there would be no fingerprints. The D typewriters were never used for official church business, and were destroyed after serving their purpose. The committee also planned and carried out pressure campaigns against enemies of the church. For example, after Lester Kinsolving ran his columns that were critical of the Temple, the committee conducted a smear campaign so that he would lose his job. As a result of their rumors and harassment, Kinsolving was eventually transferred out of California.

Terri Buford was the head of the Diversions Committee. She had an analytical mind and a strong scientific background. According to Debbie, she spent considerable effort devising plans to secure information on church enemies. One such case involved George Klineman, a Santa Rosa journalist who had been investigating the Temple. Terri contacted a private investigator and paid him four hundred dollars for a copy of Klineman's telephone bill. An examination of Klineman's long-distance phone calls revealed many placed to Treasury Department officials. The committee didn't know whether he was a T-man himself or whether he was discussing Temple finances with the government, but either way it was bad for them. In time, Diversion Committee members tunneled an entry under Klineman's house and stood around under his floorboards listening to meetings between Klineman and various church defectors. Thus forewarned with accurate information, the Temple was better able to protect itself.

Diversion Committee work became more demanding as the Temple moved into San Francisco politics. Letters were drafted by the thousands, cleared by Jones, and taken out of town or out of state to be mailed. In addition to the library of taped telephone conversations that the committee kept on file, there were extensive dossiers on all members of the church. The Diversion Committee also collected bits and pieces of information on the families and friends of current and prospective members. This was accomplished by gaining entrance to their homes and reading old correspondence and family papers. During services, Jones would casually mention obscure facts about some member and thus appear to be exercising supernatural powers.

These same files also included signed confessions of all manner of crimes allegedly committed by church members. A new member was not considered loyal unless he or she had a signed confession on file. The worse the crime confessed to, the stronger the implied loyalty. Members confessed to being violent revolutionaries; to making bombs; to planning to kill the president; to being homosexuals and child molesters. Confessions were never dated, so that they would always be "current." Some members even signed blank pieces of paper, so that other charges could be made up as needed.

For a long time, Debbie knew only vaguely what the committee was up to. Matters were handled on a need-to-know basis, and most of the work assigned to her was secretarial. She didn't ask questions or show any special interest in events that did not directly concern her for fear that others would become suspicious of her motives and attack her on the floor. Generally, Diversion Committee information was closely guarded, but Debbie did "happen" to learn of one major church caper—the bombing of a military supply train in Roseville, California, just northeast of Sacramento.

One of the most trusted members of the church had left, and Debbie was allowed to move into her room. While rearranging the furniture, Debbie discovered a packet of typed pages describing the plan for the attack. Parts of the manuscript were underlined, and the margins were filled with handwritten notations. Debbie could make out that Jones and several other members of the church had carried out the operation. She took the packet to Terri Buford, whose reaction was "Oh, my God! Give that to me!" Thinking back to that moment, Debbie feels sure that Terri was not one bit surprised to see the document in her hand. But at the time, Debbie was convinced she had stumbled onto something. She was reminded of the incident several months later during a Planning Commission meeting when a counselor was confronted with something he had done. In his own defense, he accused Jones of not having trust in him. To which Jones replied, "Do you honestly believe that I don't trust you after what we did at Roseville?" Debbie, however, was never able to tell if the Temple had actually been responsible.

There were several reasons for allowing this "plot" to become known. It would make it appear that Jones was willing to risk his own life in the cause; it would make Debbie and others similarly taken in feel that they had been trusted with an important secret, however "accidentally"; and it would be more difficult for individuals to defect if they feared being implicated for real crimes.

Jones once told John Collins that one of the Temple's major protections from serious investigation and prosecution was the very nature of the church's practices—practices so extreme that no one on the outside would believe them. Conversely, members who were allowed to learn special secrets, real facts, and methods of the church, were afraid to defect because they were convinced that the sensitivity of what they knew would make it necessary for the Temple to kill them.

In January 1974, Debbie had graduated with an Associate of Arts degree from Santa Rosa Junior College. She had made the dean's list and earned high honors. Science and medicine had always interested her, but her earlier grades were an obstacle to medical school. She decided that technical training in health services would be a good alternative, so with Jones' blessing she enrolled in the San Francisco School for Health Professions to become an operating-room technician. Dr. Layton paid her tuition. At the same time that she enrolled, Debbie moved in with Lisa, and the two of them lived together until Debbie finished her training.

Debbie kept up a hectic schedule of attending classes, church services, P.C. meetings, and working at her first paying job, clerking at a doughnut shop in San Francisco. The pace was exhausting. More than once she found herself struggling to stay awake during church meetings or in the operating room. About this time, the growing violence in the church began to frighten her. Bloody boxing matches were growing more frequent, and often they would go on until the victim could no longer rise from the mat.

Debbie was also demoralized by what Jones had done to her brother Larry. Aware that Jones had taken Carolyn away from Larry, giving him Karen in her place, Debbie now watched as Jones seduced Karen as well. He did it partly by getting Larry to admit that he had homosexual desires for Jones—a confession every male member of the P.C. was pressured into making sooner or later. The result, as Debbie realized, was the addition of another loyal eunuch to Jones' palace guard.

Debbie first began to consider leaving the church while reading *Papillon,* a story of escape from prison on Devil's Island, during a bus trip to Los Angeles. She was part of the team that leafletted the city in advance of Jones' arrival. The next day they were joined by Jones and his entourage, including Maria Katsaris. "Did you hear what happened to Bob Houston?" Maria asked. "He threatened to leave the church and wrote a letter to Jim. He was killed. Smashed between two trains." And later, in sermons, Jones himself would say, "Bob Houston wrote a hateful letter to the church. See what happened to him?"

Robert Samuel Houston, Jr., thirty-three when he died, was the son of Associated Press news photographer Robert ("Sammy") Houston. He was one of the church's hardest workers. Jones broke up his first marriage, then assigned Joyce Shaw to him. Bob was reluctant, but agreed to marry her. He worked two jobs so that he could contribute two thousand dollars a month to the church. He and Joyce ran a home for twenty-four children assigned to them by Jones, including the two daughters from Houston's first marriage. But as far as Jones was concerned, Bob Houston had a terrible problem. He was one of the brightest people around, he asked probing questions, and when he took a stand, he would not budge—not even when he was brutally beaten in P.C. confrontations.

On July 16, 1976, Bob's second wife, Joyce, bought a bus ticket and left San Francisco. On October 2, she called her husband. On October 3, Houston wrote Jones a letter, the contents of which were never revealed. On October 4, the mangled body of Robert Samuel Houston, Jr., was found on the tracks at the Southern Pacific Railroad yard. He had been working two jobs, days as a counselor at the Youth Guidance Center, nights as a switchman. His light had been left on the brake wheel of a flatcar, his glove was found on the coupler.

Ten months after his death Houston's daughters, then thirteen and fourteen, were sent by Jones to the Temple's South American colony in Guyana.

After graduating from the health services school as an operating-room technician, Debbie hoped to be offered a job in the Oakland hospital where she had trained, and it appeared likely that she would. She had done well in school, and had loved her part-time job at the hospital. Jones, however, thought that if she took the job she would become less dependent on the Temple.

Jones often arranged for Temple members to be confronted

at crucial times—just before a major school examination, or on the threshold of advancement in an outside job. The object was to upset the member by means of a long cathartic session to the point where he or she would fail or become disheartened about the new opportunity. Outside rewards focused members outwardly, and that was exactly what Jones didn't want.

In the Temple, Debbie had been working on the Diversions Committee for several months. One day she refused to use one of the regular typewriters to do some Diversions Committee typing. Consequently, she was written up in a critical report to Jones. Jones, in turn, used this report as a pretext to have Debbie confronted on the floor.

They confronted her for hours. They confronted her for living with her mother in her mother's apartment. They confronted her for being overweight and for having a "smart mouth." They even confronted her for never having been confronted before. Her punishment was to move away from her mother and live in Ukiah.

Larry was at work, and not present for Debbie's confrontation. Immediately after the session, Jones told Debbie, "You should let Larry know that you were confronted for three hours." Because Larry had himself been confronted on numerous occasions, Jones wanted him to get the message that Debbie was not receiving special treatment.

Both Karen Layton and Larry's ex-wife, Carolyn, had been present during Debbie's confrontation, and what continued to bother Debbie most about the experience was the vehemence of Karen's participation. Karen had seemed to delight in aggressively attacking her sister-in-law.

After that confrontation, Debbie returned to her mother's apartment and wrote a long letter to Phil Blakey's mother in England. Phil, Debbie's husband in name only, had been out of her life for almost three years—ever since Jones had sent him to South America to work on an agricultural project in Guyana. Debbie was fond of her mother-in-law, and wrote that she wanted to join her in England. But then she became frightened and threw the letter away, packed her belongings, and moved to Ukiah.

It was typical that Jones sent Debbie to Ukiah after she had completed her training as an operating-room technician but before she could take the state licensing examination. The same thing happened to many Temple members being educated as nurses, doctors, or lawyers. Jones did not want his people to qualify for work outside the Temple; he wanted them to be unemployable should they ever leave him, trained only for his use in the Temple and, eventually, in Guyana.

For Debbie, Ukiah was like Siberia. She worked hard "to get into Jim's good graces again," and by the end of the summer she was given a job that reflected Jones' renewed trust. She was assigned to review tapes of P.C. meetings, particularly of conversations with suspected and outright "traitors" and potential blackmail victims. Her job was to listen to the tapes, jot down what "important" things were said, and return the tapes and notes to Carolyn Layton, the P.C. member in charge of the tape files. Debbie devoted herself to the tapes project, and Carolyn in turn passed glowing reports to Jones.

Exile to a propaganda-laden atmosphere such as the Temple's base in Ukiah was a common measure when Jones sensed that his hold on a member was loosening. Or he would overload them with work, challenging them to live up to such responsibility. Or he would seduce the person, strengthening his hold through amorous flattery and sex.

When Debbie was allowed to return to San Francisco in the fall of 1976, she was put back on the Diversion Committee. Soon Jones told her he was so pleased with her work that he was going to assign her to the Finance Committee as well. She became head of the offering room, where one of her duties was to count contributions. "We were pulling in tremendous amounts of money, often twenty to twenty-five thousand dollars on a three-day weekend," Debbie recalls. "After making the count for each offering, I would walk up to the pulpit and whisper the amount into Jim's ear. If he wasn't happy with the total, he'd ask for more—there were often several offerings in the evening."

One evening, as she started to walk away, Jones called her back. "Don't ever whisper in my ear again," he admonished her. "I'm extremely attracted to you." Debbie returned to the offering room, put her head down on her arms, and cried. Upset and confused, she tried to forget the incident.

A month later, following another evening service, she went to Jones' room to give him the final count on the night's take. Rose, an elderly black woman who was Jones' personal servant, left the room and closed the door behind her. Debbie got on her knees to spread the money out on the floor. She was pointing to the various stacks of checks, bills, and coins when Jones said, "Rose shouldn't have left like that. You'd better leave the room before I rape you." Shaken, she hurriedly gathered up the offering and left.

Debbie was afraid to refuse Jones' advances. She was aware that he had had sex with other women in the church; but they had maintained that they wanted and needed Jim. Maybe they did, but Debbie didn't. She didn't know what to do.

One night, returning from a Los Angeles service on the bus, Jones purposefully sat down next to her and chatted with her until the rest of the passengers had dozed off. As the bus rolled quietly through the fog of California's Central Valley, Jones leaned his head on her shoulder. He belched, and she could smell the liquor on his breath. He began to fondle her. Debbie was surprised by his awkwardness, his working on her like a high school novice.

Jones looked around to make certain no one was watching before placing his hand on her breast. He quickly worked his way down to her pants. She froze. "When the bus stops, don't get off," he whispered hoarsely. "Wait until I call for you." The back of this particular bus had been converted for the leader's comfort into a cozy apartment with a bed, a bar, and a private bath. Jones got up and went into his compartment and closed the door.

At the next rest stop, after everyone had gotten off the bus, Jones signaled for Debbie to come into his room. She was frightened. Brusquely he undressed her halfway. There was no foreplay, and he hurt her when he penetrated. He bit her on the neck, so hard that she thought he was going to break the skin. He finished quickly. Debbie remembered to thank him for the privilege. When it was over, the bus was moving again. Jones left the room, telling her to sneak out at the next rest stop as soon as he called in that the coast was clear. She waited, huddled in the room, for what seemed like hours. Finally the bus stopped; she could hear everyone chatting as they got off at the rest stop, and as they filed back on. Jones didn't call her. The bus started moving again.

"Oh my God, are you still here?" he exclaimed when he returned to the room. He told her to return to her seat by crawling on the floor past the sleeping passengers.

A few days later, Debbie came down with an extremely painful vaginal infection. Joyce Parks, the Temple nurse, told her to see a doctor. In the doctor's office, Debbie was so embarrassed that she fabricated a story about a husband who traveled a great deal. The doctor described the infection as common among those who have sex with many different partners. More specifically, the doctor said that the disease was common to persons who have intercourse "from both the back and the front with both men and women." Lots of sailors have it, he added. The doctor treated her, and the physical infection soon disappeared. Psychologically, though, she still felt diseased.

In the weeks that followed, Debbie tried to come to terms with the episode. She even composed a letter to Jones saying, in effect, that she understood why he had done it. It was for her own benefit, to improve her poor self-image and give her some confidence. "I told him that I knew it wasn't because he had any great love for me personally. I told him that I appreciated it. I said what I knew I was supposed to say."

Several weeks later, after a service in San Francisco, Jones sought her out and told her to hide behind a pillar in the main church until everyone had left. He found her there ten minutes later, led her into the men's room, pushed her to the floor, and jumped on top of her. "He nearly broke my neck," Debbie recalls. "I couldn't imagine how this was helping me." In the days that followed she thought more and more about getting out of the church, but she had gone so far that she was afraid to leave.

The third and last time Jones had sex with her occurred one evening as she was typing up notes from a counseling session. Terri Buford stuck her head in the door and said, "Jim wants to see you right away." Debbie picked up her notes and ran downstairs to Jones' room. Just as she entered, Jones emerged from his bathroom with an erection protruding from the folds of his bathrobe. "I want to fuck you," he announced. When it was over, he gave her his condom and told her to get rid of it.

A week later, he completed his act of humiliation and entrapment by exposing her at a Planning Commission meeting. "I want everyone who I've screwed recently to stand up," he said. Eight women stood up. Debbie remained seated.

"Now, one of you isn't going to, but you'd better because you're no different from anyone else."

Debbie stood up.

"We all knew what we were supposed to say because we had seen it all before. We were supposed to say that *we* had approached *him*; that he had helped us psychologically; that he had the biggest penis we had ever seen; that he could screw longer than anybody; and that we had never had an orgasm until we had sex with him. Until that moment I had always believed that what all the others previous to me had said was true; now I knew differently."

As he had done confidentially with his son-in-law John Collins, Jones now bragged openly about his sexual endurance. He told the Planning Commission that he'd had to make love to Karen Layton for eight hours as a sacrifice for the cause. Nevertheless, he added, no one should feel guilty about approaching him for sex. As a comfort to all, he admitted that even his own daughters had approached him.

"He screwed both men and women," says Debbie. "We were all in the same boat. He did it with every man on the Planning Commission so they wouldn't leave. If they tried to, he threatened to expose them to the outside world as homosexuals."

Despite all of Jones' lusty admissions, sex was still made to appear an ugly preoccupation. Chris was a twenty-one-year-old male virgin who made the mistake of announcing that he wanted to leave the church to find a girl friend. A Planning Commission meeting was called in his honor, with all female counselors briefed on what was expected of them. Jones greeted the young man sympathetically. "We understand you want to leave us because you think you're missing out on life never having had a relationship. We understand your problem. We want you to choose any woman here that you want to go to bed with."

"Debbie Blakey," he said. Debbie was shocked to hear her name. Even Jones was surprised. Debbie was quickly taken aside and told that she was not to touch or even act warmly toward Chris, but to disrobe and just stand in front of him. Jones then told the two of them to go upstairs to one of the sleeping rooms. "I did what I had been told to do," says Debbie.

"I took off my clothes and sat down. Chris just stood there, looking shocked, not making a move to undress. I told him to take off his clothes, then we lay down on the pad. He was frightened, and couldn't get an erection. I had been instructed not to help him in any way. This is the way it is, I told him, all relationships are like this. He wasn't missing out on anything; it was all the same, here or on the outside, and there was no point for him to leave the church. We dressed and went downstairs. Chris confessed to the commission that he hadn't been able to get it up. The poor kid was then confronted by the whole group for insulting me."

The move to San Francisco brought increased pressure on members to live communally. When people joined the church, they would give their property and savings as well as their salaries or pension checks to the organization. Before long, more than a thousand people were living communally in San Francisco. Every Tuesday evening, on "Needs Night," each member would itemize and detail in writing the money they would need for the next week. People generally got ten to twenty dollars to cover such essentials as gasoline and parking. Food was supplied by the commune. Purchase of clothing was prohibited; most members were required to dress in secondhand clothes distributed by the church.

Each person was given an allowance of eight dollars per month for personal use. Normally this money was spent on snacks or a movie. There were various ploys to get extra money. A member might stop at a gas station and ask for a receipt for an alleged earlier purchase, explaining that the original had been lost. The church would then reimburse for the voucher on Needs Night.

Lisa Layton never resorted to such tactics. In fact, she seldom spent her eight dollars on herself at all. Instead she would save up the allowances and use the money to buy special treats for the Temple children. It was a source of pride to her when the little black children called her "Grandma."

The church's communal discipline was especially important with respect to its senior citizens. The Temple had recruited a large number of elderly and retired people, most of whom received government checks that all came in on the first of the month. The church kept record cards for every person, on which it was noted when a check was turned in and the check's amount. If a check was not signed over immediately, the individual was confronted. The Temple had established its own private check-cashing company under the guise of helping out its senior citizens by relieving them of the fear of having to go to a bank and possibly being mugged. After notation on the member's record card, the information was duplicated on a deposit slip to the check cashing company's account at the California Canadian Bank in San Francisco.

Hundreds of green and gold SSI and SSA checks, as well as ordinary paychecks, were cashed and deposited each month. The church would then withdraw an identical amount of cash, ostensibly for payments to its members, so the bank would not become suspicious. This cash was taken back to the church, mingled with various other donations, and redeposited in the church's own savings or checking accounts at the Bank of Montreal in San Francisco.

As communal members were forced to sell their homes, hundreds of thousands of dollars came to the church in the form of escrow checks. Statistics were kept on how much a church of this size should expect to receive annually in donations, and phony records listing this average were submitted to the government. At all times, the church kept a hundred thousand dollars in cash locked in a cabinet in the finance office to cover incidental expenses.

Late in 1976, Jones became uneasy about the swelling church coffers and decided that most of the Temple funds should be removed from the United States to avoid seizure by the government. Debbie had been working on the Finance Committee with Maria Katsaris under Terri Buford's general supervision. One evening Jones called Debbie and Maria to his room. "Debbie, will you ever leave the church?" he asked. She was afraid to tell him that she wanted out. "No," she answered. "Okay," said Jones, "because after what you're about to do, you can never leave." Jones told her to get a passport and yellow fever shots. The following weekend, Carolyn Layton drove Maria and Debbie to Los Angeles. When it was Debbie's turn at the counter at L.A. International Airport, she still didn't know where she was going. She turned to Carolyn. "Panama," Carolyn said, handing Debbie the money for the tickets.

Four members had been chosen for this first trip. Terri Buford was already in Panama and met Debbie, Carolyn, and Maria at the airport. In any secret dealings with Temple funds, Jones liked to cover himself by using more than one or two members—with each one watching and reporting on the others, group loyalty was more assured. Actually, with Maria Katsaris along, Debbie was just as glad to have Terri Buford overseeing the operation. Maria, Jones' constant mistress, was always attacking Debbie to Jones, as she attacked other women in whom he showed sexual interest. Terri was one of Debbie's closest friends in the Temple, and could be counted on to defend her performance in Panama against any lies Maria might report.

Debbie's closeness to Terri went back to early Ukiah days, and Lisa had also taken a liking to this tense, quiet girl. But while Terri was clearly fond of the two Layton women, her loyalty remained unswervingly with Jones. A nervous and insecure person who had run away from a threatening family life, Terri had earned her status as one of Jones' most trusted aides.

It turned out that there was little for Debbie to do in Panama. Terri visited the banks and set up accounts, then brought the papers back to the hotel for Debbie and the others to sign. Debbie never went to the banks herself; Terri told her that this was so that she would have nothing significant to reveal if she were ever interrogated. In fact, Terri revealed very little to Debbie of the details of the money transfer operation. Debbie remained in Panama for about four days before returning to the United States with Maria.

Eight months later, Debbie was again told to pack, this time for a two-to-eight-week trip in both hot and cold weather. She dashed around the church looking to borrow some appropriate business clothes. At six o'clock the next morning she climbed into a church car with five thousand dollars in a money belt strapped around her waist. This time there would be just two of them. Terri Buford met her at the airport and together they flew first to Panama, so Terri could change all the account numbers of recent Temple defectors, then they went on to England. In London, their business was not with banks but at the library. Terri was seeking information on the economic and banking systems of various communist countries. She was particularly interested in Rumania. Two days later Terri and Debbie flew to Paris, rented a car, and drove to Switzerland. They entered Zurich around midnight. To help preserve the anonymity of foreign investors, the Swiss do not stamp the passports of people entering for short visits, and the plan was for Debbie to return to France within twenty-four hours. They spent the rest of the night in an old nunnery that was being used as a hostel. At the bank the next morning, Debbie showed her passport to an official and signed some papers. She left immediately for France.

Debbie returned to the United States alone; Terri would travel through Eastern Europe for another month before returning. Debbie flew home from France by way of Montreal and Seattle before touching down in San Francisco. She took this circuitous route because Terri had been worried that United States customs officials would read Debbie's passport and notice the two trips to Panama and, since the French did stamp passports, the missing day in Switzerland. It looked too much like a drug smuggler's route. The customs people examined her suitcase carefully, but they did not interrogate her.

With the move to San Francisco, Jones took his people en masse into the city's body politic. Knowledgeable observers consider that he may have swung the close mayoral race of 1975 in favor of George Moscone. Jones put some eight hundred Temple members on the street as precinct workers to get out the vote in areas where the winning candidate piled up twelve-to-one margins. After the election, Moscone tried to show his gratitude by appointing Jones to the city's Human Rights Commission. Jones turned the appointment down—not enough power and prestige. In October of 1976, he was nominated to a seat on the Housing Authority Commission, with the promise that he would be made chairman. Jones accepted, and moved into the chairmanship on February 24, 1977.

Housing Authority meetings were usually quiet affairs. Attendance was sparse, and many who did attend could be found dozing off to the drone of bureaucratic readings. Not so after Jones was appointed. He arrived with a full retinue, mostly elderly black women. (They and other temple members did not, of course, appear at these meetings as "Temple members." Jones wanted the meetings filled to give the impression that he had wide public support. "The purpose," says Debbie, "was to show strength both within and without, and it worked.") The cheers were thunderous whenever Jones made a point. Housing Authority meetings overnight became lively, well-attended attention-getters. And Temple members didn't hesitate to let the press, and especially popular local columnists, know about the events.

As in Mendocino County, Jones wanted to cover himself in the district attorney's office. In San Francisco, the candidate he favored was Joe Freitas. After Freitas was elected D.A., he took Jones' suggestion and hired Tim Stoen as Assistant D.A. Stoen was placed in charge of the voter-fraud unit. Even today, there are suspicions that many Temple members voted more than once during the 1975 fall elections.

But then problems arose. Jones could not quell the undercurrents of mistrust running through the black community, whose religious leaders, by and large, had no use for him. The reason was simple. Jones had mounted a major effort to build a large black membership in the Temple, and black leaders were suspicious of his attempt to develop a power base within their constituency.

Another problem came up in regard to the San Francisco school system. All the children the church had adopted were placed in a few schools, and transported to them in church cars. The idea was to have as many Temple children together in the same school as possible. The problem was that the church had to provide phony addresses for the children, or assign many children to the address of a single church member. When a school would notice that ten children were supposedly living at one address, an investigation would follow and complaints would result. Although Jones' political power was of some help to him in silencing these complaints, as the church became more actively involved in the city's affairs it became the focus of increasing scrutiny and criticism.

With this increase in outside attention, Planning Commission meetings became even more tense and violent. Jones began to step up his litany of governmental menace, until it got to a point one night where with all seeming logic he presented his congregation with a choice of mass suicide or destruction by the U.S. government.

It began with his calling Debbie and four other counselors together for a secret meeting. He reminded them that several key members had defected, and told them that he was afraid they would reveal damaging information. He thought the Temple might be raided, and said he wanted to discuss ways to have the entire membership of the Planning Commission killed rather than captured. It was decided at this meeting that the most efficient method would be for all the members to board a chartered plane flown by a commercial pilot. When the plane reached a specified altitude the pilot would be shot in the head. Nothing was resolved at this secret meeting, so the six adjourned until the entire P.C. met later in the evening.

At that meeting, Jones announced that the Temple was at its end. The church was cornered. They could not go any further. "Tonight," he said, "we will sit here and die together." Even Debbie was not certain whether Jones was simply testing the group or whether they were really to die then and there. Several people became frantic. Jim asked everyone to stand and make his or her last request. A woman asked for a final cigarette. Two young men said they wanted to fuck someone before they died. Others stood and expressed relief that they were about to die; they said they were sick of life. Debbie knew how they felt. "I wasn't afraid myself," she recalls. "I was too tired of living."

Suddenly two members entered the room carrying trays with little bottles of liquid and stacks of small paper cups. Bottles and cups were handed out, and the first to receive and drink the liquid promptly collapsed. With that an older woman stood up, announced that she wasn't going to die, and ran for the door. A guard drew a pistol and shot her at close range. The gun was loaded with blanks, but the power of the blast cut her side and she fell in a heap. After a moment of silence, when all eyes had turned back to Jones, he announced that this had been a "tryout" in order to see what would happen.

Mass suicide would remain their ultimate recourse in escaping a hostile and misunderstanding world, but there was another option for Jones and his Temple followers: Guyana. Since his first visit in 1963, and another in 1973, Jones had been preparing his people for the establishment of a jungle settlement, a utopian Promised Land. They would found a model community—interracial, self-sufficient, free of racism, sexism, and ageism. The Promised Land would be called "Jonestown." Two years earlier the Temple had leased 3,852 acres from the government of Guyana, and a small vanguard had left San Francisco to finish clearing that land and establish a colony.

The transfer of people and supplies to Guyana quickened in the spring of 1977. Jones' concern about a raid deepened into paranoia. The FBI had raided the Church of Scientology, and he thought that Peoples Temple would be next. Financial records and large amounts of cash were removed from the Geary Boulevard building, as was a large cache of guns and ammunition. These were stored in a warehouse under a made-up rental name. One night, Jones thought there might be a raid on the warehouse and ordered the entire store of guns and ammo dumped into San Francisco Bay. Soon, however, the church began collecting another arms cache. A Temple member secured a license as an arms dealer. A list of stores that sold guns was drawn up and different members made purchases at each place, enabling the Temple to amass many guns and enormous amounts of ammunition without attracting attention. These arms were again stored in a rented warehouse; but now they were periodically removed and shipped to Guyana in huge crates, packed with farm equipment. After most of the arms had been shipped, Interpol somehow learned of the operation and informed the Guyanese government. U.S. customs officials in Miami later examined several Temple crates; but by then it was too late.

For security, Jones decided that all tapes and files should be destroyed. Since all P.C. meetings, church services, confessions, and confrontations had been secretly recorded for years, the amount of material was staggering. When Jones saw how much there was, he changed his mind. The tapes of the traitorous defectors were kept intact. Files on members containing confessions were edited, and only incriminating documents were retained. Debbie and two other workers spent days erasing thousands of tapes with an industrial magnet. When the task was completed, everything that remained was shipped to Guyana.

"I could have found my own file and destroyed it," Debbie

says, "but I wasn't thinking clearly. I was too tired from over-work and lack of sleep."

Members were now moving to Guyana at a steady rate of seven per week. Each went loaded with cash. U.S. citizens are allowed to carry five thousand dollars in cash out of the country. It was a simple and convenient way for the Temple to ship church money into Guyana. Departing members were given different amounts so it would appear that the cash was their own. Roughly thirty thousand dollars a week in American currency was shipped to Jonestown in this manner.

Lisa Layton, for one, was anxious to join the exodus.

Annalisa recalls a night she spent at her mother's apartment during this period. The telephone rang at 3 A.M. It was a message from the Temple: "Jim can see a fire." Everyone, wherever they lived, had to move all furniture and clothing away from heating vents. It was a telephone-tree call—Lisa had to call ten people on a list who, in turn, would telephone ten others. "The reason for this," Annalisa explains, "and Mom felt proud to know the real reason, was that some day they might need to escape quickly. With such good practice at waking up at night and passing along messages they could move before the gestapo arrived. It was the same rationale for all of the long bus trips. The group would be well practiced in moving together. And the reason the babies and children were required to sit through all the marathon meetings, missing meals, sleep, and study time, was to teach them to sit quietly in case this escape had to be done in silence."

It was hoped, however, that the exodus to Jonestown could continue gradually. In June of 1977, Jones found ample cause to accelerate the process.

The sharpest outside scrutiny of Peoples Temple came from the press, first and foremost in the reporting of Marshall Kilduff, a bright young reporter for the San Francisco *Chronicle*. If any one person blew the whistle on the Reverend Jim Jones, it was Kilduff, backed by a courageous editor, Rosalie Muller Wright.

No doubt Jones made it easier. He was going crazy. He had always spoken about the impending nuclear holocaust; now he began to preach of imminent destruction by the CIA and FBI. Key members of the group had already defected, including Jones' son-in-law John Collins. Beatings were becoming more brutal, and the membership was assuming the aspect more of a frenzied mob than a church congregation. But it was Kilduff who, with the help of Phil Tracy, pulled all the information together and published it in an explosive article in *New West* magazine. Oddly enough, his own newspaper had refused to print the article. Part of the reason was that the paper's city editor had attended staged church meetings and retained a great respect for Jim Jones.

Kilduff had to sell the story three times. When his own paper wasn't interested, he took the story to *New West*. Kevin Starr, then the editor, accepted the article but then changed his mind. He explained to Kilduff that the story would jeopardize the Temple's programs in drug rehabilitation, care of the elderly, and legal aid for the poor. Kilduff went to *San Francisco* magazine. There, editors Nino Tosi and Karen Evans were excited about the article and accepted it, but asked for an expanded rewritten version. Word got out quickly. Within a day, a contingent of Temple members was staging what amounted to a sit-in in Tosi's office. They demanded that the story be withdrawn, insisting that Kilduff was biased and the article untrue. Unshaken by these demands, Tosi and Evans decided to proceed, but they never had a chance to publish the story. In an unrelated but bitter internal debate over editorial and advertising policy, the entire editorial staff of *San Francisco* magazine resigned. Once again, Kilduff was left without a publisher.

In the meantime, however, Starr had resigned as *New West*'s editor. Kilduff thought the new editor, Rosalie Wright, might be more receptive. She was. Not only that, she already had a contributing editor, Phil Tracy, working on a similar article. Tracy had been staying in San Francisco with a friend whose sister was a member of the church. From his conversations with her, he became interested in Temple affairs. He asked her if she could get him into a church service. What she ended up getting him were three other Temple members who questioned Tracy about his own religious and political beliefs. The Temple doors remained barred. Tracy's reporter's curiosity was definitely piqued.

Wright put Kilduff and Tracy together. Within hours after

Wright sent a *New West* photographer to catch Jones at a Housing Commission meeting, the telephone calls from Temple members and friends of the Temple began. At first the callers were friendly, they just wanted some information. Did Ms. Wright know about the Temple's community work? Was she aware that an unfriendly story might jeopardize all this, might even endanger the lives of Temple members and Jones himself? As the days wore on, the calls became harsher. There were attacks on Kilduff's integrity and professional credibility. Finally came the demands that the story be killed entirely. The atmosphere around the *New West* office was much like that of an armed camp under siege.

Jones himself was among the first to call. "I've heard good things about you from Steve Gavin [the *Chronicle* city editor]," Jones told Wright. "I know you'll be fair." Wright immediately suggested sending Kilduff over to the Temple for an interview. Jones declined. Kilduff was too biased, he said. Wright countered by offering Jones his choice of any *New West* staff writer. He selected Tracy, and agreed to an appointment for Friday, June 3, 1977, a week away.

During that week the magazine received a deluge of letters and telephone calls at both its Los Angeles and San Francisco offices. Even the magazine's new owner in New York, Rupert Murdoch, received his share, with one of the calls coming from Debbie Layton. California's Lieutenant Governor Mervyn Dymally called. He said he had heard the magazine was doing a negative story on Jones; he wanted to point out that Jones was doing good work for the people of San Francisco. Milton Marks, a California state senator, wrote to Murdoch on Jones' behalf. At the height of the Temple's campaign, the magazine was receiving fifty phone calls and seventy letters a day.

Rosalie Wright, however, was not budging. Jones and the rest of the Temple leadership were catching on to this fast. For once, their intimidation was not working. They fired off another letter. Jones wrote this one himself, but did not sign it. It said in part, "The current editor [Wright] of *New West,* although undoubtedly conscientious, does not seem to understand the precarious faith people from disadvantaged backgrounds have in the system, and their proclivity toward militant reaction to what they might perceive as an unfair or unwarranted attack."

"I'm not ready," said Wright at the time, "to label that a

threat, but I have to admit I feel threatened. How would you interpret 'militant reaction'?"

Several days later, the office of the magazine was burglarized and files on the Peoples Temple story were rifled. There was little doubt in anyone's mind that the burglars were members of the Temple.

Wright began receiving telephone threats at her home in the middle of the night. "Don't do it!" the caller would say harshly, and hang up. Wright and her children went into hiding.

On July 12, Wright called Jones and read him the entire article before sending it to press, a standard journalistic courtesy. "We confronted him with everything in the piece," she said. As she read each charge, Jones replied tersely: "That's a lie. . . . That's not so. . . . That's absolutely wrong. . . . No comment. . . ."

Two weeks before the *New West* article was due to appear, Debbie started making plane reservations for Jones, one every successive day, so that he could fly out of the country at a moment's notice. On July 13, he was ready to fly to Guyana. From the San Francisco airport he made one last call to one of the Temple's most prominent supporters, defending himself and the Temple against the charges that were fast becoming public. He claimed that he was not running away; he was needed at the South American settlement. He would be back, and then all of these ridiculous lies would be exposed for what they were.

One of Jones' deepest fears was the effect the *New West* article would have on certain Temple members. "Jim was never concerned about old black women reading the exposé," says Debbie. "He was more worried about educated whites reading it, people of practical use who filled middle-level positions in the Temple. For this reason, just before the article came out, he encouraged a number of educated whites with professional skills to emigrate to Jonestown."

Ironically, the media campaign that Jones and the Temple members created in the end gave *New West* a stronger story. After reading about the commotion, the magazine's tenacity, and Wright's firm stand, phone calls of a different sort began to come in. These were anonymous at first, the callers volunteering "background" information, as well as adding more specific charges to the growing file.

Wright, Kilduff, and Tracy told the callers they were not interested in anonymous charges and innuendo. But a few called back and agreed to meet in person, to be photographed, and to tell their stories for publication. They also agreed to be tape-recorded.

Their outpourings about life inside Peoples Temple included the gamut of Jones' activities and practices: the orchestrated cures; the self-imposed humiliations; the physical beatings; the letter-writing campaigns; the questionable money transfers; the threats of reprisal for defection; Jones' political connections. Those connections ran from the White House to Governor Brown to San Francisco Mayor George Moscone and a flock of state senators and assemblymen to leftist leaders like Huey Newton, Angela Davis, and Dennis Banks.

Although the article was a major bombshell, the city administration assumed a posture much like that of the proverbial ostrich. Mayor George Moscone said he had read the article and found it to be "a series of allegations with absolutely no hard evidence that the Rev. Jones had violated any laws, either local, state or federal."

After suggesting that anyone with any evidence take that evidence to the appropriate law enforcement officials, the mayor continued, "The Mayor's office does not and will not conduct any investigation into the Rev. Jones nor the Peoples Temple."

The Temple itself, at Jones' direction from Jonestown, issued its own rebuttal, filled with platitudes of good works. The church "represented the heart of Christian social-gospel teaching, taking for our text the Acts of the Apostles, in which the disciples of Christ formed a totally just society based on the sharing of all wealth, in contradiction to the selfish materialism of prevailing society. . . ."

The Temple also noted that these "persons who are now coming forward" had originally been the ones who "pressed us to take extremist actions"; that some were "even involved in manufacturing weapons"; advocated "violent revolution" and "terrorism"; mistreated people in their charge; stole money from the church; "and even sexually molested their children."

"But in the face of it all," the rebuttal concluded, "we plan only one course of action: to proceed with our work."

What really confounded those who pressed for an investigation of the Temple was the fact that even with Jones in Guyana, the liberal and new left politicos of the city stood by him. On Sunday, July 31, the Temple in San Francisco held a rally in support of Jones. Jones spoke to members of his congregation and supporters via telephone relay from Guyana. He was very pleased about who had turned up. "I will be here when you are under attack," State Assemblyman Willie Brown told the congregation, "because what you are about is what the whole system ought to be about." Art Agnos, another assemblyman, declared, "I am proud to stand with you." Also appearing were two of the city's gay leaders, supervisor Harvey Milk and the leader of Gay Action, Howard Wallace. Human Rights commissioners Enola Maxwell and Sylvester Herring, San Francisco NAACP president Joe Hall, and one of the city's most powerful black ministers, Cecil Williams of Glide Memorial Foundation, also attended.

"I know some of you are wanting to fight," Jones' voice crackled over the telephone hookup, "but that's exactly what the system wants. It wants to use us as sacrificial lambs, as a scapegoat. Don't fall into this trap by yielding to violence, no matter what kind of lies are told on us or how many.

"Peoples Temple has helped practically every political prisoner in the United States. We've reached out to everyone who is oppressed, and that's what is bothering them. We've organized poor people and given ourselves a voice. The system doesn't mind corporate power for the ruling elite, but for the first time, we've given some corporate power to the little man and that's an unforgivable sin. And that's the whole problem in a nutshell."

Without Jones' overriding presence, discipline among Temple members remaining in San Francisco fell off sharply. And as a corollary effect, relations among members of the Layton family became more normal than they had been in years. Although it was to prove a brief turn, they came together. Larry, his influence on the Planning Commission all but dissolved, had been working at a variety of non-Temple jobs while completing his residency as an X-ray technician. He now moved in with his father, and a modicum of communication was restored between Dr. Layton and his son, although Larry's loyalty

to Jones never wavered. Larry was drawn even more closely
back to his mother, as was Debbie. When Jones let Lisa and
Debbie know that they were expected in Guyana, he also decreed that Larry should stay in San Francisco. Like other members with steady jobs and promising earning futures, Larry
could be considered a reliable source of income to support the
Temple's holding operation in the Bay City.

Carolyn Layton, Terri Buford, and Debbie had been left in
charge of that operation. Carolyn was the overall supervisor,
Terri handled public relations, and Debbie was in charge of
finances. The books were a shambles. Debbie was told to
reorganize them, but about all she could do was close out the
various Temple accounts, except for the one at the Bank of
Montreal. The triumvirate was supposed to confer nightly, but
they rarely met.

Rumors in the church increased. Negative thinking set in
and meeting attendance began to dwindle. After the most committed members moved to Guyana, only about two hundred
peripheral people continued to attend. Each evening, Debbie
reported everything to Jones by shortwave radio. She was told
to add a zero to attendance figures when broadcasting them.
If two hundred people attended, she reported two thousand.
These figures were recorded and rebroadcast to the residents
at Jonestown to bolster their confidence in the strength of the
home operation.

When Lisa Layton had developed a bad chest cold in 1975,
she didn't want to get it treated because she felt that would
show a lack of trust in Jim Jones' healing powers. After urgent
persuasion by Debbie, she reluctantly agreed to see a doctor.
Her cold was diagnosed as pneumonia. Now, in August 1977,
one month after Jones left for Guyana, Lisa again complained
to Debbie about a persistent cough that had been troubling her.
Again, Debbie urged her to go to the hospital. An X-ray revealed a small spot on her lung.

Debbie spent that night with Lisa at her apartment. The next
morning she drove her mother to Kaiser Hospital in Oakland
where doctors would perform a bronchoscopy, taking a piece
of lung tissue for a pathological examination.

"She seemed anxious," Debbie recalls, "but afterwards we

went over to the Watergate where she had once lived. She loved that place, thought it was so pretty. So we had a little picnic there and then returned to San Francisco. Two or three days later she telephoned me. She was speaking in a little waif of a voice. She said, 'Debbie, I have cancer.' I could tell she was very frightened. She was calling from the hospital. She said that they had to do surgery but would only have to remove a third of one lung. She was relieved by that."

While in the hospital before her operation, Lisa felt near death. She told Debbie that it had always weighed heavily on her that years before she had revealed Debbie's teenage confidences to her father. Lisa had been afraid of being caught in the middle, of being accused of condoning and supporting Debbie's "immoral behavior." Debbie reassured her over and over that there was no need for her to feel guilty. Several times she excused herself to go and cry in the hallway. Her mother had become very precious to her.

The spot was larger on a subsequent X-ray, and two weeks later, when the surgeons operated, they found the cancer to be extensive. They removed Lisa's left lung.

Lisa had always been terrified of cancer. When she woke after the operation, Debbie was with her. "Loyal people don't die of cancer, do they?" she asked. "Jim won't let me die of cancer, will he?"

Debbie wanted to explain that cancer had nothing to do with being loyal to Jim, but found that she couldn't say it.

"No, Mom," she replied instead. "Jim loves you."

Debbie went to the hospital each day and massaged her mother's legs. "You know," Lisa said one afternoon, "it's funny. I used to be your mother, and I hate to put this on you, but I'm so dependent on you, Debbie. I don't want you to leave my side when I go to Guyana."

When Lisa got out of the hospital, she moved into the church. She had her own room, right down the hall from Debbie. Debbie fixed it up with some of Lisa's favorite furniture, and plants all over. Lisa had lost a lot of weight, so Debbie brought her extra food, all the treats she could afford. They spent a lot of time together, planning their trip to Guyana.

Lisa couldn't wait to go to the "promised land." After her cancer operation, she asked her physician to let her know the earliest possible date at which she could travel. She visited

Annalisa often, and expressed her hope that Annalisa would join her someday in Guyana. She also warned her older daughter that she might have to leave on such short notice that she wouldn't have time to telephone. Annalisa did not want to think about her mother's departure. She gave Lisa a pot of azolla, a small fern, to provide nitrogen fertilizer for any rice paddies they might have in Guyana.

Early on the morning of December 7, Debbie and Lisa telephoned Annalisa from New York with the news that they were en route to Guyana. Annalisa cried on the phone. She told her mother that she was afraid this would be the last time they would ever talk together. Lisa cried too, but she assured Annalisa that when the time was right, meaning after the nuclear holocaust, they would all be back. Lisa also said she was certain that Annalisa would join them in Guyana before that happened.

Annalisa had wanted to arrange a code, to ask her mother to write the word "really" in her letters if she was saying something that wasn't true. But Lisa was so excited about the trip that Annalisa didn't have the heart to express any doubts to her mother. Tearfully, each one hung up the phone. Annalisa lay down beside her husband, Ray, and cried. The telephone rang again two minutes later. It was Lisa. The azolla were turning brown and dying, she said. What should she do with them? "Leave them," Annalisa said. "Good-bye, I love you," said Lisa. "Good-bye, I love you," Annalisa said, and slipped back into her husband's arms.

Larry's wedding to Carolyn Moore in Davis, 1967

Annalisa's wedding to Ray Valentine in Berkeley, 1967, with Dr. Layton on the right

Larry and Carolyn Layton in Berkeley, 1967

Larry with Karen, the marriage photo he sent to his family in 1969

Lisa Layton with her first grandchild, Lori Valentine, Berkeley, 1969

Karen and Larry with their "son," Bruce, Berkeley, 1971

Peoples Temple, Redwood Valley: the church Larry helped build (COURTESY SAN FRANCISCO EXAMINER)

Larry standing before the Peoples Temple bus, 1972

Lisa Layton and Annalisa Valentine, before Lisa joined the Temple, Berkeley, 1972

The Temple on Geary Boulevard during an evening service
(COURTESY SAN FRANCISCO EXAMINER)

Lisa at the Berkeley house after joining the Temple, 1973

Philip Blakey, Debbie's first husband, in a photograph sent to her from Jonestown

8

The Promised Land—II

Jones had told Debbie to pack enough clothes for two months in Guyana, long enough to get her mother comfortably settled. The plan was that Debbie would then return to San Francisco to continue work on the Temple finances, then go back to Guyana for another two months, and so on in a continual rotation.

Lisa and Debbie left San Francisco on December 6, 1977, with almost five thousand dollars each and twelve crates of goods for Jonestown. Every Temple member leaving for Jonestown was expected to take an extra trunk or two for the community. Sometimes the person would know what was in the trunks, sometimes not.

Lisa and Debbie had a seven-hour layover in New York, and Debbie took her mother out to dinner at an expensive restaurant. They had almost ten thousand dollars between them, and who knew when they would ever have a chance to be alone together again.

Like every Temple member who came through New York, they had been instructed to buy as much duty-free liquor as they could legally take into Guyana. They didn't know that the alcohol was to be used as gifts to Guyanese officials.

The following day, when Lisa and Debbie stepped off the plane and into the one-story wooden customs building in Georgetown, Guyana, it was one o'clock in the morning. Because they had so much luggage they were the last from their plane to go through customs—they didn't get out until 3 A.M. But that was part of the plan. In the small hours, the energy of customs officials is as low as anybody else's, and they tend to be less nosy about poking into crates and footlockers.

They were met at the airport by five of the Temple's Georgetown staff. Along with their twelve crates, they squeezed into the rear of a small van for the trip to Georgetown headquarters, a large yellow house in the Lamaha Gardens section on the outskirts of the city. When they arrived at the house it was four in the morning—no welcome awaited them, no showers or hot drinks, not even a bed. Lisa and Debbie stretched out on a dirty rug on the concrete floor of the radio room for a few hours' sleep, covered with a sour, mildewed sheet to protect them from the mosquitoes.

Lisa and Debbie arose with the rest of the household at six and went upstairs for a breakfast of boiled rice with milk and sugar. There Paula Adams collected their passports and locked them in a strongbox for "safekeeping." Debbie had expected to keep hers, but there was nothing she could do. She was beginning to realize that status in the San Francisco Temple had nothing to do with status in Guyana, and that she would have to prove her loyalty all over again.

As it turned out, they stayed almost a week in Georgetown before going up the river to Jonestown because the Temple boat, the *Marceline*, was being repaired. Although Lisa was anxious to finish her journey, she fell in love with Georgetown. She and Debbie went for walks, went to see an East Indian movie with English subtitles, spent long hours talking and just being together. Lisa had never been in a tropical country before, and she was delighted to see horses and cows grazing in the front yards of the brightly painted Victorian-style wooden buildings. The climate was especially good for her health. The soft, warm breezes and slight humidity eased her cough and allowed her to breathe more freely. And the people were so friendly and open. If Lisa and Debbie, out for a walk, looked hot and thirsty, they were likely to be invited into someone's home for a glass of water or a Pepsi or even a rum drink.

Of course, Debbie was still on Temple buiness while they were in Georgetown. On their fourth evening in Guyana, Debbie, along with Sharon Amos, Deborah Touchette, Paula Adams, and Mike Prokes, attended a reception at the Pegasus Hotel in honor of a group of Cubans who were doing volunteer work in Guyana, something of a Cuban Peace Corps. The Temple members were to propagandize the Cubans about their cause. A young Cuban doctor took a fancy to Debbie and asked her to dance. She hesitated, because she hadn't danced in years, and furthermore it was against Temple rules. But Paula gave her the cue that she'd better do it—that was what they were there for.

Once out on the dance floor with the handsome Cuban, Debbie found that she was enjoying herself very much. After several long dances, she felt herself drawn to him; he made her feel pretty. Suddenly she realized, actually for the first time in her life, that she *was* pretty. She wasn't fat and dumpy anymore, she was thin—and she was attractive to men.

On the way back to the house in the Temple van, however, it became clear that her enjoyment had drawn resentment from the others, especially Paula and Sharon. She thought maybe they were jealous because they hadn't been asked to dance as much as she had. The tension was so bad that she knew they were going to write her up—report her to Jones. So she wrote the incident up herself, changing only her reaction to what happened. As she described it, this Cuban doctor wouldn't leave her alone, and she was nice to him out of her sense of duty and loyalty to the Temple, because that's what she thought she was supposed to do. But actually, she reported to Jones, it was an ordeal.

When she talked the incident over with her mother, Lisa was very supportive. She said, "Debbie, it's not your fault that a man liked you. You had to be friendly to him." Still, Debbie was frightened; she felt that she was going into the interior with a mark already against her.

On December 8, the day after they arrived in Georgetown, before word had reached them that they were to stay in the city while the *Marceline* was being repaired, Lisa wrote a letter to her father, Hugo Philip:

"Dear Papsch: Debbie and I arrived yesterday in Georgetown, Guyana. We first flew from San Francisco to New York and then from New York direct to Georgetown where our friends met us. We arrived here at midnight, and then it took us a long time to go through customs.

"Georgetown is an interesting little city, especially after one goes a little way out of the middle of the city.

"This afternoon we will board a ship and journey to Jonestown. We will be on the ocean for 4 hours and then go up the Kaituma for 20 hours. Then a short journey in an auto (Land-Rover). The climate is beautiful. It is warm but not too warm—a light wind always wafts. I feel so much better here.

"Jonestown is in the vicinity of Matthews Ridge. We will live in a great beautiful house called 'Peoples Temple.'

"Before I left I divorced Larry.

"Hugs and Kisses, Lisa."

Debbie had not seen Phil Blakey since Jones had sent him to Guyana late in 1973, and she was looking forward to spending time with him—especially now that she had lost weight and was feeling so trim and attractive. During the week they spent in Georgetown, Debbie talked several times with Phil on the radio. He sounded eager to see her, and when she spoke with Jim Jones he would say things like, "It will be nice to see you and Phil together again." Even when she was still in San Francisco, Jones had given her the hope and understanding that when she came to Jonestown she and Phil would be allowed to live together. Phil was not only the captain of the Temple's shrimp boat, but he also had become their expert on tractors. He had been too busy to leave Jonestown, but he would meet them when they got off the boat in Port Kaituma and drive them the rest of the way in.

As much as they enjoyed Georgetown, Debbie and Lisa were not sorry when the time came to board the *Marceline*.

They were anxious to reach the interior. The films they had
seen at the Temple in San Francisco showed a thriving community, full of busy, smiling friends. As the *Marceline* got
under way, Debbie fantasized about the little house she would
share with Phil, about fishing on the river, hiking in the jungle,
swimming in the lake.

The trip took longer than usual—sixteen hours on the ocean
and ten on the Kaituma River. Lisa had one of the six bunks
in the cabin, but most of the passengers slept on the open deck.
During their night on the ocean a storm struck. Rain poured
down, and the wind blew the waves over the deck. Debbie
didn't get seasick, but she was one of the few passengers who
didn't. Soaking wet and cold, she and a young black boy pulled
a tarp over themselves and huddled together through the night.

About eleven o'clock the next morning they started up the
Kaituma River. From the deck of the *Marceline* the passengers
got their first close look at the jungles of Guyana. It looked
and sounded exactly like a jungle in an adventure movie. (In
fact, *Lost Horizon* was filmed only sixty miles from Jonestown,
in a wild area inhabited mostly by small bands of Amerindians.)
The Kaituma River at that season was wide, brown, and muddy,
the color of root beer. Exotic birds flashed through the thick
underbrush. Overhead, the sky was a deep, dense blue. Every
five miles or so they would come upon a clearing—a couple
of wooden houses or grass huts with canoes tied up alongside,
barefoot children in shorts hanging off the sides of the docks
while their fathers fished.

On that trip upriver, Debbie's fears were reawakened when
the captain announced, "OK, everybody who is bringing in
letters from the outside, we are going to collect them now.
Any communications at all have to be checked and cleared.
And I mean all of them, because your luggage is going to be
searched."

The *Marceline* docked in Port Kaituma at one o'clock in
the morning. From the deck they could hear Phil's voice in the
crowd on the bank. Two men helped Lisa up the ladder to the
top of the high, steep river bank, then Phil climbed down to
the deck. Now, with her husband before her, Debbie felt reserved and nervous, especially with the rest of the Temple crew
standing around watching and laughing. The two stood looking
at each other. Debbie thought that Phil had grown; she hadn't

remembered him being so large, or so handsome. Finally he said, "Well, how are you?" In answer she put her arm halfway around him and gave him a quick embrace and a pat on the back. Then everybody got to work unloading the scores of suitcases and crates they had brought from Georgetown.

Finally they all piled into a stake-bed truck for the last leg of their journey to Jonestown. Including the passengers from the *Marceline* and the Temple members who had come to help with the unloading, about twenty people were perched precariously atop the luggage, continually clutching at each other to avoid falling off as the truck lurched from rut to mud slick to pothole. Lisa sat in the front seat with three others. After almost an hour of driving through the black jungle they could see Jonestown in the distance. It looked like a huge city of lights, like Los Angeles from an airplane at night, and Debbie felt an upsurge of hope—maybe the films they had seen and the reports they had heard were true; maybe Jonestown really was that modern utopia of a socialist community. Then they began to pass the makeshift cabins with tarps for roofs, and her spirits sank. When they came to the huge central pavilion, her memories took over, eclipsing the rest of her anticipation—she recalled the endless meetings, the all-night harangues. Debbie felt sick. Oh God, she thought, it's the church again.

Most new residents of Jonestown had no idea of what to expect. Many, in fact, had never lived outside the ghettos of North Oakland and the street culture of San Francisco's Fillmore district. What they found in their new home was a very different kind of jungle.

The Amerindian word *guiana* means "land of waters." The rivers and jungles of Guyana teem with wildlife. Monkeys and deer are the most common, but tapirs, sloths, anteaters, capybaras, armadillos, and iguanas also abound. More dangerous are the ocelot, puma, and jaguar, and the giant anaconda and poisonous bushmaster. The rivers swarm with piranha and caimans; sharks and giant stingrays patrol the coastal waters.

As in other equatorial lands, temperatures in Guyana are high, averaging from 79 to 82 degrees the year round. Rainfall is heavy, and the humidity hardly ever slackens, though an occasional northeast trade wind would cool the Jonestown settlement, located near the coast. The vegetation of the country is as varied and exotic as the names imply. Mangrove and saltwater grasses grow offshore. Coconut and other palms dot the wet savanna behind the coastal areas, along with trees like the greenheart, the wallaba, the giant mora and crabwood, the balata and other latex-producers, and the siruaballi and huba-balli, which provide handsome woods for cabinetmakers.

About 51 percent of the population of Guyana is of East Indian origin, the descendants of indentured servants who were brought from India to Guyana when slavery was abolished by the British in 1834. The second major ethnic group, about 33 percent of the population, are the Afro-Guyanese, the descendants of slaves emancipated in 1834. The indigenous people, the Amerindians, make up less than 5 percent of the population, and live mostly in the interior of the country.

In fact, the Amerindians are just about the only people who do live in the interior. The jungle is so dangerous and inhospitable that 95 percent of the Guyanese people live on the coast, occupying just 4 percent of the country's land.

Jonestown was a struggling community carved from this lush but inhospitable wilderness. Jim Jones must have liked what he saw when he first visited Guyana—then British Guiana—in 1963, because in December 1973 he and a contingent of Temple members approached the Guyanese government with a proposal beneficial to both parties: He and his group would pioneer an area in the interior of the country where the government had been unable to convince its own citizens to settle. Peoples Temple would supply all of the labor and money necessary to clear and develop the area—all they needed was land. Jones was proposing a visionary model community that would be completely integrated with the Guyanese population. The maximum population of the proposed community was to be two hundred people.

In many ways, Guyana and Peoples Temple were ideally matched. The country's socialist government was seemingly compatible with Jones' Marxist-socialist philosophy. About 75 percent of the members of Peoples Temple were black, and Guyana's population was almost entirely nonwhite. The religious mix of Hindu, Christian (Anglican, Roman Catholic, and Methodist), and Moslem seemed likely to be receptive to a religious community. The official language of the country was

English. The people were very poor—living would be cheap. The country was relatively close to the United States. And— possibly an important factor in the mind of the man who viewed himself and his followers as refugees from a fascist oppressor— historically Guyana had a long tradition of harboring fugitives, from the penal colony in nearby French Guyana and most recently from the United States.

In 1975, the government of Guyana officially leased to the Peoples Temple 3,852 acres, of which about 3,000 had the potential to be developed. The land decided upon was located near the Venezuelan border, in an area where the national boundaries had been in dispute for years. The Guyanese government felt that the Temple would help establish their claim over the area. For his part, Jones saw the possibility of switching allegiances should relations with Guyana deteriorate.

Although the lease was not signed until 1975, a small group of Temple members, including Phil Blakey, had begun work on the land in 1973. A colony was built up slowly, until by the beginning of 1977 about 130 young workers had cleared away a substantial amount of jungle and had put up several simple huts and a radio shack. When Jones fled the increasing pressure on Peoples Temple in San Francisco, plans for a mass exodus were stepped up—between January and September of 1977, more than 800 persons poured into Jonestown.

The agricultural base of the community was nowhere near able to support this six-fold increase in population. Medical facilities and schools were nonexistent, and housing was completely inadequate. Jonestown was a long way from being self-supporting, particularly in view of the fact that a large percentage of the new immigrants were either school-age children or "seniors"—consumers rather than contributors in the ecology of the community, at least in terms of long hours of hard labor in the fields. In addition, there were immediate food shortages—the soil was not as fertile as had been hoped, and the new farmers were agriculturally ignorant. For example, in their first season the settlers plowed straight up and down the hillsides, rather than contouring the furrows, so that the heavy rains soon washed away most of the precious topsoil.

It was into this setup for disaster that Lisa and Debbie Layton stepped on December 14, 1977.

Lisa was taken directly to her cabin, while Debbie went up to the radio room to report to Jones and to hand over to Carolyn Layton the ten thousand dollars they had carried in. Jones was not particularly friendly. He said "Good to see you" and turned away. As they chatted in the radio room, Debbie sensed a coldness and reserve on the part of Carolyn and Maria Katsaris, which made her feel very uncomfortable. She soon learned that a class structure had developed in Jonestown, based partly on how close a person was to Jones and partly on how long the person had been in Guyana. In fact, when she had been there a little while herself, she felt a certain disdain for new arrivals, knowing the naïve hopefulness they brought with them and the shock and bewilderment that awaited them.

By the time Debbie was shown to the cabin she was to share with eight other women, it was almost morning. After less than two hours' sleep, her first full day in Jonestown dawned.

Lisa's early letters from Jonestown to Annalisa, Tom, and Laurence seem to reflect a strong sense of commitment, purpose, and community. Actually, all outgoing mail was checked by censors and rewritten to leave out any negative comments or observations. Also, Lisa was characteristically rosy-eyed in viewing anything to do with Peoples Temple, and at least in her first months at Jonestown, no doubt exploiting her as a happy messenger to her many American correspondents, she was favored with special treatment. On December 17, 1977, just three days after their arrival in Jonestown, she wrote to Annalisa:

"Jonestown is like a huge farm in a beautiful setting. In the center are dining and cooking areas. The huge ovens are not in the kitchen but out of doors and we are using our own wood. There are many bungalows clustered here and there. Some made out of wood and painted, others with side walls made of trulie. Very attractive! The roofs are tin and all houses are 3–4 feet above ground. There are wooden walks (planks arranged crosswise) connecting all buildings and everything is immaculately clean. The toilet houses are separate from the building where one showers. After coming from the toilet house one comes to an area with many sinks with running water and liquid soap diluted in bottles and a person seeing to it that all children wash their hands (and adults too for that matter, but they seem to do it automatically). There are larger dormitory buildings for young people and older children. There is a large nursery and the children go home with their parents in the evening. There are several large green tent-top buildings for school. It is like a warm to hot summer, but there is always a breeze which makes it comfortable. It is much less humid than Georgetown.

"Everyone has a job. Karen for instance works with children in the morning (and likes it!) and in the fields in the afternoon. I am going through a book on medicinal herbs to see if any may be useful to us and grow here.

"Could you possibly get hold of a modern book on herbs that grow in Guyana or any scientific literature on the subject?...

"We are a truly egalitarian society here and I am so grateful to be part of it. It is like coming to a different world. And aside from everything else my chest feels good.

"I took a walk with Karen yesterday to the forest and into the forest to a bubbling brook. The forest wasn't anywhere as dense as I had pictured it. So many beautiful plants. We walked through fields where eddoes, sweet potatoes, and pineapple and banana trees were planted."

To Laurence she wrote in March 1978:

"Hope all is well with you! I am doing fine. This is such a beautiful place. Rolling farmland wherever you look, with the forest in the distance. We are raising a tremendous number of crops—3 kinds of bananas, pineapple, rice (mountain rice), cassava, sugar cane and every imaginable vegetable plus some you have never heard of. Dasheen—is purplish and tastes just like potatoes. Papaya—makes excellent vegetable and pies. Cutlass beans which are like extremely large flat string beans. They are especially good marinated. We have horses, cows, pigs, chickens and ducks. Food-wise we are almost self-sufficient. It is nice to see Phil and Debbie together. Phil very seldom is on the boat now. He is running some of our farm machinery, plowing and cultivating land.

"I am working in our medical department part time. Have plenty of time to rest. We are expecting our X-ray equipment to arrive shortly. One of our older members here is an X-ray technician."

And on March 28, 1978, she wrote to Annalisa:

"I am fine and busy, with plenty of time in between to rest. . . . A few weeks ago I caught on to the fact that my cancer has metastasized into the hyler lymph nodes, which also were removed (it said so in the report from Kaiser which I carried with me to give to Larry Schacht). I am sort of glad that I didn't catch on any earlier. Debbie knew that the cancer had metastasized but asked Dr. Clark not to tell me—which was good. All I know is that I am feeling fine and gaining weight. You have no idea how glad I am to be here. Well, I take that back. I think you do know!

"We had a drought here. It hardly rained for 3 weeks and we had to organize bucket brigades to save our vegetables. Thank goodness it has started raining again.

"By the way, our bread and rolls here are out of this world. We use quite a lot of cassava flour with wheat flour—tastes just like regular bread—only better. We use a lot of rice. Rice with cheese melted into it is delicious."

Much of what went into Lisa's letters was sheer fabrication, and some of the rest was exaggeration. For example, her description of her stroll in the "forest" with Karen—it was impossible to walk in the area, it was much too dangerous. Aside from biting and stinging insects and the poisonous snakes, the jungle was so dense that the casual stroller would be hopelessly lost within a few hundred feet. There simply were no footpaths through the jungle. And as for being self-sufficient in food crops and livestock, the colony was falling further behind its actual needs all the time.

Lisa's early special treatment was most apparent in her housing. When she first arrived she was assigned to Marceline Jones' house, one of the nicest in Jonestown. Marceline lived separately from Jones, in a different part of the settlement. When Lisa had been there for a couple of months, Marceline returned to Jonestown and Lisa moved into another house, smaller but still very pleasant. She lived there by herself, and then invited a friend, an elderly black woman who also suffered from cancer, to share the place. Debbie helped her fix it up until it was so comfortable and bourgeois-looking that it was appropriated for a guest house—the same guest house that such future visitors as Charles Garry and Mark Lane would consider typical of Jonestown.

Finally, Lisa was moved into a cabin with four other seniors. It was at this point that Lisa, who had always valued her privacy, discovered that she hated living in a commune. But she understood the reasons and necessity for communal living, and she felt terribly guilty for hating it.

Debbie in those days was working the radio from seven in the morning till seven at night, and she hardly ever got to see her mother. When they did get together, Lisa would tell Debbie of her fears. Debbie encouraged her mother to talk only to her; she knew the consequences if Lisa's complaints were to get back to Jones. Lisa was afraid of the violence in the public meetings, and she worried that the children were made to work such long hours in the fields. And she especially dreaded Debbie leaving her, to work in Georgetown or to return to the United States, as planned, to manage the Temple finances there. So far from her home and the rest of her family, she had grown very dependent on Debbie, and her awareness of that dependency added to her guilt.

And so, ridden with guilt, depressed and lonely, fearful and sick, Lisa kept faith with her paradise.

Lisa's daily life in Jonestown, essentially that of an invalid, was relatively easygoing. Debbie's was far more typical. Like almost every able-bodied resident, she worked in the fields for the first month and a half she was there, until she was transferred to radio duty. The schedule was brutal. The day began at five-thirty with a breakfast of rice and gravy or biscuits and syrup. By six-thirty everyone was at work in the fields—hoeing, planting, cultivating, harvesting the crops under the tropical sun, or picking papayas and wild greens in the bush. The harvest was loaded into big burlap sacks that had to be carried the mile or more back to the settlement.

Actually, come lunchtime, it was better to be working farther from the settlement than close in. Those who were expected to be too far out to return to the community for lunch took sandwiches, which were at least filling, and they got to spend the lunch hour sitting down. But those working within a mile of the mess hall had to walk back and spend half their time standing in line for a couple of pieces of bread and a bowl of watery rice soup. Then it was back to work in the fields until about 6 P.M. Dinner was usually more rice, with beans. This was the schedule six days a week, Monday through Saturday. Sunday was a half day—everybody got to knock off at two in the afternoon. However, no lunch was served on Sundays.

Debbie and Lisa arrived in Jonestown two weeks before Christmas, but the day came and went without celebration. In Jonestown's monotonous calendar, one day passing into another, people didn't even know it was Christmas. It was just another workday, and the food was as bad as ever.

Besides being nutritionally inadequate to support such intense physical effort, the food didn't taste good. There was no attempt at seasoning, and the rice was frequently infested with small white grubs that when boiled were indistinguishable from grains of rice. It was impossible to keep the hordes of flies and hard-shell black beetles from alighting on your plate—if you protected your bread, they would land in your soup. One morning at five-thirty when the flying black beetles got stuck in Debbie's biscuits and syrup, and drowned in her coffee cup, she just threw the whole mess in the garbage. But the rule was, you had to eat everything on your plate, and if you got caught throwing food away you could be punished. And of course, you needed all the nutrition you could get just to keep working in the fields.

Vegetables were served two or three times a week, and on Sundays everybody got an egg. Chicken was served once a month. But the culinary high point came every week on Sunday evening, when the entire population would line up to receive a cookie from the hand of Jim Jones. The cookies, made from cassava flour, were the only sweets allowed in Jonestown, and they were doled out by Jones himself.

Jones did not share the diet of his followers. His refrigerator was well stocked with fruit and meat. While everyone else in Jonestown lost weight, Jones was actually getting fat.

Not only were people losing weight—one man went from 220 pounds to 185 in a month—they were getting sick. By February 1978, half of Jonestown was down with severe diarrhea and high fever. Debbie and Lisa were both sick. Debbie began to recover her strength after a couple of weeks, but Lisa's health continued to decline. The only treatment they received was plenty of liquids—water and tea—until they were well enough to return to the usual diet of rice and gravy and beans.

The thing that bothered Debbie most was that, while people were eating so poorly, she knew that sixty-five thousand dollars in Social Security checks were coming into Jonestown monthly.

And a lot of cash—maybe as much as three million dollars—
was hidden away down there too. When Debbie was still in
San Francisco, she had received an urgent message from Jonestown to send down mothballs, lots of mothballs. All the money
stored away in trunks had started to mildew, and the insects
were eating it up.

The toilet facilities and living quarters were as inadequate
as the food. For a population of more than one thousand, the
outhouses offered eighteen holes for the women and ten for the
men. In the sleeping quarters, the bunk beds were shoved right
up next to each other. Suitcases, clothes, and personal effects
were stored in the rafters of the low-ceilinged huts. Fourteen
people lived in a twelve-by-twenty-foot cabin. Few complained
about the lack of privacy, though, because the punishment for
complaining was to be stripped naked in front of the whole
community.

As it had been in San Francisco, a constant feature of life
in Jonestown was surveillance. Only here, in addition to everyone writing up reports on everyone else, there were armed
guards, sentries who wore their guns openly over the shoulders
of their khaki uniforms. This "security alert team," about fifty
strong, patrolled both the perimeter, to keep the inhabitants in
and unwanted guests out, and the main area where people were
working. If they happened to catch you taking a break because
your back was hurting, or if you were just a little slower than
the rest of your crew, you would be written up and called on
the floor that night, or put on the "learning crew."

It was very easy to get on the learning crew; being late to
a meeting, for example, or not eating all the food on your plate,
or having a bad attitude would do it. No excuses accepted, no
one exempt. The learning crew was supervised by three members of the security alert team. Being on the learning crew
meant you had to run everyplace—run to the fields in the
morning, run back to camp for lunch, run down to the piggery
and back. You could lose five pounds in one day. People on
the learning crew slept in a special dorm with an armed guard
outside, ate at a separate table, were not allowed to speak or
smile or laugh.

The beatings that had become commonplace in San Francisco continued—usually for any form of outspoken complaint
or protest—and new forms of punishment were instituted. A

child who broke the rules would be taken to a well in the forest. Two adults would be waiting down in the well, treading water in the dark. The child would be thrown into the well and the two swimmers would grab his feet and legs, pulling him down while he screamed with terror. All the way back to the settlement the child would cry, "I'm sorry, Father. I'm sorry, Father. . . ."

Adults were punished with a day or more in the "box," a sunless underground cubicle. The food and water of the person being punished would be reduced to liquid in a blender and fed in that form; vital signs would be checked once a day. The victim would be interrogated over and over until the responses were satisfactory to the questioner.

For especially recalcitrant cases, there was the "extended care unit." This eight-bed unit, separate from the medical clinic, was established in August or September 1978, and pretty much replaced physical beatings as the method for keeping troublemakers and potential defectors in line. People who continually violated the rules, or who wanted to leave Jonestown, would be kept locked up and drugged for a few days or weeks; when they were released, their "behavioral problems" had vanished. As one ex-Temple member put it, "People who wanted to leave were fed drugs like Thorazine so they would 'come to their senses.'" Other drugs in the Jonestown pharmacopoeia included sedatives, painkillers, and relaxants—Quaaludes, Demerol, Seconal, Valium, Nembutal, morphine—enough to fill the ordinary needs of a city of sixty-five thousand people.

Given the continual surveillance, and the potential for punishment in every action, personal relations understandably suffered. People tended to talk mean to each other, to stand about ten feet apart, and not to smile very much. New relationships were discouraged. If a man and a woman were seen talking to each other they might be called on the floor for flirting. Romantic ties were considered counterrevolutionary. But if a couple were really determined, they could go before the relationship committee and tell why they wanted to be together. The relationship committee was composed of eight people of all ages, from young children to seniors. The ground rules for the would-be couple were simple: For the first three months, talk only—no physical contact; then, for six months, the couple could live together—that is, share a cabin with several other couples—and have sex; after the six months, they could get married—if they still wanted to. In practice, very few relationships survived the first three-month period. People who valued their status with Jones, or who just wanted to stay out of trouble, steered clear of such involvement.

Shortly after Debbie arrived in Jonestown, she and Phil decided to try living together, as they had planned. After all, they were legally married, even if their marriage had never been consummated. Both had been through a lot, had changed a lot, but the basic affection was still there. No sooner had they reached their decision, however, than they were confronted for it. In a public meeting, Jones announced that some recent arrivals from the United Sates were still enticed by the world, flirting with people and probably even drinking. Debbie guessed he was talking about her evening with the Cuban doctor; she was glad she'd already written herself up. And Jones did go on about that incident, proudly stating, "Our women can get anything they want. There is a Cuban official who is infatuated with Deborah," as if the man were high in the government and not just a young doctor.

Finally Jones got to the point. "I have a note here," he announced, "that Debbie Blakey wants to live with Philip and another *white* couple in one of our cabins." He soon changed the subject, but Debbie knew that there was no chance that she and Phil would ever live together in Jonestown.

The next day Debbie was approached by the head coordinator of Jonestown. "Debbie," the woman said, "you know I've always thought of you as a daughter." Never having been especially close to the woman, Debbie decided she'd better guard her words. "Do you really want to live with Phil?" the woman asked her. "Why do you want to try to start up a relationship that's never worked before?"

Debbie knew that Jones had told the woman to talk to her. She said that no, she didn't really want to live with Phil, she just wanted to get out of the dorm where she was living, so she had asked Phil if she could move in with him. Of course, she said, she wasn't interested in living with him to have sex or anything like that, it was just that dorm life didn't agree with her.

She told the same story to Carolyn Layton, so it would be sure to get back to Jones in a couple of different ways, and the matter was dropped. She was sorry, and Phil was very upset that she changed her mind about living with him, even after the public confrontation. But she was formulating a plan to escape from Guyana, and she couldn't afford to be in Jones' bad graces.

Debbie had already gotten in trouble with Jones at least once. The day after she arrived in Jonestown there was a political meeting of the People's National Congress in Port Kaituma. The PNC was the party in power in Guyana, and the prime minister, Forbes Burnham, a black, was speaking at this meeting. Jones wanted an interracial Peoples Temple contingent there, and Debbie was assigned to attend. After the speeches, soda pop and beer were served. Debbie saw a young child handed a beer, which she didn't think he should drink, so she traded him for her soda. She drank about half the beer, which she didn't even like.

As soon as the party got back to Jonestown, Jones was on the loudspeaker, saying, "I understand some counterrevolutionary people took a drink of beer at the PNC meeting. I want every one of you to come up to the radio room and tell me why you did it." Debbie's first thought was not to go up there, but she knew that someone had already reported her. So she went to the radio room, where Jones was waiting alone, and told him about trading drinks with the young boy. He said, "Well, that's pretty bad, but I'll forgive you." So Debbie went on about her business, thinking that the incident was closed.

The next thing she knew Jones was on the loudspeaker saying he was still waiting, and that *everybody* who had been to the PNC meeting should come to the radio room at once. So they all came running, and Jones launched into an attack on those who had drunk beer at the meeting. Debbie, standing on the outside of the circle as the confrontation got heavier and heavier, finally walked up to the microphone and said, "I took a drink of beer at the meeting, I'm sorry, it was counterrevolutionary." She volunteered to put herself on the learning crew for two weeks, but Jones told her, "No, you don't have to do that, you just got here."

Although she was tempted to refer to her earlier conversation with Jones, she knew that would only get her into further trouble. She had to accept the clever way he had manipulated her, leading her to believe that she had been cleared of the charge of beer drinking so that she would not at first come forward when summoned with the others, but would reveal herself only after the confrontation had subjected the others to threats of punishment. The impression left was that Debbie had hung back while the others were being harangued, implying that she thought she could get away with breaking the rules, no doubt considering herself better than everybody else.

The loudspeaker was the most consistent and pervasive feature of life in Jonestown. While people were working, eating, or trying to sleep, Jones would be on the microphone five, six, seven hours at a time. The first full night that Debbie and Lisa spent in Jonestown, Debbie fell into bed exhausted. No sooner had she fallen asleep than Jones' voice blared over the loudspeaker. He had read a book, and now he discussed it, point by point, endlessly. Debbie tried to cover her ears, but the sound was too loud. She soon learned that sleep was a precious commodity in Jonestown, but she never got used to the blaring loudspeaker.

Five nights a week "services" were held that went on until two or three in the morning, or even all night, until it was time to go to work in the fields. One night a week was devoted to socialism class, followed by an oral test. Failure to answer appropriately was punishable by a stint in the learning crew.

For a while on Sunday nights, the one free evening of the week, people would get together to visit and play music and dance. But one night Jones looked in on the gathering and the next morning he was on the loudspeaker, and then every day for a week, about how capitalistic, degenerate, and counter-revolutionary such amusements were. He questioned the loyalty of everyone who had attended the dances. Needless to say, that was the last occasion of Sunday-night parties.

To Debbie it was obvious that Jones had deteriorated in the six months since she had last seen him, when he fled San Francisco. Physically, he was a wreck. He had gained a great deal of weight, and he complained constantly of such a number of serious ailments that it was a wonder he was still on his feet at all. He claimed to have cancer, a heart condition, a fungus in his lungs, and a recurring fever of 105 degrees. He dosed himself with painkillers, tranquilizers, and amphetamines, which only added to the incoherence of his speech. Psychologically, his behavior was almost continually manic. He would talk nonstop for hours at a time, launching into incomprehensible tirades, ranting out his paranoid vision. As his delusions took a tighter hold on his mind, Jones and his inner circle became more and more irrational.

Certain subjects could be counted on to drive Jones into a frenzy. His most frequent tirade was on the issue of custody of John Victor Stoen.

John's parents, Grace and Timothy Stoen, had been among the most trusted members of the church in Redwood Valley and San Francisco. They had known each other before joining the church. In fact, on one of their first dates they had attended a Temple service. Both had come with an intense desire to be of service, to make a difference in the world, and Peoples Temple offered them an opportunity to make that kind of commitment. The couple were married by Jones in the Redwood Valley church in 1970, and both quickly rose in the hierarchy of the organization.

Grace Stoen, who was only nineteen when she joined the church, soon became the Temple's bookkeeper and chief counselor, as well as one of Jones' chief confidantes. Between them, Tim and Grace probably knew as much about the inner workings of the organization as anybody except Jones himself.

John Victor Stoen was born early in 1972. Like other Temple children, he was raised more or less communally. Jones took a special interest in the child, including him in many family activities with his own sons.

As beatings and public humiliation became commonplace in the church, Grace grew disenchanted and was finally repelled by Jones' "paranoid world vision." In July 1976 she defected from the church, leaving her husband and her four-year-old son with the Temple. Four months later, Jones sent John Stoen to live in Guyana. In February 1977, Grace filed in San Francisco Superior Court for divorce and for custody of her son. Timothy, who by this time had also defected from the Temple, joined her in seeking custody.

Jones by then had some legal grounds for his claim on John Stoen—in 1974 and 1976 Grace had signed documents turning custody of her son over to the Temple, and Timothy himself had signed a piece of paper requesting that Jones father a child with Grace because he wanted his offspring to be sired by "the most compassionate, honest, and courageous human being the world contains."

Jones' contention that he was John's biological father was denied by both Stoens, and in August 1977, the Superior Court ruled these documents invalid and granted to Grace Stoen custody of her son. It also ordered Jones to appear in court. Of course Jones didn't show, so Grace's attorney, Jeffrey Haas, flew down to Georgetown to set in motion the extradition proceedings that they hoped would return their child to them. There was some question as to whether or not the Guyanese court would honor the decision of the U.S. court.

Naturally, Jones had a different version of the story. He claimed that Grace had approached him and begged him to father her child, and that Timothy had not only agreed but had added his plea to hers; witness the paper he had signed. According to this account, once the child was born Grace became demanding of Jones' time and energy, and paid little attention to her son. The boy spent most of his time with the Jones family, and was treated as one of his children.

The defection from the church of two such popular and high-level members as Timothy and Grace Stoen posed a threat to Jones' absolute control. No doubt he thought he could prevent them from speaking out against him as long as he was holding their son in Jonestown.

When the Stoens' attorney, Jeffrey Haas, arrived in Georgetown to bring legal proceedings against the Peoples Temple, the real depth of Jones' instability began to emerge. The radio messages from Guyana to San Francisco were frenzied and hysterical. One morning Terri Buford, Jones' public relations officer in San Francisco, received radio instructions from Karen Layton to place a telephone call to the Guyanese deputy prime minister, Ptolemy Reid, who was visiting the United States, and deliver the following threat: ". . . unless the government of Guyana takes immediate steps to stall the Guyanese court action regarding John Stoen's custody, the entire population [of Jonestown] will extinguish itself in a mass suicide by three thirty P.M. that day." Debbie, who was then still in San Francisco, later learned that Temple members in Guyana placed similar calls to other Guyanese officials.

In response to Jones' message, Temple members in San Francisco managed to contact attorney Charles Garry, who was in Detroit for a speaking engagement. Garry reached Marceline Jones, who was also in the United States, and they arranged to meet in Chicago. According to Garry, "I made a telephone-radio patch to Jonestown. I told him it was madness. Jim said the people had demanded suicide and that he, as their leader, had to give in." The attorney then arranged to have Huey Newton, Angela Davis, and Dennis Banks speak with Jones on the radio, to reassure him and plead with him.

Garry then drove to Indiana to explain the situation to the wife of the Guyanese ambassador to the United States, who was visiting a friend there. She contacted her husband, and within a couple of hours the Guyanese court action had been stopped.

According to Debbie, this was not the only time Jones used the threat of mass suicide to hold the government of Guyana at bay. There were other occasions when Jones got his way by saying, "We'll kill everybody, and you'll have eleven hundred dead people on your hands."

The colonists had been primed for suicide since their San Francisco days. In Jonestown, at one point, the favored scheme was for a "killing squad" to shoot the colony's elderly people and children before killing themselves. The plan was that people would be given a tranquilizer, then a drink of alcohol, before being shot.

By the time the Stoens carried their custody case to the courts of Guyana, Jones' paranoid monologues were no longer purely rhetorical. Jones harangued his followers constantly about their impending mass suicide for the cause. Besides the Stoens, the conspirators against him included the CIA, the FBI, Interpol, the government of the United States, and the families of many Temple members who had come to Guyana. He convinced his followers that, through their association with him, they too were targets of the conspiracy. And not only his followers—he also cultivated fear of the CIA and the American government in officials of the Guyanese government, holding up to them the example of what had happened in Cuba at the Bay of Pigs.

Black Temple members were told that if they returned to the United States, they would be put into concentration camps and killed. White members, he said, would be arrested as enemies of the state, tortured, imprisoned, and killed because of their association with Jones and with the black members of the Temple.

Two hundred miles from Georgetown, with no newspapers, no radio, and no letters, surrounded by dense jungle, the residents of Jonestown were isolated both physically and psychologically. Jones would read articles from the newspaper over the loudspeakers, but he would never let anyone see the papers themselves. He was their only source of information. Some people, like Debbie, might question his word, but no one could know enough to reject what he said with certainty. When he announced, for example, that the population of Los Angeles was fleeing the city because of severe drought and famine, they had no reason to doubt that it was so. He also told them that the KKK was marching in the streets of Los Angeles, and that Marshall Kilduff had been assassinated by the Temple.

Even if they left Guyana, most were convinced that they would have no place in the whole world to flee to. Because their lives were so wretched and fear-ridden, almost no one in Jonestown was capable of challenging the idea of mass suicide. As Debbie says, "Life at Jonestown was so miserable and the physical pain of exhaustion was so great, the suicide rehearsals were not traumatic. We had become indifferent to whether we lived or died."

At least one night a week, Jones would declare a state of emergency—what he called a "white night." As Debbie described it in an affidavit after her escape, "The entire population of Jonestown would be awakened by blaring sirens. Designated persons, approximately fifty in number, would arm themselves with rifles, move from cabin to cabin, and make certain that all members were responding. A mass meeting would ensue. Frequently during these crises, we would be told that the jungle was swarming with mercenaries and that death could be expected any minute.

"During one 'white night,' we were informed that our situation had become hopeless and that the only course of action open to us was a mass suicide for the glory of socialism. We were told that we would be tortured by mercenaries if we were taken alive. Everyone, including the children, was told to line up. As we passed through the line, we were given a small glass of red liquid to drink. We were told that the liquid contained poison and that we would die within 45 minutes. We all did as we were told. When the time came when we should have dropped dead, Rev. Jones explained that the poison was not real and that we had just been through a loyalty test. He warned us that the time was not far off when it would become necessary for us to die by our own hands.

"During another 'white night,' I watched Carolyn Layton, my former sister-in-law, give sleeping pills to two young children in her care, John Victor Stoen and Kimo Prokes, her own son. Carolyn said to me that Rev. Jones had told her that everyone was going to have to die that night. She said that she would probably have to shoot John and Kimo and that it would be easier for them if she did it while they were asleep."

On some of these occasions, Jones would order the entire congregation to gather on benches in the pavilion area to discuss how they were going to die. These gatherings could last a day or even two days. Meals would be served in the pavilion, but no one was allowed to sleep, or to leave the area—except to be escorted to the bathroom by an armed guard. By the end of one of those sessions, most people had given up any lingering resistance to the idea of suicide.

To convince the more religious-minded of his followers that they had nothing to fear in self-inflicted death, Jones taught that if they committed *revolutionary* suicide, and under his divine guidance, they would be reincarnated; death was only a passage to another life. As long as they believed in him, they would not cease to be. And just to make sure that they all stuck it out together, Jones taught that the debt incurred by individual rather than collective suicide would be so heavy that the person would be reincarnated a million years in the past and have to go through it all again.

Lisa Layton was not blind to what was happening in Jonestown, but her reaction was more one of bewilderment than dismay.

As Debbie recalls, "Mom was becoming weak, and I got it cleared with Carolyn for her not to have to stay in the long meetings. But she was frightened to get up and leave after the first few hours of those nightly marathons. She was afraid of being confronted for walking out. She thought the meetings were far too long and far too violent. And she was concerned about other things, about the tapes that never stopped playing at night, and how tired and poorly fed we were. She would say, 'Oh, Debbie, you're in those fields so long—all of you children. You need more rest and more protein.' Mom would complain about it, but only to me, never to Jim. I would listen to her and try to explain why Jim was doing these things. I wanted her to tell me her fears so she wouldn't tell anyone else. Sometimes I invented reasons for what was going on, to reduce her concern."

Letters to Jonestown from friends and relatives in the States were read and censored before being passed on to the recipient, or else were simply thrown away. And control on outgoing mail was just as tight. The discipline of the days of the San Francisco letter-writing campaigns stood Jones in good stead. There is a sameness about the letters that came out of Jonestown—an almost hysterical cheerfulness and unrelenting insistence on the perfection of the new life the people had found.

"This is a dream come true. This is a whole world—clean, fresh, pure. . . ."

"I am so happy, and that terrible feeling of insecurity is gone. . . ."

"Jonestown is pure democracy in action."

"Nestled in the most exquisite forest surroundings, we have every convenience—plus more; the best in social services any community anywhere can offer!"

"All around Jonestown, tall green trees surround us. Just imagine never hearing the sound of a siren. It's so peaceful and quiet here. At nighttime a person will feel comfortable knowing that they don't have to worry about being murdered or robbed in their sleep. . . ."

"It's so peaceful; everyone looks so much better and feels better for not having to worry about where their next meal is coming from."

In fact, the residents of Jonestown were forced to copy from blackboards whole paragraphs of praise, filling in the names of family members where appropriate. Many people who received such letters recognized them as phony. One woman in San Francisco received a note from her father "that Ray Charles could see wasn't in his handwriting."

Every day, someone in Georgetown would be on the radio to San Francisco relaying reports of how beautiful and perfect everything was in the Promised Land. And when a group of concerned relatives in the United States accused Jones of human rights violations "including prohibition of telephone calls, personal visits and the censorship of mail," about a dozen people took turns on the radio in Georgetown to proclaim their happiness and loyalty to their leader, and to denounce their relatives.

That radio testimonial was broadcast to the San Francisco office of Peoples Temple attorney Charles Garry, who soon became the first of the few outsiders allowed to visit the community for extended periods of time. In November of 1977, he reported on his week-long stay in Guyana in the following glowing terms.

"I saw a community where there is no such thing as racism. No one feels the color of his skin, whether he's black, brown, yellow, red, or white. I also noticed that no one thinks in terms of sex. No one feels superior to anyone else. I don't know of any community in the world today that has been able to solve the problems of male sex supremacy completely. That does not exist in Jonestown.

"I also saw something else: There is no such thing as ageism. The community is comprised of the little children, the teenagers, the young adults, the old adults, the senior citizens, all together.

"Why are these people so happy? They are learning a new social order. They are learning an answer to a better life. When I returned to the States, I told my partners in the office that I had seen paradise. From what I saw there, I would say that the society that is being built in Jonestown is a credit to humanity."

Actually, Debbie recalls that Jones was furious at the necessity of inviting Garry down for a week, because there was only one sufficiently nice place for him to stay—Jones' own home. So Garry stayed in a comfortable house with his own refrigerator, shower, bathroom—even toilet paper, a luxury the rest of the colony did without.

The whole community benefited from the visit—their work hours were shortened, and there was fried chicken on every plate. As the saying goes, Charles Garry got the "Angela Davis tour of China." As a result of this trip, he urged Jones to open the community to others in order to dispel the ugly rumors about the place that were increasingly current in San Francisco.

Garry was not the only visitor to be impressed to the point of lyricism. The Reverend John Moore and his wife, Barbara, the parents of Larry Layton's first wife, Carolyn, visited their daughters Carolyn and Annie in Jonestown in May 1978. Jones didn't really trust the Moores, but he allowed them to come for a fairly extended visit, partly to remind his followers that important people from the outside still respected him, and partly because he was sure that the Moores would return to the States with a glowing report. They proved him correct. At a press conference on May 28, 1978, Moore stated, "The two words that came to mind, immediately as I was there and as I tried to reflect upon my experiences, were 'impressive' and 'amazing.' . . . I had a feeling of freedom. Neither in Georgetown, where there were about twenty-five or thirty people living, coming and going all the time, with total freedom, nor at the project itself . . . did I have any feeling that anybody was being restrained or coerced or intimidated in any way."

Jones had things so well orchestrated that it was virtually impossible for anyone from the outside to get at the truth of the situation. Most visitors flew in for only a couple of hours; very few were allowed to remain overnight. When Guyanese or American officials visited, the guards would hide their guns and replace their khaki uniforms with jeans and T-shirts.

Richard McCoy, the American consul in Guyana, made three visits to Jonestown, in August 1977 and in January and May 1978. On each occasion, he had to submit in advance a list of the names of the people he wanted to talk with, usually colonists whose concerned relatives had contacted the U.S. embassy. The Temple's insistence on having the list in advance was explained by the possibility that the people McCoy wanted to see might otherwise be up the river fishing, or playing bingo in Port Kaituma. Of course, those to be interviewed would be thoroughly coached in the correct response to any likely question. And during the actual interviews there would always be someone around, engaged in an innocent-looking task—like a senior sweeping the area—with the responsibility of eavesdropping on the conversation. Under those circumstances it would have been difficult indeed for any colonist to express to an American official a desire to leave the settlement.

The last visit by an American official before Congressman Leo Ryan and his party arrived took place on November 7, 1978. Douglas Ellice, the American consul, and Dennis Reece, vice consul, reported on their observations. "Mr. Ellice and Mr. Reece shared the same general impressions as follows: The members they met appeared to be in good health, mentally alert (considering the advanced age of some of them), and generally happy to be in Jonestown. They all seemed to be absorbed in their general duties such as shop work, teaching or gardening. No one indicated any desire to return to the United States."

Earlier in the year, however, at least one American official had been less sanguine. Frank Tumminia, the State Department desk officer for Guyana, reported on his visit to Jonestown with the American embassy's Deputy Chief of Mission John Blacken: "One of the things that struck me at the time and upon which I remarked to Embassy staff as well as to Department officials, was my feeling that many of the people with whom I met and spoke appeared drugged and robot-like in their reactions to questions and, generally, in their behavior toward us visitors."

Before she had been in Jonestown a week, Debbie knew that she had to get out. At first she wasn't too worried, because Jones' own plan from the beginning had been for her to return to the States to help complete the Temple's financial transactions in San Francisco. But then, after Jones assigned her to the Jonestown-Georgetown radio, where from seven in the morning until seven in the evening Debbie would transmit messages from Jones to the Georgetown headquarters—instructions about dealings with various Guyanese ministers, and feedback on all kinds of problems and activities—he decided that Debbie knew too much to be allowed to return to the States. As he explained it, she would be in too great a danger of being betrayed to the government and put in jail.

•

That was when she started planning her escape from Guyana.

Jones had earlier decided that it would be good for the Temple's public relations with the Guyanese people to stage a "cultural program" in Georgetown. An evening of Americans singing and dancing in the capital city would scotch the rumors that Jonestown was a prison camp from which people were not free to leave, and the Guyanese people would see that the place couldn't be so bad after all. The name of the program was "A Cooperative Feeling."

A group of teenagers was to go into Georgetown for the event, and Debbie hoped to be assigned to accompany them as a chaperone. Rather than count on luck, however, she began dropping hints to Jones that the Temple's Georgetown operation was disorganized and that his instructions were not always followed. The implication was that if she were in Georgetown, she could clean up the act at headquarters. But she had to be subtle about it—it wouldn't do to let anybody know that she *wanted* to leave the jungle community—so she began to talk up what she would be sacrificing by going. And Jones had other reasons not to worry: Debbie would be leaving her passport behind, and Lisa would still be in Jonestown.

Up until the night before the group was to leave for Georgetown, Debbie didn't know whether or not she was going. At about two o'clock in the morning of March 28, she was told to pack her things; the boat would leave at 11 A.M., and she was to be on it.

Saying good-bye to Lisa was the hardest thing Debbie had ever done in her life. Maybe she should stay in Jonestown with her mother until she died, she thought, rather than leaving her hostage to a madman. But she knew that if she didn't go while she had this chance, she would never get out.

About her parting from Lisa, Debbie remembers, "I had all my things packed and I went to Mom's little house on the morning I was to leave. I told her I was going to Georgetown and she began to cry. I could hear them screaming at me, 'Come on, come on, we gotta go.' At that moment I thought, I can't leave my mom. Then she said, 'I'll probably never see you again,' and I knew that she was not referring to her own death but to the likelihood that I would not return. I think she hoped I would try to escape, but we never said a word about it. It was simply an implied understanding between us that I would not come back. We were of the same blood. She had left Germany, not knowing if she would ever see her parents again, and I was leaving the Temple.

"When I was thirteen years old I wrote a poem called 'I Am the Mirror of My Mother'—'She looks at me and sees herself.' We had so many parallels that I used to think sometimes that she would be angry with me because I was mirroring her childhood. She saw my rebellions coming, and she feared them because she had done the same things."

9

The Escape

Debbie spent the entire boat trip from Jonestown to Georgetown trying to devise a plan of escape. She knew that she would need help from the outside, and her sister, Annalisa, seemed her most likely contact.

A couple of days after Debbie arrived in Georgetown, the Temple presented its "cultural program." That evening she told the rest of the Georgetown staff to go on to the performance, that she would stay to monitor the radio. Her offer was gratefully accepted.

As soon as everyone had left for the Cultural Center, Debbie went down to the radio room and called Annalisa by radiophone collect. But the instant she got through to her sister it occurred to her that the phone might be tapped, and she was suddenly afraid to tell the real reason for her call. Debbie assured Annalisa that she and Lisa were fine, really doing well, and hung up quickly, promising to call again soon. Annalisa was at first puzzled and then concerned by this uncommunicative long-distance call.

A few days later, Debbie slipped away from Temple head-quarters to place a call from the Pegasus Hotel. The lobby phones were out in the open, so that anyone could overhear the conversation, and the phone connection was so bad that Debbie had to raise her voice to make herself heard. Quickly she told her sister that she wanted to leave Guyana, but that she didn't have her passport, and she was afraid to go to the embassy to get a new one lest the Temple find out. The two of them sketched out a plan. Annalisa would write to Debbie saying that she and Ray would be coming to South America with their children—it was true that Ray would be making the trip in his professional capacity as a United Nations expert on nitrogen fixation—and that they wanted Debbie to travel with them to baby-sit for the two Valentine children. She would ask Debbie to meet them in Caracas, Venezuela, and travel with them through several South American countries on a U.N.-sponsored trip, meeting high government officials and other important people. They hoped that the implied contact with the elite and powerful would impress Jones enough so that he would give Debbie permission to go along. The trip would last about a month, and she would end up back in Georgetown.

Actually, Annalisa and the children were not planning to accompany Ray; he would be traveling alone on his U.N. business, ready to help if needed.

In a series of hasty letters and surreptitious phone calls, Debbie and Annalisa worked out the details of the plan. An-nalisa would arrange the flight reservations, and it would be up to Debbie to take care of the passport situation. She had six weeks to do it. Debbie asked her sister to keep the scheme secret from everyone, including Dr. Layton and Tom. She was afraid that her father and brother might blow her cover by trying to contact her to offer help, or that they might even rush down to Guyana to try to rescue her.

On April 20 the plan was launched when Annalisa phoned Debbie at the Georgetown Temple with her initial request that Debbie help take care of the children on their proposed trip. She followed up that call with a letter outlining their itinerary. Debbie discussed Annalisa's request with Karen Layton, and radioed Jones to ask his permission to travel with her sister. Jones told Debbie that the letter sounded phony to him; he speculated that Annalisa might be setting up a kidnapping at-tempt to deprogram her. Afraid of seeming too eager, Debbie agreed that it sounded suspicious. As soon as she could, she called Annalisa again to ask her to send more documentation.

On April 26, Annalisa sent Debbie an impressive telegram, giving details of their itinerary, including Pan Am and Varig flight numbers and a Holiday Inn reservation number in Caracas. Annalisa's fertile imagination had created a month-long circle tour. Leaving Georgetown May 12, Debbie would meet them in Caracas, and they would all then travel to Port of Spain, Colombia, Peru, Brazil, and back to Caracas, before Debbie returned to Georgetown. Actually, the ticket that would be waiting for Debbie in Caracas would take her straight to Los Angeles.

Debbie phoned Annalisa on April 29 to report that Jones still did not believe the trip was for real. Getting into the spirit of her role, Annalisa told Debbie to let Jones know that she would not take no for an answer. This trip meant a lot to her, and she expected Debbie to be there to help her with the children.

At about that time Annalisa thought she had better let her father in on their cover story. She was afraid that Jones would send a radio message to have Larry check out Debbie's trip. She assumed that Larry's loyalty would lie with the Temple rather than with Debbie, and that he would do whatever Jones told him to do. Annalisa didn't tell her father that the whole trip was a ruse, knowing that Dr. Layton would be more convincing to Larry if he believed what he was saying. Then she phoned Larry herself, describing the plans for the trip. She wanted to make sure that the stories the Temple heard in San Francisco and in Guyana matched.

On May 10, just two days before Debbie's scheduled flight, Annalisa sent a final telegram, confirming Debbie's travel arrangements to Caracas. Now she had done all she could do—except wait for a phone call from Debbie. She could only hope that the call would come from Caracas, and that her sister would be safe at last.

From the time Debbie arrived in Georgetown, less than two months before the scheduled date of her flight to Caracas, she was immersed in Temple business.

The Georgetown headquarters of Peoples Temple was located about five minutes by taxi from the center of town. It fulfilled the expectations she had used as a pretext to Jones: the place was a disorganized mess. No one was in charge of the house, the vehicles, the radio, appointments, or schedules. A firm hand was needed, and Debbie—whose aim was to make herself so indispensable that she wouldn't be sent back to Jonestown—stepped right in and started organizing and arranging. Her first act was to set up a huge communal calendar in the kitchen; the overworked residents of the Georgetown branch of the Temple had so many appointments, many of them with officials of the Guyanese government, that it was hard to keep track of where everybody was at any given moment.

In most communal living situations the kitchen is the nerve center, so Debbie set about straightening out the chaos and eliminating the waste she found there. Menus had to be planned and perishables purchased accordingly, so that good food would not spoil and have to be thrown out. Cooking and cleaning schedules had to be established. Even shelving and storage needed organization. When this was accomplished she turned her attention to the radio room, where Jones had actually placed her in charge.

One of the problems in the Georgetown-Jonestown communications setup had been that when a delegation—routinely composed of three members, since hardly anyone was allowed to go alone on Temple business—returned from visiting a Guyanese official, and if Jones was not immediately available by radio, they would hold on to their information or report in the hope of relaying it to him themselves, instead of giving it to the person on radio duty. Debbie changed all that. As soon as people got back from an appointment she simply told them, "Hey, give me your information, I'm going to make sure it gets relayed." Because she was known to be close to Jones, people had no problem with telling her everything they'd learned. Or she would have people relay their own information—as long as it was done immediately. That way, Jones could find out what was going on almost as soon as it happened, and give feedback and instructions on the spot. He had been feeling paranoid and anxious about being out of touch with Georgetown. Now he relaxed a little, and complimented Debbie on her efficiency in relaying messages.

If the reorganization of the radio room impressed Jones, the reorganization of the entire Georgetown operation impressed Marceline, who had come to town to give a speech at the

Cultural Center about the conspiracy against the church.

"You know, Debbie," she said, "this place has never been so organized as since you've been here. I think you should stay."

"No, no," Debbie protested, "I have to go back to Jonestown."

But Marceline got on the radio with Jones and told him, "Look, Jim, Debbie has done such a great job of organizing this place, I don't think she should leave."

At that point Debbie's place in Georgetown was secure. She had made herself indispensable. She was exactly where she wanted to be—positioned for flight.

Debbie had other duties in addition to taking charge of the household and the radio room. Temple members were assigned on a rotating basis to beg in the streets of Georgetown. Each team of two was expected to bring in a hundred dollars a day, seven days a week. It was Debbie's responsibility to collect that money at the end of every day.

Another important part of her work in Georgetown was to visit various officials on church business. Because of her position of trust in the organization, she was frequently picked for the more sensitive assignments—visits to Guyanese government offices and to the Russian embassy. Having some diplomatic access was, of course, a critical part of her plan; sooner or later, she would find an opportunity for an unaccompanied errand to the American embassy.

Escape from the racist oppressor in the United States had been one of the original reasons for the establishment of Jonestown. Now, believing themselves hounded even in the jungles of South America, their desperation sustained by the increasingly real alternative of mass suicide, Jones and his followers explored other avenues of escape. Afraid that the government of Guyana would be unable to resist the mounting pressure of conspirators from the United States, Jones spoke of emigrating with his flock to the Soviet Union. Temple representatives in Georgetown had met with Russian officials in December 1977 to arrange for a delegation to visit the USSR, and in Jonestown Russian language classes had become compulsory, with everyone reciting Russian phrases before each meal of rice and gravy.

Russian consular officials did visit Jonestown, and the community was written up by the Soviet news agency Tass; but however hopeful Jones may have been about the colony's chances of emigrating, the Russian consulate in Guyana remained less than encouraging. Jones ordered the Georgetown staff to apply more pressure. By then Debbie was there, and while she welcomed the diplomatic contact, her involvement in the Temple's stepped-up Russian campaign added to her rising tension while she hoped and planned to get out of Guyana.

Another Temple delegation arranged to meet in late March with Soviet embassy official Feodor Timofeyev. It included Terry Carter Jones, Sharon Amos, and Debbie Blakey. Sharon Amos' typed report to Jones on that meeting reveals a continuing reluctance on the part of the Soviet officials to commit their country to welcoming the proposed emigration.

"Regarding the need for exodus," Amos wrote, "he [Timofeyev] doesn't see the need for such a situation developing right away, not within a year at least.

"Regarding a possible delegation going to the USSR, he said it was a possibility that he could help, no problem getting visas at any time, but when asked if it would be possible to arrange meetings with officials, he said that would have to be coordinated and might take a little bit of time. He is waiting for response back from Moscow to the letter he sent a week ago with our requests.

"He said that it was a difficult thing to arrange (the exodus), but when I cried and said 'It would be very painful for the door to be shut against the children, we adults don't matter so much but we need safety for our children,' he said that the USSR had taken in 5000 Spanish children (from Spain) and they had been taken care of and then later returned to Spain, so he felt it was worth pursuing. . . .

"He said the first time he had talked to us about a possible exodus [the previous December], he had written Moscow saying that people might at some time want to come, but he said there was no answer as of yet on this, or he didn't want to tell us?

"He said it was not a simple question.

"In regard to a delegation going to Moscow he didn't think

the Secretary of the Communist Party could see us but others might be able to be arranged and Timofeyev could help make the arrangements."

Debbie has her own memory of that meeting: "We were at the Russian embassy on the ploy that mercenaries were coming in to kill everyone in Jonestown and we had to get out of the country. We had told the first secretary that we had to talk to the chargé d'affaires. He asked us why, and we said, 'We can't go into it with you, it's an emergency, people's lives are at stake.' He left the room. We all knew that we were in a very touchy situation, the pressure was terrific. I started clowning around, saying things like, 'This furniture is nice, we should give them our old beat up stuff and take theirs.' Terry Carter Jones, who was sitting next to me, cracked up, but everybody else got very upset, especially Sharon. Their feeling was, how can you be laughing at a life-and-death time like this. I said, 'I'm sorry, we really shouldn't be laughing, because when they leave the room they are probably taping us,' and then Terry and I cracked up all over again. When we left, Terry said, 'There's something about you, Debbie, you can make any dying situation into a joke.'"

Jones spoke also of emigrating to Cuba. That might be easier, he felt, because everybody could get on the Temple's boats instead of having to be airlifted.

In such an event, Jones said, explosives would be planted under every building in Jonestown, to be detonated by the last people to leave the settlement. He wanted to make certain that nobody else would profit from their years of labor in the jungle. The community had practiced planting the explosives at least once, before Debbie and Lisa arrived in Jonestown.

It was for this possible eventuality of a sudden departure, or more broadly "if anything happened in Jonestown," that Temple members in San Francisco were trained in the use of handguns. They were told that they would be left responsible for killing "traitors" in the United States.

Many of the problems faced by the Temple in Georgetown seemed to have been transplanted straight from San Francisco.

Far from escaping the conspiratorial vision that had developed in the United States, Jones and his followers found an even lusher climate for their paranoia in the foreign atmosphere and smaller, more closed society of Guyana. The Stoen case in particular continued to plague Jones. In constant fear that he would lose custody of John Stoen, now six years old, Jones ordered his trusted aides in Georgetown to put pressure on government officials to influence the case. These tactics—together with Jones' threat of mass suicide if the boy were taken from him—were successful. After months of delay, the judge who was presiding over the custody hearing refused to rule on the case and sent it back to Guyana's chief justice for reassignment—even though Grace and Timothy Stoen had already won their custody battle in the U.S. courts. The judge gave as his reason the extreme harassment to which he had been subjected.

Heavy lobbying by Temple members also forestalled an investigation of Jones' activities by the Guyanese police. In payment for such favors, Temple members took an active part in local party politics on the side of the ruling party, the People's National Congress. There were rumors that Jones had promised to deliver a thousand illegal votes in one important election. Even more so than San Francisco, Georgetown was small enough that a relatively minor degree of sophisticated political manipulation could make a difference in official policy.

Relations were friendly with several top government officials; some were visited almost daily. Jones would get on the radio and issue a couple of hours of instructions about what the Temple delegations should say. Then Marceline Jones, Sharon Amos, Mike Prokes, Tim Carter, Debbie Blakey, or whoever else was in authority in Georgetown at that time would go and spend hours talking to the government ministers as directed. The tactics varied from regular gifts of imported liquor to "crazy niggering," the near-hysterical argumentation and claims of outside menace such as Sharon Amos tried on the Russian consular official. Usually a compromise was reached in favor of the Temple.

On at least one occasion when Debbie was present in the office of a high government official, the topic of discussion was the threat of raids on Jonestown by mercenaries and the necessity of arming the settlement—in other words, to bring more arms into Jonestown. By then Jones had curtailed the smuggling of guns from the United States and was feeling inadequately protected. If he could get Guyanese officials to approve the purchase of guns in Georgetown for shipment to the interior, he would not only have his protection but also a convenient breach of law with which to blackmail the government.

The influence of Peoples Temple on certain Guyanese officials extended also to customs and immigration practices. This relationship made it easy for Temple members to enter the country, and difficult for would-be defectors to get out. Many shipments of money and goods for the agricultural project were inspected perfunctorily if at all.

Cover-ups on customs violations didn't necessarily have to come from the top. Debbie recalls that when a particularly important or patently suspicious shipment arrived, Karen Layton and Paula Adams—both attractive blondes—would go out to the airport and flirt with the guards and the customs officials until they didn't care what they let through. Another Temple tactic was to pack Kotex on the top of boxes that wouldn't stand close inspection, on the theory that the customs men would be embarrassed to look underneath. A lot of American dollars entered Guyana safely tucked away beneath layers of sanitary napkins.

Given the aggressiveness with which Debbie moved into the small, tight Temple community in Georgetown, there were bound to be jealousies and personality conflicts. The Temple custom of everybody writing up reports on everybody else reveals that at least two of Debbie's co-workers did not agree with Marceline Jones' evaluation of the job she was doing.

Bobby Stroud's report to Jones read:

"Debbie Blakey is very moody. One day she has a good attitude, the next day she's a bitch; she takes it out on people here, with a sharp and sarcastic tongue. If I have had a bad day—and come home like that—she's the first one to say something about it; but no one can say anything to her without her attitude getting in the way."

Debbie's sister-in-law, Karen Layton, agreed with Bobby Stroud:

"Debbie is very difficult to deal with. She often likes to 'bite peoples' heads off' just by her nasty attitude. Sometimes she is so kind and thoughtful and other times she is short tempered and pissy. I have not found her that helpful in organizing here. She works well in different areas, such as she'll go in the kitchen and cook, or clean up the house or rearrange furniture, etc. But as far as overall coordination, I don't find us working together that well. I back off from her because she gets pissy. Richard and Jack, Bobby, Sharon and Tim C. have all mentioned to me that they think her attitude is pissy. She's just short tempered and irratable. . . ."

In addition to writing up reports on each other, Jones required written self-criticism from everyone in the Georgetown group. Debbie refused. She had stayed cool up to now, but the strain of waiting and trying to work out her escape, together with the pettiness and backbiting of the other members of the group, made her nervous and short-tempered. She could no longer entirely restrain her anger and hostility. She knew she had to get out soon, or she would blow it completely.

In that atmosphere of duplicity and institutionalized informing, Jones' paranoid view of the world seemed no more than realistic. And there was some real evidence on certain of Jones' "conspirators." It was true, for example, that the FCC was sporadically monitoring Peoples Temple radio communications from Georgetown to San Francisco. This was in response to the complaints of other amateurs, who claimed that Temple operators were violating FCC and international regulations prohibiting business negotiations by radio. Temple operators were also accused of operating outside the prescribed amateur bands, and of using "clear text cryptography," coded messages disguised as routine communications.

According to Debbie, most of what went out on the air was in code. Every Temple officer had a code name, and so did every country referred to. The United States was Rex, the Soviet Union was Shirley, Cuba was Nettie. So if Debbie wanted to relay to San Francisco the information that Mike Prokes had visited the Cuban embassy and had a productive meeting with a high-ranking official, she would say, "Harry went to Nettie's house today and talked to her mother. She was very nice."

For the heaviest top-secret transmissions between Georgetown and San Francisco, the code was even more complex,
and involved switching frequencies several times during a message. There was even a code for switching frequencies. If the
operator said, "I've got to go see Mary," that meant to go up
81 kilocycles. If she said, "I have to water the plants," that
meant to go down 31 kilocycles. When both operators were
on the new frequency, the operator would say, "OK, go up
35."

By the time Debbie arrived in Guyana, the Temple was no
longer smuggling guns and money. The messages that she
relayed between Georgetown and Jonestown dealt mostly with
the daily activities of the Temple communities there. In the
earlier days, however, the message "Send us more guns and
ammunition" might have gone something like this: "Give Lilly
a message for me. Hold on, I have to go see Mary." (Go up
81 kilocycles.) "Tell her to send—wait, I have to water the
plants." (Go down 31 kilocycles.) "OK, meet you at 15." (Go
up 15 kilocycles.) "Fishing poles and toys for the kids."

Of course, such procedure was in violation of all kinds of
international and FCC regulations concerning amateur radio
transmission, and was bound to draw official attention to the
broadcasts. And, of course, such attention was regarded as
further proof of a conspiracy against the Temple.

By now it seemed that no one was benefiting from the Peoples
Temple Agricultural Project, the clearance and development
of the Guyana jungle—not the residents of the colony, not the
Guyanese people, not the Guyanese government. Officially,
the government still welcomed the Temple as a "beneficial
organization," feeling that it was in their best interest politically
to continue to offer Jones their support and assistance. Not all
officials were so kindly disposed, however; some issued veiled
warnings to Temple delegations not to push so hard for favors
and publicity. And the Guyanese people themselves were
clearly growing more hostile. The popular attitude seemed to
be: "Who are these Americans to come down here and take
what should be ours? What would happen if we went to the
United States and started begging on the streets there?"

Rumors and gossip flourished. Peoples Temple was out for
itself, to get what it could off the Guyanese. The members

didn't want to integrate into Guyanese society. Visitors to the mysterious jungle community were discouraged. And those who lived there were not allowed to leave.

One member who wanted to leave was hanging on in the eye of the storm. It was becoming clear to Debbie that the scheme she and Annalisa had concocted was not going to work. No doubt cautioned by the manifold risks of the deteriorating situation in Guyana, as well as the continuing reports of Debbie's irascibility, Jones would not give permission for her to meet Annalisa in Caracas.

With less than a week to go before her scheduled date of departure, Debbie decided to go through with the plan without clearance from Jones. That meant she would have to keep her preparations secret from her associates in Georgetown. It was too late to get further word to Annalisa or Ray—Debbie was now constantly involved with other matters in Temple business. But she knew she could count on Annalisa to have a ticket waiting for her at the Pan Am office on May 12, and she would just have to trust to luck and take care of the rest herself.

The first time Debbie tried to approach the American embassy about her passport, she became frightened at the last minute that Jones would learn of her defection.

The opportunity came with her assignment to conduct three young Temple couples whose children had been born in Jonestown to the office of the American consul, Richard McCoy, for information on getting birth certificates. McCoy asked each of the young parents in turn, "Are you happy? Do you want to leave Jonestown?" Dutifully—with Debbie sitting there to report to Jones on whatever they said—each one reaffirmed his or her desire to remain in Jonestown, and to raise their children as Guyanese citizens.

Before the meeting Debbie had told the couples that she was to deliver a confidential message to McCoy. When they had all filed out of the room, leaving her alone with the consul, she said, "I have a message for you . . ." and then she stopped. Richard McCoy was a regular visitor to Jonestown, and she was hearing once again Jim Jones' frequent boast: "I can get any information I want out of Dick McCoy." McCoy was scheduled for a visit to Jonestown a couple of days before her planned departure. What if he were to remark casually to Jones, "It can't be as nice here as you say, someone has already approached me about leaving."

"Jim wanted to thank you for taking so much time with us," she continued lamely. "We really appreciate it."

McCoy assured her that it was his job to be of assistance to U.S. citizens living abroad, and patted her on the back as he held the door for her.

I really blew it, Debbie thought as the door closed behind her. What a chicken. How am I ever going to get out of here?

A few days later, Debbie found herself in McCoy's office once again. This time she and Sharon Amos and Terry Carter Jones were there, on Jim Jones' orders, to tell the consul that Tim Stoen and the CIA were planning an aerial raid on Jonestown; that armed mercenaries were ready to attack from the jungle; and that Jonestown needed more guns to protect itself. McCoy's response to Sharon Amos' account of the perils faced by the jungle community apparently was not satisfactory, and she burst into tears. His reaction to her "crazy niggering" was, "Come on, Sharon, don't give me that." And a little later, "Hell, if the planes come over, shoot 'em down."

Debbie, silent throughout the meeting, kept trying to make eye contact with McCoy, to establish rapport and separate herself from the group.

When Jones heard the report on that meeting, and particularly the comment about shooting down the planes, he was furious that it hadn't been taped. Taping all conversations had been standard procedure in San Francisco, but not in Guyana until now. Jones ordered Sharon, Terry, and Debbie to return to McCoy's office, this time with a concealed tape recorder, and get him to repeat the statement. It would then be banked for future use in justifying antiaircraft fire from Jonestown. "Why, McCoy told us to shoot them down!" Jones would say.

The next day Annalisa's final telegram arrived—fortunately, Debbie was at headquarters to receive it herself. It was also the day Dick McCoy and Sharon Amos were scheduled to fly into Jonestown on a one-day trip. They were to return on May 12, the same day that Debbie was booked on an 11:55 P.M. flight out of Georgetown. She still felt uneasy about approaching McCoy concerning her passport before his Jonestown trip, for fear that he would give her away to Jim Jones, but she knew that she would have to see him as soon as he returned— and that she would have to arrange to see him alone.

For once, luck was with her. Rather than flying back with Dick McCoy, Sharon Amos remained in Jonestown. So Debbie and Terry Carter Jones were to go alone to see McCoy, to try to trick him into repeating his statement about shooting down the planes and to tape-record it.

Early on the morning of May 12 Debbie called McCoy's office to try to set up an appointment for that afternoon, but the line was busy. She had to go downtown anyway, to run some errands, so she told Terry that she would stop by McCoy's office to make the appointment. She arrived there at about ten o'clock, only to be informed by the secretary that Mr. McCoy was in a meeting with Ambassador John Burke, and that he would be back in about half an hour. Debbie waited in the hall. When McCoy returned she followed him into his office and said, "I've got to talk to you about something extremely confidential."

"Well, then, close the door," he replied.

Debbie pulled the door shut and sat down in front of the desk. "I know you're not going to believe this, but I want to leave Peoples Temple, leave Guyana. My sister wired me a ticket, and it's for tonight." McCoy suggested that she write out a brief statement of her reasons for leaving the Peoples Temple; witnessed by McCoy's vice consul, Daniel Weber, this sworn statement would become a part of the official file on the Temple. In longhand, Debbie quickly wrote out what seemed to her to be the most important facts about the situation in Jonestown.

Georgetown, Guyana

I, Deborah Layton Blakey, hereby swear that the following statement is true and correct to the best of my ability.

I have decided to leave the Peoples Temple Organization because I am afraid that Jim Jones will carry out his threats to force all members of the Organization in Guyana to commit suicide if a decision is made in Guyana by the Court here to have John Stoen returned to his mother. I know that plans have been made to carry out this mass suicide by poison that is presently at Jonestown. I also know that plans are made to kill the members who are unwilling to voluntarily commit suicide. I believe that this plan will be carried out. I also believe that the Organization will physically try to prevent any attempt to remove John Stoen from the custody of the Organization. In part for the above I have decided to leave the Peoples Temple.

s/Deborah L. Blakey

Sworn to this 12th day of May 1978

Daniel P. Weber
American Vice Consul

McCoy later told Debbie that he knew what she had to tell him as soon as he saw her sitting alone in the hall. He had never been visited by a Temple member alone; they always came in groups. Now, however, all he said was, "Don't worry, I'll take care of everything." He gave her the forms to fill out for an emergency passport, and took her picture with an ancient Polaroid. While she was completing the forms he excused himself to confer with Ambassador Burke, leaving her with Vice Consul Dan Weber. When McCoy returned in half an hour he stamped her brand-new passport and tried to give it to her.

"Don't I have to have a tax clearance too?" she asked. "I think you have to have a tax stamp before they'll let you out of the country. I know I had to get one for Carolyn Layton when she went to Nassau."

"No, this is all you need," McCoy assured her. "You don't have to have anything but your passport." Again he tried to hand it to her.

With almost twelve hours to go before her flight, Debbie knew that if she were discovered carrying a passport she would be in trouble, since her original passport was known to be locked up with a thousand others in a trunk in Jonestown. She asked Dan Weber to hold the new passport for her. Weber would be driving her to the airport to catch her plane, and they arranged to meet at nine o'clock that evening at the Pegasus Hotel.

By this time it was past noon. Quickly Debbie set up an appointment for Terry Carter Jones and herself for two o'clock. She next warned McCoy that they would try to trick him into repeating his statement about shooting down the airplane. Then she called the Georgetown headquarters to let them know the time of the meeting.

Her next task on that frantic day was to race over to the Pan Am office to pick up her ticket, then get it back to Dan Weber so that he would be holding both of her documents. But the ticket wasn't there. She gave the attendant Annalisa's phone number and begged him to try to find out what had gone wrong. By that time it was too late to do anything else but meet Terry for their scheduled appointment back at the consular office.

That meeting was shorter than the one several days before. When Debbie and Terry tried to get him to repeat his comments, McCoy looked directly at the purse in which Terry had concealed a tape recorder and said, "I know what you're getting at. I'm not going to repeat it. I only said it in jest." At that point Debbie became frightened that McCoy's bold response would betray her. She excused herself to go to the bathroom and instead ran to find Dan Weber to ask him to try to get her ticket cleared with Pan Am.

As they were leaving McCoy's office Terry said to Debbie, "Either he's broken our code and listens to our transmissions, or he's CIA. Either way, he's damned smart." The simple solution—that Debbie might have told him why they were there—didn't occur to her until much later.

Their next stop was the Russian embassy, where they told essentially the same story they had told McCoy, and requested once again that the colony be allowed to emigrate to Russia.

It was after four by the time they got back to the house. As Debbie walked up the stairs she was greeted by a group in the radio room. "Dick McCoy phoned for you," someone called out. Oh my God, she thought, he's blown it.

"You shouldn't have taken your panties off in front of him," one of the men said. Debbie started breathing again. If they were joking around, it couldn't be all that serious.

"He just said you left some documents there and you should pick them up from Dan Weber tomorrow." Debbie took that to be a code message, telling her that the plan was off for tonight and on for tomorrow. For the rest of the afternoon she kept trying to get out of the house to phone McCoy, but one person after another demanded her attention.

Finally, at eight-thirty, her chance came. She had been assigned to pay a friendly visit to Dr. DeCosta, a dentist who had contributed free dental work to Jonestown residents. Every so often during her time in Georgetown, she had dropped by his house with a bottle of Johnny Walker Black Label from Jim. A group of people were going out to the airport to meet new arrivals from the States, and she asked them to drop her off at Dr. DeCosta's house. Deborah Touchette offered to go with her, but she said, "No, I'm just going in for a minute, I'll be real quick. Jim just wanted me to see him."

As soon as she got to Dr. DeCosta's home, Debbie asked to use his phone. Dick McCoy wasn't at the embassy, and he wasn't at home. Finally, she tracked him down at a party at the Marine base. It was now 9:15.

"Where are you?" he asked.

"I'm at Dr. DeCosta's house, about five blocks from the Temple house."

"Don't you know Dan Weber is waiting for you at the Pegasus right now?"

"Oh no! I thought it was off until tomorrow."

"Tomorrow?"

"That's what your message said."

"Oh good God. I said that only because I couldn't very well tell them you should come by the office tonight. Dan's got your ticket—it was there at Pan Am all the time—and he's waiting to take you to the airport."

"I don't know if I can make it. I have to go home first."

"Can't you go straight from where you are?"

"No, I don't have anything with me. I have to go by the house. Can you call Dan and tell him to wait for me? I'll be there as soon as I can."

"You get going, I'll call him. But hurry."

Hanging up the phone, Debbie turned to Dr. DeCosta. "I know you're not going to understand this," she said, "but I need your help. Will you please drive me home, and then to the Pegasus Hotel? I'll explain later."

On the way to the house she told him, "Just wait for me in the driveway, and if anybody asks what you're doing tell them I've gone upstairs to get some clothes for your maid to try on."

As Debbie ran up the stairs to her room all she could think was, "This is crazy." She grabbed her wallet, a pair of jeans, her toothbrush and deodorant, and rolled them up in a towel. She unlocked the strongbox, took out an American hundred-dollar bill, and headed for the door. On the stairs she ran into Karen Layton. They had a brief conversation about the radio schedule, then Karen asked, "Where are you going?" "No place," Debbie answered. She walked out the front door and jumped into the waiting car. She urged Dr. DeCosta to hurry. As they drove to the Pegasus Hotel, she explained, "I'm leaving tonight, I'm going back to the States. If anyone from the church asks, just say you dropped me off at a friend's house. Don't tell them anything else, please."

Dr. DeCosta was a kind man, and a calm one. "Okay, Debbie," he said, "don't worry. I won't tell them anything." There was a small plastic bag in the car, and he gave it to her to put her things in. She gave him her father's address in Berkeley, promising to write and explain everything.

Dan Weber was still waiting for her at the Pegasus Hotel. It was about ten o'clock; her plane was scheduled to take off in two hours. She and Dan ran out to his waiting car. The drive to the airport would take almost an hour. It would be close, but she could still make her flight.

At the airport customs gate, she spotted the Temple members waiting to greet the new arrivals coming in, as it happened, on the same plane that she was to leave on. Debbie stopped short. Dan, not noticing, kept on walking. He turned to address a comment to her, but she wasn't there. He found her hiding behind a pillar. "Come on," he said, "what are you waiting for?"

"They're from the Temple, they're going to see me."

Dan couldn't understand her fear. "Come on, I'm here." They walked right up to the group at the customs gate. One of the girls looked at Debbie quizzically. Debbie put a finger to her lips, indicating that she was on a secret mission. Since no one in the group knew who Dan Weber was, maybe they wouldn't realize until they got back to the house that she really wasn't supposed to be at the airport.

Things did not go smoothly with customs, either. "How long have you been in the country?" the official asked her. Debbie, with her brand-new passport, didn't know what to answer. "Five months," she said.

"Five months? And you don't have a tax clearance? You can't travel out of the country without a tax stamp."

"But I have to get home," she wailed, and then was inspired to add, "My father is dying!"

The official wasn't moved. "Well, he'll just have to live another day for you," he said.

Dan Weber went off to make several phone calls, which led to Dick McCoy calling the head of the airport. Debbie kept up a conversation with the customs men, smiling and flirting, because she knew that as long as she was talking to them, nobody from the Temple group would approach her.

McCoy and Weber made themselves unpopular that night—a couple of white foreigners throwing their weight around—but finally it was decided that Debbie would be allowed to get on the plane. The decision came about two minutes too late. The plane had already taxied down the runway; they watched it take off.

Debbie convinced Weber that she could not go back to the house in Lamaha Gardens: She was about three hours overdue—they would send her immediately back to Jonestown, and she would never get out again. She was hoping that Dan would invite her to spend the night at the embassy or at his house, but she didn't feel up to pressing the issue. He had already done so much for her. So, after trying to arrange a flight reservation for her the next day, Dan drove her back to town, to the Tower Hotel. They didn't get there until about three in the morning. Debbie wanted to register under a phony name, but she couldn't because she had to show her passport. "Look," she told Dan, "the first thing they're going to do is try every hotel in town. They'll come in and say, 'Is Debbie Blakey here? We have to find her—her father is dying.' Then the kid behind the desk will say, 'Wow, yes, she's in room so-and-so,' and it'll be all over." Dan told her not to worry, that he would tell the clerk at the desk not to let anybody know she was there unless he or she had an American embassy passport.

Debbie still wasn't happy with the arrangement, but she paid her $60 Guyanese and registered. In addition to the American $100 bill she had taken, she was carrying $100 Guyanese—about $67 American—money that had been collected for the church that she hadn't had time to deposit.

Dan led the way up the stairs to her room, looking into every dark corner. As soon as he left, with a promise to return at eight in the morning, Debbie called down to the desk for cigarettes. She spent most of the night sitting up, smoking and thinking. At about six o'clock she tried to call her father in Berkeley. The phone rang and rang in the empty house. Christ, she thought, of all the times for him to spend a night out.

When Dan Weber arrived the next morning she told him, "I don't have to go myself for the tax clearance, you can go for me. I've done it for other people lots of times."

"No," he said, "it'll go faster if you come with me."

"But the Temple knows why I had to stay over. They were at the airport last night, and they'll be waiting for me today."

"Don't worry," he reassured her. "I'll be by your side."

She checked out of the hotel and they walked over to the post office, a large building housing several offices, including the passport and tax-clearance offices. They were standing in line when Deborah Touchette walked up to her and said, "Debbie, what are you doing? What's wrong?"

"I don't want to discuss it."

"You know you can leave Guyana anytime you want to. Just talk to Jim about it, that's all he asks."

"You know the truth and I know the truth," Debbie said, "and I don't want to discuss it."

The conversation ended inconclusively when they reached the head of the line. Deborah Touchette walked away, and a tax official ushered Debbie into a large room by herself. Dan Weber showed his embassy identification, but the guard at the door wouldn't let him accompany her, so Debbie went in alone. She was sitting there staring at the floor, waiting for her name to be called, when someone came in and sat down in the chair next to hers. She looked up. It was Deborah Touchette, ready to continue their conversation. Debbie could see Dan Weber outside the door, arguing with the guards, but they still wouldn't let him in. It figures, Debbie thought. She's black and she's been in Guyana five years; she can get in anyplace. Dan was watching them through the window in the door, unable to get in to help her.

Deborah Touchette picked up the discussion right where it had been dropped. "We called Jim and he wants to know why you're leaving. The least you can do is tell him that much. It's his birthday, you know. Your leaving on his birthday is killing him. It's already caused him to have a heart attack. At least write him a note, tell him why you're going."

Debbie didn't want to put anything in writing, but she finally agreed to dictate a note, spelling out her reasons for leaving the Temple. She explained that she wasn't vindictive or hostile, she just had to get out of Jonestown, out of the church, out of Guyana, back to the United States where she could have a life of her own, settle down and have a family. She talked about the brutality of life in Jonestown, the severity of the punishments she had witnessed, and how the situation had gotten out of control.

When she had finished, Deborah Touchette asked her to come back to the house so she could talk to Jones on the radio, explain to him directly her reasons for leaving.

Debbie was incredulous. "Are you crazy? No way am I going back to that place."

"Then will you call on the telephone and I'll relay on the radio? You know Jim loves you, you owe him that."

"I'll think about it," Debbie conceded as the tax official finally called out her name.

Once she was actually sitting across the desk from the tax official, Debbie got her clearance fairly quickly. In all, though, she and Dan had spent hours at the post office. When they left for the short walk back to the embassy, it was raining with tropical intensity. In spite of the umbrella they shared, both were soaked within a block. They were followed by a Temple van, and another one was parked outside the embassy.

Dick McCoy greeted her and escorted her to an office where she could wait until it was time to go to the airport, in about four hours. While they were making plans for getting her safely on the plane—her reservation on the flight still wasn't confirmed—the phone rang. McCoy answered it. "No, she isn't here, I think she spent the night at the Tower Hotel," he said, and hung up. He turned to Debbie. "That was Karen Layton. She wanted to know if you were here."

"She knows damned well where I am, they followed us to the front door. Now she knows you're lying for me." McCoy just shrugged.

McCoy was leaving that night for Washington on official business, flying out on the same plane as Debbie. This new flight was direct from Georgetown to New York, rather than connecting in Caracas for Los Angeles. He gave her a pillow and suggested that she try to get some sleep while he went home to pack, but she was too keyed up and afraid to do more than put her head down on the desk. She was still debating whether to call Jones; McCoy and Weber had advised her to do what she thought was right. At about two o'clock she decided: If I don't call they'll think I'm hiding something. If I do call, they'll at least know I'm not afraid of them, or out to hurt them. So she called the Lamaha Gardens house, and Deborah Touchette got Jones on the radio. The first thing he said was, "Ask her why she's leaving." So Debbie ran through her reasons again. Jones agreed with her that punishments might sometimes have been too severe; but people need a lot of structure, he argued, until they can understand all the consequences of their actions.

"And what about your mother?" he demanded. "This will kill her. You'd better call Annalisa and tell her everything's cool, you're not coming back right away after all, then get on back here and tell your mother to her face why you're leaving her."

Debbie almost wavered at that point. Though she thought she had already resolved the issue, the question returned to her—how can I leave my mother to die in that hellhole? But she knew beyond any doubt that if she returned to Jonestown she would never leave there alive.

When he saw that his most powerful argument was not going to work, Jones became abusive. He called her egocentric, naïve, and ignorant. Debbie thought, Man, if you're trying to be my friend, you're saying all the wrong things.

He began to plead, to beg for her sympathy. Today was his birthday. His life had been hard, full of pain. If she let him down on his birthday it would kill him. But Debbie had heard the threat of a fatal heart attack once too often.

Again Jones switched tactics. "Will you just wait long enough to talk to Marceline?"

"I'll talk to her on the radio right now."

"No, wait for her. She'll come into town."

"How long will that be?"

"About a week."

"I can't wait that long."

As soon as one argument failed, Jones was ready with another. But he was sounding more and more desperate. "Please, just stay until the Russian thing is finalized. Don't leave now. This is too important. Can't you just stay until this is finalized?"

Debbie was silent. There seemed no point in responding.

"You know you can't go back to the United States. You'll be arrested." (This whole conversation, of course, was actually being spoken and relayed in code. What Jones had said was, "You'll see Bobbie on Rex's doorstep.")

Debbie wondered. For all she knew, she really might be arrested. After all, her name was on several foreign bank accounts, accounts that might be illegal. Sensing her hesitation, Jones pressed his momentary advantage. "At least go to England instead of back to the States. You'll be safer there, and we'll send you some money."

"What am I supposed to do in England?" Debbie asked.

"Go from there to Russia. You can help prepare the way for our people when we all come."

"Do you mean to say that you would trust me to represent you in Russia?"

"Debbie, I trust you. I've always trusted you. You're just tired, you've been working too hard and you're feeling paranoid."

She thought, You lying dog, you're the one that's been following me around all day. But suddenly she *was* tired and confused. She didn't know what she should do anymore. If they were going to arrest her in the United States, maybe it would be better to go to England. And then, Jones was urging her to go to the Russian embassy in London and ask for help in getting to Russia...

"I've got to go now," she said.

"What are you going to do?"

"I don't know. I'll go to England. No, I don't know what I'm going to do. I'm in such a mess, I just don't know."

"Well, where can we reach you?"

"I'm staying at a friend's house, I can't give you the number."

"Will you call us every six hours?"

"Yes, okay, I've got to go now."

As soon as she hung up the phone Debbie realized that
things had gone too far to change her plan now; in two and a
half hours she would get on the plane for the United States.

Dan Weber came into the room. "It's two-thirty, Debbie,"
he said. "Time to head for the airport."

Dan drove the car up to the back door of the embassy and
hustled Debbie out of the building. He had brought her a sand-
wich, which she nibbled as they drove. At the airport parking
lot she couldn't spot any Peoples Temple cars or vans. "That's
funny," she said, "I wonder where they are."

"They're probably not going to follow you anymore, they
must have given up," Dan said. He went into the airport to
check on her reservations, while Debbie sat in the car with the
doors locked. When Dan came back he told her that she was
on emergency standby, and that Dick McCoy would make sure
that her name was at the head of the list.

They sat in the car and talked. Debbie told Dan some more
about what she had seen and experienced in Jonestown, and
about her fears for the safety of those remaining in the jungle
colony. It was hard for him to believe what she was telling
him; he kept shaking his head, saying, "I don't know, Debbie,
it doesn't sound quite right."

Then Dan told her about his days in the Peace Corps, and
how he came to be with the embassy in Guyana. He asked
about her plans, what she wanted to do in the United States,
and she told him about her training as an operating-room technician. She hoped to get back into surgery, she said, but she
was afraid that Temple members would send hate mail to every
employer or potential employer to prevent her from getting a
hospital job.

At that point Dick McCoy drove up. He and Dan conferred
briefly, and then he went into the airport to check on the standby
list. At last he stepped out of the building and waved victo-
riously. Dan said, "This is it." As she got out of the car, Debbie
caught a glimpse of Terry Carter Jones walking into the airport.

With Dick McCoy and Dan Weber at her side, Debbie
picked up her ticket and started for the customs gate. Suddenly,
Karen Layton pushed through the crowd and ran up to Debbie.
She grabbed her in a big hug, put her head on Debbie's shoul-

der, and started crying, sobbing convulsively. But when she looked up, her eyes were dry. Boy, Debbie thought, you are not a good actress.

Karen was pleading with her, "Debbie, write to us. We love you. Jim loves you. Don't do this to us."

"Okay, okay, Karen," Debbie said, half hugging her and half pulling away. "I have to go now." She walked through the customs gate with relief; only passengers were permitted beyond that point. But suddenly Terry Carter Jones jumped out from her hiding place, her face an angry mask. "Debbie, what do you think you're doing?" she demanded. Debbie just stood there looking at her.

"Do you want to talk to her?" Dan Weber asked Debbie. "You don't have to if you don't want to."

"It's okay," Debbie said, and Terry started crying, genuine tears. She and Debbie had been close friends. When she could speak again, Terry's message was the same as Karen's had been. "Please, please, just wait until our plans are finished. Don't do this to Jim, he's dying—you're killing him."

Debbie almost started crying herself as she hugged Terry. "Look," she said, "I can't, can't stay. I have to have a life of my own. I have to go now."

Debbie broke free of Terry's embrace and started through customs. She and Dan Weber made their awkward good-byes, exchanging little pats on the back. "Good luck, honey," he said. Then Dick McCoy ushered her through customs. As she walked out to the plane she could feel Terry and Karen watching her, and for a moment she wondered if she was going to be shot in the back.

Before the plane was in the air, Debbie was asleep in her seat.

Later that afternoon, Terry filed the following report to Jones:

Seeing Debbie at the Airport:
    I waited inside where the passengers go through right before they board the plane. As Debbie walked through I popped up and said it would ease the mind of the one who loves you the most if you just keep in touch. She nodded slightly. At that point I started to cry and said why are you

doing this to Jim. She said I'm not doing anything. I said can you imagine how he's feeling right now, he is so sick, Debbie. She said I just need to be on my own, I didn't agree with things going on out there. I said but it's not his fault, you never gave him a chance. You never told him. It's not his fault that we aren't perfect; you can't blame him for that. She said I'm not blaming him. I just don't like some of the things going on out there. I said you've never told him. You've never given him a chance. . . .

We asked her please talk to Lisa. It would kill her. She said Lisa doesn't have to know. Just don't tell her. I don't want her to know I'm gone. I said what do we do, just say you're living in Georgetown the rest of your life? At this point, Dan Weber said you'd better be going so we hugged her goodbye and repeated the first message. Daniel W. then turned to us and said do you need a ride home? We said no we were waiting for some people to come for the interior. He waited until the plane took off. It was half hour late in leaving.

She never flinched, never batted an eye, but she was the one who approached us to hug her. She hid in the car with Dick McCoy and Daniel W. until the last possible minute, then Dick M. left first and walked up the around about way and then she walked up with that other puke.

Because the plane was so full, Debbie and McCoy were not able to sit together. As soon as they were airborne, McCoy made his way back to where Debbie was already sleeping. He gently shook her shoulder. "Are you all right?" he asked.

It took her a moment to figure out where she was. "I'm okay," she said. "Can I talk to you now?"

"Sure, or would you rather wait till New York?"

"No, I don't know if you'll have time there. Let's do it now." She climbed over her seatmate and followed McCoy to the front of the plane. They talked for almost an hour, standing up near the pilot's cabin. The first thing Debbie wanted to know was, "Are they going to arrest me when we land in New York?"

"Don't worry about that, I already checked and there aren't any warrants out for you. You might be subpoenaed to give testimony, but you're not going to be arrested."

During their conversation Debbie kept thinking of more

things she wanted to tell McCoy. Once again she found herself talking about her fears for her mother and the hundreds of others still in Jonestown. She gave him a detailed account of what she knew of the Temple's illicit financial dealings, and of how they had smuggled guns and other contraband. She told him that all of his "spontaneous" interviews with Jonestown residents had actually been setups. She gave him the names of people who wanted to leave, and told him that he should speak with them alone, away from listening ears. But he would have to be very careful. If he went into Jonestown and tried to take people out with him, they could all be shot. And again she warned him that Jones' threats of mass suicide were not idle, but terribly real. Finally, she asked him, "What should I do with this information when I get home? Should I go to the press?" Part of Debbie's reason for leaving Jonestown was to make sure that the world knew what was going on there. McCoy urged her not to contact the press, but to let the State Department handle the situation without any more publicity than the incident was already likely to get. He also pointed out that previous press reports had not accomplished anything.

Back in her seat, Debbie wondered why she wasn't crying. She felt as if she should cry. She wanted to cry, but the tears wouldn't come. Thinking about her mother and the friends she had left behind, she fell asleep again.

When she awoke they were forty-five minutes out of New York. She went into the bathroom and changed into her clean slacks and a sweater that Dick McCoy's wife had sent with him for her, combed her hair, and washed her face. Whether she was coming home to freedom or to jail she really didn't know; but she wanted to be ready for either.

When the plane landed she tried to be one of the first off. Dick McCoy had told her that the customs official would check her name in a book, and if they were going to arrest her they would do it then. She could see McCoy ahead of her in line. The line inched forward slowly, and when her turn came the woman at the gate checked her name, smiled, and waved her through.

Dick McCoy was at her side. "Welcome to the land of the free," he said.

10

The Oracle

For Debbie, the "land of the free" meant that she was free in New York City, on her own, exhausted and disoriented, alone and afraid. Her first act was to telephone Annalisa to tell her to try to reach Larry in San Francisco and prevent him from going to Guyana. She was certain that he would be ordered to Jonestown now that she was known to have defected. She also knew that once he was down there, Larry would never be allowed to leave.

Dick McCoy called a Howard Johnson hotel and reserved a room for her, then put her on a bus for the hotel with a good-bye hug. "Don't worry," he told her once again, "you'll be home soon."

It was 11:30 P.M., and except for her naps on the plane Debbie hadn't really slept for three days. She felt stunned, drained of all energy and emotion. She gazed out the window of the airport shuttle bus at the blur of lights and activity; her eyes refused to focus. She managed to check into the hotel, to make the appropriate responses to the desk clerk and the bellhop. Safely in her room, she fell into bed without even a thought for dinner or a bath.

When Debbie heard the phone ring the next morning, she had no idea where she was or what was going on. She lifted the receiver and after a few seconds put it back in its cradle. At that point she realized where she was and remembered her wake-up instructions to the desk the previous night. When it rang again she answered it. "Five o'clock," said the operator. Debbie stumbled out of bed and took a quick bath. At six o'clock she was back on the shuttle bus to the airport. After picking up the ticket that Annalisa had prepaid for her, she still had two hours to wait before her flight. She browsed in the airport gift shop and bought a delicate necklace—the first time in several years that she had indulged her taste for pretty, feminine things. She thought about buying lipstick and eye shadow. Her hair was cropped very short, in line with the dictates of Temple fashion; she would let it grow long. At least she wasn't fat anymore. Would men find her attractive? she wondered. And how could she possibly hope to find a man who could understand her and what she had lived through?

Once she was safely on the plane, exhaustion overcame her again. She evidently looked so done in that the stewardess took her back to the last row, which was empty of passengers, raised all the arm rests, and gave her a blanket so she could lie down across the seats and sleep. But as soon as she fell asleep she jolted herself awake with a loud scream. She tried again, but every time she drifted off she would wake up with a start of fear, so she gave up and went back to her seat.

There was a two-hour layover in Denver, where she bought a plastic shopping bag for her wallet and extra clothes. By the time they were airborne again, Debbie felt sick of planes. She thought about having a drink to help her sleep, but decided no, it wasn't worth it. She hadn't had an alcoholic drink since the trouble she'd gotten into over a beer her first week in Guyana.

Finally the plane landed in Sacramento. It was eleven-thirty on the morning of May 14. Less than forty-eight hours earlier she had still been in Georgetown, and escape had been only a hope and an uncertain plan. Walking down the ramp she caught sight of Annalisa and felt the tears rising in her eyes. She tried to hold them back, but when she saw that Annalisa was crying too she had to let go and cry herself. But only a little; there was too much to tell to waste time on tears.

During the drive to Annalisa's house, Debbie started telling the story of the last few months. The only thing she held back on was Lisa's condition. She didn't want to alarm Annalisa any more than was absolutely necessary, and she still hoped that they would somehow be able to help Lisa escape from Jonestown.

Almost as soon as they walked in the front door of the Valentines' house in Davis the phone rang. Annalisa answered it, listened for a moment, and hung up without responding. She turned to Debbie, frowning. "That was somebody claiming to be from Pan Am. They said they were concerned because my sister had two flight reservations out of Guyana, and they wanted to make sure that you'd gotten in touch with me."

"That wasn't Pan Am," Debbie said.

"I know it. The airlines aren't concerned about who gets where."

When Annalisa's husband, Ray, heard what Debbie had to say, they realized that it wasn't safe for her to stay with them. Annalisa was known to have been her only contact outside Georgetown. The three of them talked it over and decided that Debbie should go and stay with Tom in Los Angeles. She slept for an hour, until Annalisa woke her at five-thirty to drive back to the airport. Annalisa fixed her a cup of coffee, which she drank hiding on the floor of the car in case they were being followed. Before leaving, she had studied herself in the mirror. Her eyes were so bloodshot that she was afraid she would be picked up at the airport as a drug addict.

As soon as she had received the phone call from Debbie in New York, Annalisa had started trying to contact Larry, to warn him not to go to Guyana until he had talked with Debbie. She reached him at eight o'clock on the morning of May 13 at Herrick Hospital in Berkeley where he was completing his residency as an X-ray technician. She told him that Debbie had left the Temple and was on her way to San Francisco, that she was very frightened not only for her own safety but the safety of everyone in Jonestown. It was urgent, Annalisa said, for Larry to hear what she had to tell him before leaving the country.

"I'm not planning any trips," Larry responded coolly. "Have Debbie call me. She knows my phone number."

About noon Annalisa phoned her father to let him know that

Debbie was safe in the United States and would soon be arriving in Sacramento. She did not pass on what Debbie had told her about Jonestown.

That morning Larry had called his father to say he would be coming by to mow the lawn. It had been the cause of an argument between them a week before, when Larry was still living in Dr. Layton's house. When his father had requested that Larry do the lawn, Larry had replied that he had other things to do. Dr. Layton had insisted that if he were going to live there he would have to do his part. Larry had left the house, both of them angry, the lawn unmowed. Dr. Layton hadn't seen his son since.

When Larry arrived shortly after Annalisa's call, he appeared to be drugged. He mowed the lawn half-heartedly, then, still dressed in his hospital uniform, dazedly jumped in the swimming pool. Dr. Layton was frightened by this bizarre behavior, but then the phone rang again. It was for Larry. Dr. Layton called him to the phone. Larry listened for a moment, responded noncommittally, and quickly left his father's house.

That evening Larry boarded an airplane in San Francisco on the first leg of his trip to Guyana.

Tom Layton and his girl friend, Grace Corse, met Debbie at the Los Angeles airport. At first Tom hardly recognized his sister, she was so thin and her hair was cut so short. They had decided that the safest place for Debbie would be at Grace's grandmother's home in nearby Altadena. As they drove east on the Santa Monica Freeway, Debbie began to tell them a story that Tom would not have believed, except that his sister was telling it to him. This was the first Tom had heard of the sexual abuses that took place in the Temple; that Jim Jones had been responsible for the breakup of Larry's marriage to Carolyn; that Jones had finally gone mad.

Debbie's exhaustion verged on hysteria. The story poured out of her, she couldn't stop talking. Finally Grace gave her a glass of cherry wine and firmly put her to bed. Debbie was asleep almost instantly. Tom and Grace sat up talking. A horrible fear occurred to them: Larry might be sent down to kill Debbie. They didn't know that he had already departed for Guyana. It was decided that no one else should know where Debbie was hiding. They definitely would not tell Dr. Layton.

He might inadvertently reveal her whereabouts to someone in or close to Peoples Temple.

Almost as soon as Annalisa walked in the door after dropping Debbie off at the airport, the phone rang. It was Larry, calling from Georgetown, Guyana. He wanted to know where Debbie was. Annalisa said she didn't know. "Why did she leave?" Larry asked. "I've been to the interior, everything is cool there. It's fine for her to leave, but I don't understand why she wanted to."

Annalisa was noncommittal. She knew that Larry could not possibly have traveled to the interior and back to Georgetown in the time he had been in Guyana. Obviously Larry was saying what Jones was telling him to say.

Half an hour later Larry called again, to tell Annalisa that Lisa would not be told that Debbie had defected. Annalisa saw this as an attempt to warn Debbie not to talk openly about the conditions in Jonestown.

Annalisa and Ray did not sleep well that night. Ray had assembled his shotgun, and several 12-gauge cartridges were lined up on the night table.

In Los Angeles, Debbie didn't sleep well, either. She dreamed that she was trying to lead her friends in an escape from Jonestown, and that Jones was chasing her through the jungle. She woke up at two-thirty in the morning and lay there until five o'clock, staring at the ceiling. Finally she managed another couple of hours of sleep. At eight o'clock she went downstairs to breakfast. It was such a thrill to be able to have eggs and orange juice—delicacies she had seldom tasted in recent months. The food smelled so delicious, she found her appetite returning. As she ate hungrily, she and Tom began to make plans. Today, she would go with him to California State University at Dominguez Hills, where he taught anthropology. They could talk there, and she could use the untraceable university tie line for some phone calls she wanted to make.

At six o'clock on the morning of May 15, Laurence Layton received a phone call from Larry in Georgetown, asking where he could reach Debbie. Dr. Layton said that she was with Annalisa in Davis. Then Larry wanted to know why Debbie had left Guyana and the Temple. Unable to think of his son as the enemy, Dr. Layton responded that Debbie had gotten out because Jonestown was an armed camp, that all mail was censored, that Lisa was unhappy, that all her money had gone to the church, and that he, Larry, should not go to Jonestown. In effect, Dr. Layton revealed to Larry, and to whoever else might be listening at the other end, that Debbie was indeed talking, perhaps telling everything she knew, at least to her family. Actually, Dr. Layton didn't know that much about what was going on in Jonestown. Debbie, Tom, and Annalisa were still trying to spare him the worst of that shocking knowledge.

For the rest of that day Larry called Annalisa repeatedly, asking to talk to Debbie. Annalisa kept telling him that she didn't know where Debbie was. It was obvious that Larry didn't believe her, but there wasn't much he could do about it, except to keep calling.

Debbie wanted to make contact with others who had left the Temple, so that they could exchange useful information. One of the first people she telephoned from Tom's office was John Collins, Jim Jones' ex-son-in-law. She and John had been friendly in the San Francisco days—at least as close to friendly as the Temple allowed. John's parents and sister were still in Jonestown, and she wanted to give him news of them. John had called his sister Sarah one night when Debbie was working in the radio room; Sarah had been sent for, and a group of staff members had stood around her and told her exactly what to reply to John's questions.

Debbie reached John easily enough in San Francisco, but she had a hard time convincing him that she really had left the Temple. He finally agreed to fly down to Los Angeles to see her that same day, on the condition that Debbie and Tom meet him at the airport alone. If anyone else were there with them, he said, he would not approach or speak to them. He wanted to believe that Debbie had really left the Temple, but at the same time he was suspicious and afraid that she might be trying to set him up for a kidnapping. Tom was similarly worried that John might be a Temple informer.

As John had requested, Tom and Debbie sat inconspicuously in the PSA lobby, waiting. Suddenly John came up behind them. He had been watching to make sure they were alone.

He talked with Debbie for several minutes before he agreed to accompany them back to Grace Corse's grandmother's house, where Debbie and Tom were staying. The suspicion remained mutual. While John and Debbie caught up on news of friends and family in San Francisco and in Jonestown, Tom drove a circuitous route so that John wouldn't know where they were going. That evening, John called Grace Stoen at a pre-arranged time. If he hadn't, she would have called the police and told them that he had been abducted by the Temple.

Debbie, John, and Tom decided that their next step should be to contact Dick McCoy, who was still in Washington for his quarterly debriefing. Debbie realized that she hadn't given McCoy all the information he should have before returning to Guyana. For one thing, she wanted to tell him more about the guns in Jonestown, and how they had been smuggled in. And she wanted to emphasize her warning to watch his step when he visited Jonestown; she knew he could get himself shot. Also, they hoped that McCoy would be able at least to take a message to Lisa, and maybe even help her get out of Jonestown.

The next morning they tried to call McCoy in Washington. He couldn't be reached, so they left an urgent message for him to call back. They had to wait until two P.M. before McCoy returned the call. The conversation was frustrating. McCoy didn't want the information Debbie had for him. He told her that if she had firsthand knowledge of any illegal activities, she should call the FBI and the Bureau of Alcohol, Tobacco and Firearms. Debbie said that he should be the one to make those calls, since his word was bound to carry more weight than hers, but he replied that the matter really wasn't under his jurisdiction. And he didn't volunteer any specific information about whom in the FBI and the ATFA she should contact.

Then Tom got on the phone to ask about the possibility of going along with McCoy on one of his periodic visits to Jonestown. No, McCoy answered, that would not be possible, because he traveled on a plane chartered by the U.S. government, and there would be insurance problems. "Well then," Tom asked, "what if I arranged my own flight—could I then go into Jonestown with you?" McCoy agreed that would be possible, but warned Tom that the residents of Jonestown were under no obligation to let him in, and that if Tom's relatives there didn't want to talk to him there was nothing that he, McCoy, could do about it.

Tom hung up the phone, shaken. It was becoming clear that official help would be hard to come by. And yet, as far as getting Lisa out of Jonestown was concerned, their only options were official ones. They decided that the best course would be for Tom, Annalisa, and Debbie each to write a brief letter to Lisa, begging her to walk out of Jonestown under the protection of Dick McCoy. They would assure her of a plane ticket and a place to live in San Francisco, and of their love and support. They would ask McCoy to take the letters with him on his next visit to Jonestown, and to make sure that Lisa got to read them in private. And they would ask him to bring the letters back, to assure that they didn't fall into Jim Jones' hands.

It didn't seem like much of a plan, but it was the best they could come up with. McCoy had told them that his next trip to Jonestown was scheduled for the first week in August—two and a half months away, a long time to wait. Their more immediate concern became how to help Debbie wake up the government and the public to what was happening in Jonestown. Tom decided it would be wise to record Debbie's information, and began to interview her on tape.

When John flew back to San Francisco that evening, all three of them felt frustrated, angry, and despairing. The next day John called to tell Debbie that Grace Stoen had recommended a lawyer in San Francisco who worked with people who had left the Temple. Debbie had decided she needed a good lawyer. She didn't feel confident enough to make the Washington phone calls McCoy had suggested on her own.

Debbie had several reasons for wanting to go back to the Bay Area. She felt out of touch in Los Angeles and she hadn't yet seen her father. Except for Tom and Grace, all of the people she felt close to and wanted to work with were in the Bay Area. But perhaps her most important reason for returning to San Francisco was to prove something to herself. She had left the Temple in order to live her own life. By staying in hiding in Los Angeles, she was continuing to let the fear of Jim Jones dictate that life.

Tom was nervous about Debbie emerging so soon. He remained unconvinced that she would be safe in San Francisco; and he wanted to finish the taped interviews while the material was still fresh in her mind. But she was determined, so Tom dropped her off at the Long Beach airport on the afternoon of

Saturday, May 20. She was to spend a few days in the Bay Area, then return to Los Angeles to finish taping with Tom.

The day after Debbie flew up to San Francisco, Grace Stoen drove her over to Berkeley to see her father. Dr. Layton was bitter and angry, especially with Larry. He told Debbie and Grace that he had changed his will to exclude Larry. As far as he was concerned, his younger son had died twelve years earlier. Grace tried to assure him that there were other people who could understand what he was going through, people who were being hurt in the same way he was. But he was inconsolable, and not just about Larry. Debbie too had hurt and abused him. And his wife had left him and was dying in the jungle.

Debbie stood up well to her father's expressions of pain. The next day, when she told Tom about their visit, she sounded almost cheerful. In a sense, the experience had made her feel she had finally come home. Instead of returning to Los Angeles, she decided to stay in San Francisco.

Debbie lived for almost a month with Grace Stoen and her fiancé, who had also been a member of Peoples Temple. Understanding her fears and anxieties, they told her about the problems of readjustment they themselves had faced after leaving the group. But now, they emphasized, they were leading normal lives, and both had regular jobs. They took Debbie out for meals and on shopping trips, building up her confidence and ability to cope with all those aspects of society from which she had been isolated for seven years. They put her into contact with others who had escaped the Temple. Tim Stoen encouraged her to make her information public; he felt that her story would be the beginning of a "Watergate of the cults." And Al and Jeannie Mills, a Berkeley couple who were active in working with people who had left the Temple, as well as with relatives of those in Jonestown, gave her three hundred dollars to buy clothes. In March 1980, the Millses were murdered in their Berkeley home. That crime is still unsolved.

As soon as Debbie was settled in San Francisco, Tim and Grace Stoen and Jeannie Mills took her to see the Stoens' lawyers,

Jeffrey Haas and Margaret Ryan (no relation to Congressman Leo Ryan). The two attorneys had a strong interest in Debbie's information because they had met with nothing but frustration in their attempts to have John Victor Stoen returned to his parents. They hoped that Debbie's story would lead to a break-through in the case, since she was the only person to have left Jonestown in the past year and could therefore speak as an eyewitness rather than from hearsay. Together, they drew up an eleven-page, thirty-seven-point affidavit for her to sign, detailing the situation in Jonestown and her reasons for fearing a mass suicide.

Once the affidavit was written, however, Debbie began to have second thoughts about going public. For one thing, she had to be very careful not to say anything that might make her vulnerable to prosecution for illegal activities that had taken place while she was active in the Temple. For another, she was worried that her action would cause reprisals against Lisa and Larry in Jonestown. She talked the problem over with Tom, with John, and with her attorneys, and finally decided that she had no choice; she had to tell the world what she knew. She could only hope that the publicity would protect rather than harm her mother.

During the second week in June the two lawyers mailed copies of the affidavit, together with a strongly worded cover letter, to three different divisions of the Department of State, as well as to Secretary of State Cyrus Vance and the heads of the other government and intelligence agencies concerned. Debbie was also interviewed by Tim Reiterman of the San Francisco *Examiner,* and by Marshall Kilduff, who with Phil Tracy had written the explosive *New West* story the year before. Kilduff's article on Debbie in the *Chronicle* caught the attention of Congressman Leo Ryan, who was already actively interested in the unfolding story of Jonestown and the Peoples Temple.

Reiterman decided against covering the story for the *Examiner*. Later he told Debbie that he had not believed her. He was one of the journalists who was seriously wounded at the Port Kaituma airstrip on November 18.

Shortly after Kilduff's article appeared in the *Chronicle,* Dr. Layton received a phone call from Joe and DeOna Ajax, old family friends from Utah days. Joe Ajax was a ham-radio operator, and for over a year he had been listening in on the strange transmissions from the Peoples Temple in Guyana. He learned that Lisa Layton was there, and one night he and his son Denny linked their transmitters together and blasted through to Jonestown with an illegal burst of power. He asked to speak to Lisa, and she was called to the radio.

Ajax found the conversation strained and off-key. For one thing, Lisa would say nothing of the present. She spoke only of their shared experiences thirty years in the past. And she seemed to use the word *help* a lot. She asked him if he remembered how she had *helped* him recover from an illness by prescribing an old German remedy.

After reading about Debbie's affidavit, Ajax and his wife wondered about that strange conversation. Could Lisa have been trying to ask for help? That was when they called their old friend Laurence Layton. When Annalisa and Tom heard the Ajaxes' story, they drafted a letter to Lisa. Through a series of references to people who had been instrumental in helping her to escape from Germany forty years before, they encoded a message to their mother: They had received her call for help, and they were working on an escape plan for her. The letter was mailed, but of course they had no way of knowing whether or not Lisa ever got any of the letters they sent her.

Reaction from Jonestown to Debbie's public charges was immediate, and soon enough, Lisa was heard from again via radio. In a statement relayed by shortwave from Guyana, two Temple members identified as Lisa and Larry Layton insisted that, "These lies are too ridiculous to refute," and "We are treated beautifully here."

It must have been terribly upsetting for Lisa to learn that Debbie had left Guyana and the Temple without calling to say good-bye to her, whatever her premonitions that last morning with her daughter in Jonestown. Whenever anyone left the church, it was Jones' policy to make sure that the remaining family members shared the guilt for the treasonous action. It seems certain that her letters to Annalisa and Debbie during this period were dictated by Jones in his frantic efforts to get Debbie back to Jonestown. Debbie also received numerous letters from other Temple members, usually unsigned and all saying the same thing: Come back, Debbie; Jim loves you; Jim will forgive you. As the letters continued, they became more accusatory in tone: "We know what you have done—about the money—that could have been understood and forgiven. But we don't understand what you are doing now. . . . We would like an explanation as soon as possible. We don't understand why you have done these things to the ones who have loved you the most."

All of these letters were sent to Annalisa, or to Debbie in her care. The first letter from Lisa was so upsetting to Debbie that she did not read those that followed until several months later.

On June 4, Lisa wrote to Annalisa:

"I think it would be great if you could visit, but this is just about the worst time of the year. It is the rainy season and it's raining cats and dogs. The time to visit is in the fall when it is sunny and the rain is gentle here and there. I would have to get on the boat and go to Georgetown, which is rough when you get on the ocean. Else you would have to fly to Matthews Ridge.

"I love it here. It is living with a purpose that is the all important thing to me. Doing my own thing and just being concerned about myself and my family is a thing of the past, before I knew better. And I do know better now.

"Got a letter from the old man saying Debbie is doing well. Glad to hear she is happy, or thinks she is. Personally I feel that this is the place for her. Now and always. . . .

"It surely was good to see Larry. He and our portable X-ray equipment arrived just about the same time and he has been taking a lot of X-rays since his arrival. He surely knows what he is doing."

To Annalisa, June 27:

"To make a long story short I have had a bad reaction to what Debbie has done. It is absolutely beyond me how she can come up with all these lies and twisted stories. I didn't know for a while that she had left, my friends tried to protect me. But after a while they had to tell me and it caused me to get sick. . . .

"Mostly I cannot understand what happened to Debbie's mind. Everyone here is so good and loving with me, but it doesn't heal the wound of Debbie's action.

"Hope you will be able to help Debbie. Something is drastically wrong with her. I don't know if you can stop her from what she is doing. I can never come to terms with people being deceptive.

"I'll write you again when I am less upset. Love, Lisa. P.S. Larry has been a big help to me. He feels just like I do."

To Debbie, July 6:

"I have been in extensive care for 2 weeks now. I got sick after I heard that you left and how you left. It was a terrible shock to me and somehow I have not been able to get over it. I am receiving the best of medical care. Even though, I cannot get rid of the feeling of a great loss. It is with me at all times. Actually what you have done is worrying me into the grave. That is pretty strong language but it is true. . . .

"You know that we are socialists and making a beginning in a new land. You also know that what we have done with our agriculture is spectacular, and could not have happened without cooperation. It looks to me that you really did not understand socialism in its beginning stages. You gave up ¾ up the hill—and that is a shame.

"Right now we are planning to build 100 more houses. Phil keeps at picking up lumber for us. Larry is working ½ time with X-rays and the rest of his time with the Alaskan sawmill. Also we are getting another sawmill to speed up production. There are constant changes and improvements.

"The best thing that could happen to me personally is your return. Others have left in the past and come back. You know how forgiving Jim is.

"What I cannot understand is that after leaving us you turned around and told lies and twisted stories. I read copies of the papers that were sent to us by either you or Stoen. Why did you participate in their evil efforts? Were you afraid that something might happen to you if you had asked Stoen not to bother you? I wish you would stop harming us. And I wish you would come back. People have left before and returned and were lovingly received by Jim and all the rest of us. I surely hope you won't go back to your old patterns, because you won't make it this time.

"I love you. Mom."

Lisa's letters were disturbing to Annalisa not only for their contents, but also because her handwriting seemed to be deteriorating. Her last letters, in fact, were printed rather than written in Lisa's old-fashioned European script.

Tom, Annalisa, and Debbie renewed their efforts to contact their mother. When Ray Valentine went to Guyana as a U. N. consultant on soil fertility, they sent letters with him in the forlorn hope that he might find some way of delivering them. They drafted new notes for Dick McCoy to take to Lisa in Jonestown. Annalisa wrote:

"Please take this opportunity to come back. Debbie has a job and an apartment and you can live with her. She is as solid and responsible a person as you have described her to be. Her constant goal since she came back has been to get you back. Tom and I also have been working toward this goal. Your children miss you.

"I understand it will be awfully difficult to decide to leave, but you will just have to walk away with Dick. I love you dearly. Annalisa."

And of course they continued to send letters to their mother through the regular mail, cheery family letters.

On July 7, Tom called Dick McCoy at the U. S. embassy in Georgetown to try to get a commitment from him not only to deliver their secret letters but to speak privately with Lisa, and to offer her the opportunity to leave Jonestown with him if she wanted to. McCoy told Tom that he couldn't do anything unless an official request came from the Bureau of Consular Affairs, and that even then he couldn't force Lisa to read their letters if she didn't want to. In effect, he was telling Tom that he would have to be ordered in writing by Washington before he would consent to relay a message to Lisa in Jonestown.

After a series of lengthy and frustrating calls to Washington, Tom finally convinced a State Department official to send a cable to McCoy instructing him to contact Lisa Layton and "attempt to ascertain her welfare and also inform her that if she so desires [her son] will provide her with an airplane ticket for her return to the United States and will meet her in New York." McCoy was also instructed to "report results via direct cable to Dr. Thomas Layton."

No mention was made in the cable of ensuring the privacy of McCoy's conversation with Lisa, or of delivering to her any of the letters from her children.

McCoy's response to this cable and to the Laytons' letters to him was a severe disappointment to Tom, Debbie, and Annalisa. On July 28 he wrote to Debbie:

"As you know, I will be leaving Guyana in the very near future. At this time I am not sure whether I will be able to get up to the community before I leave. . . .

"However, I am sure that my replacement will plan a trip as soon as he can after his arrival. This trip would probably take place some time in late August. He and I will have an opportunity to discuss the situation and I will, of course, fully discuss the entire situation involving your mother before I depart.

"I also just received a telegram from, I believe, your brother Dr. Thomas Layton. Please inform him that both you and he will receive a report of the results of the visit."

It was a dead end to their one realistic hope. None of the Laytons was contacted again, either by Richard McCoy, or by his successor, Douglas Ellice.

There was one other possible avenue of communication: the radio. Tom, Debbie, and Annalisa had hesitated to try to get in touch with Lisa via shortwave because they were afraid that she would be punished for their attempt. In early August, however, an opportunity was handed to Tom and he was quick to seize upon it. Laurence Layton had decided to try to retrieve some of the family belongings that Lisa had taken and "loaned" to the San Francisco Temple. He particularly wanted back an etching signed by Albert Einstein, and some furniture that Lisa had promised to Annalisa. Deciding on a brash approach, Tom phoned the Temple to ask what day they should be there with a truck to pick up their belongings. A Temple spokesman said that he would have to check with Lisa in Jonestown to find out her wishes in the matter.

A couple of days later Tom received a phone call; the Temple had Larry on a radio patch from Jonestown. Larry told his brother that he would ask Lisa about the furniture. Tom asked how Lisa was, and Larry reported that she was healthy and happy, and that she was teaching a class in German at the Jonestown school. Tom said that sounded just great, and he couldn't wait to visit; would Christmas be all right? Larry, caught offguard, said yes. Acting as though the visit were all set, Tom switched the conversation to what he could bring that might be helpful to Larry and Lisa in their work in Jonestown. Larry suggested that Lisa could use some German language records for her class. Tom said that sounded like a good idea, he would be sure to bring them when he visited Jonestown in December.

At the end of the conversation, Larry again told Tom that he would ask Lisa about the furniture. They never heard anything further from the Temple about that subject, but Tom was satisfied with the way the conversation had gone; an "invitation" to Jonestown seemed a big step forward, and Tom resolved to go ahead with plans for the trip.

Meanwhile, in Jonestown, Lisa was actually a long way from being able to teach a class in German. Back in San Francisco, Jones had assured her that he would be able to cure her cancer. But she had never really regained her strength after the operation. Early in July, Lisa—now very sick and weak—was moved from her dormitory in Jonestown to a hospital in Georgetown, where she was tended by her daughter-in-law, Karen. In two memos to Jim Jones, dated July 15 and July 16, Karen reported on Lisa's health.

"July 15, Lisa Layton:

"Very weak, walks to bathroom and is tired when she comes back. It's only 2 doors down from us.

"They have been giving her anti-diarrhea medicine since she's been here so her diarrhea has stopped. I'm not sure what the medicine is but will find out.

"She gets nauseated much of the time and has to get shots. The shots are 'Gravol' and help her. She eats a little each day. I weighed her yesterday and she weighed 88 lbs. . . .

"Her attitude is positive. She made a negative statement which Tim reported on to you as I had told Tim and he passed it on. Anyway, other than that she speaks praiseworthy of Jim and PT each day. I've read 'Cities Without Crisis' to her. Now I'm reading Elizabeth Gurly Flynn and a book on the Nixon dictatorship to her. . . .

"She still is hoping what she has isn't serious."

"July 16, Re Lisa Layton:

"Today Lisa is feeling a little better. She let me wash her hair which is the first time she's had enough strength to let me wash it.

"Her talk continues to be positive and praiseworthy of Jim. She has said many things against Debbie, including that she thinks Debbie has a criminal mind. Said she doesn't know how Debbie could do all this shit against us, & talked about how terrible it was. We talk a lot about what Jim has done for us, how she would still be living in bondage with Old Man Layton were it not for Jim, etc. Of course I gear a lot of the conversation but she adds a lot too. . . .

"She said last night she's not worried about anything because she knows Jim is with her. Said even thru her cancer surgery she didn't have the slightest anxiety because she knew Jim was with her, so she's not going to start worrying now. She said Jim told her a couple of months ago that she had no cancer in her body, although she thought for a moment and then said she couldn't remember if that was before Debbie left or afterwards.

"She did say today that she's lonely. Said all her life she's never been close to anyone, not even her own children. Said she's closer to me than she's ever been to anyone, even her children. Said how grateful to Jim she is that he let me come and be with her—doesn't know what she'd do without me.

"I assume it has already been passed on to you that Dr. Searwar told me the other day that he saw what looked like a couple of masses in her lungs. He said too he thought the cancer had spread to the liver because it was hard and enlarged, & he thinks that's what's causing the stomach trouble she's having. . . .

"I asked Dr. Searwar not to tell her [his diagnosis] & he read Larry's letter which said the same. About the 3rd day he saw her he told her she had an enlarged liver. Then day before yesterday he came in & told her that her present condition was caused by her previous condition in her chest. (I about shit!) So yesterday I caught him at 7 A.M. & told him I didn't want Lisa to know as she was terrified of cancer. He said he thought she already knew . . . because her condition was 'terminal.' I said 'we' knew, but 'she' did not as our Dr's letter had explained (& as I thought he understood). So when he came in on his round he made no comments about her condition. This morning he came & Lisa asked if he had conferred with the other Dr. on her chest X-ray, he said yes, & they found nothing. . . .

"Anyway, Lisa has an amazing ability to <u>not</u> face reality, & even when he (Dr.) told her her condition was from her previous chest condition, she told me he most likely was mistaken. She told me to tell him she thought she had a bacterial infection. She said 'he's probably just guessing anyway.'

"She's said several times she wishes she could go to sleep & never wake up, as she's so tired of feeling sick. Perhaps she's not as afraid of death as she is of suffering from cancer. I don't know, but it is sad seeing her so miserable."

In early August, Lisa was transferred from the hospital in Georgetown back to Jonestown. Of course her family in the United States had no way of knowing her condition. Not until October was there any further word of Lisa. Then, October 16, Dr. Layton received a phone call from Leah Tow, Karen Layton's mother. Two days later, on October 18, he drafted a chilling letter to Tom, Annalisa and her children, and Debbie. This letter was never mailed; like many of Dr. Layton's introspective documents, it was left lying around the house where someone would be sure to find it and read it—like a note in a bottle, a silent cry for help. In this instance Tom, who had recently moved nearby to teach at San Jose State, found it in a dresser drawer in his former bedroom.

"Dear Children/Grandchildren: Today is the 37th Anniversary of your mother's and my wedding day Oct. 18, 1941 in State College, Pennsylvania. Now it is half a lifetime later; we are parted and alone and your mother is terminally ill in the jungles of South America with Jim Jones and his Peoples Temple cult. The day before yesterday—Monday Oct. 16—I was called by Mrs. Leah Tow, Mother of Karen Layton (Laurence John's wife). Leah Tow told me that she had been called by phone by a Dr. Don Freed that he had just returned from a visit to Peoples Temple Jonestown, Guyana where he had spent 4 hours talking with Lisa Layton. He said that Lisa is terminally ill and has been in a hospital, that she is comfortable, cheerful and well taken care of, that Karen Layton is caring for her but that she knows that she is dying! Dr. Freed is convinced that Jim Jones and the Temple people are doing fine work, are sincere, and well liked in Guyana. This is all the news that we have. Laurence L. Layton."

On October 30, both Tom and Annalisa wrote letters to Lisa. Tom's was a chatty family letter, detailing his move from Los

Angeles to San Jose, and reporting the Valentines' harvest of corn and squash from their garden. He concluded:

"We all miss you and wish that you would return to California for treatment. Should that be possible both Annalisa and I have plenty of space. I appreciate your offer for me to visit. When last we talked over the radio Larry suggested a Christmas visit and I am now attempting to arrange for it. Larry suggested I bring some German teaching materials and I will do so. I have wanted to visit you for a long time and I am happy that it is finally working out. Please let me know if there is anything special that I should bring with me that might make you more comfortable."

Annalisa's draft of her final letter to her mother read in part:

"I know Debbie's name must be very high on Jim's enemy list since she was trusted, then left, and his tirades against her must bring you a lot of sorrow. I want you to know that she arrived in this country with a small plastic bag containing a pair of pants, an emergency passport and one dollar. Tom and I supported her until she got a job. In no way did she take a cent from the church. You must believe that, Mom. . . . You told me often what a levelheaded, honest, sensible, good person Debbie had become. She still is. She is a pleasure to be with, and she, Tom and I have become quite close. All three of us think of you more than you can imagine. . . .

"I often think of myself as a mother compared to you as a mother (which is really the only way I knew you). I feel like you were always understanding and supportive and had 100% trust in me. Did you ever give me hell for being self-centered or nasty to Larry? I get in a bitchy mood and no one is spared my wrath. I don't remember that happening with you. Maybe I just forgot such scenes, as will my kids—hope, hope? I certainly remember having a lot of restraints on what I could do and wear, but those I always attributed to Dad. Anyhow I often wonder what I should do to have my children think of me as I thought of you at that age. Did you think of your mother much as you were rearing us?

"Our physical separation isn't everything because I feel mentally you are part of what I am and how I react and think. So you see, although I miss you and really want to visit with you, I still have 34 years of you which will always be with me. By the way, why didn't you make me better at expressing myself and a better speller while we were at it. . . .

"Dad grieves terribly for Larry. I guess Larry was his favorite child, perhaps because he could never quite reach him. Any how Dad feels betrayed because Larry helped the church locate Debbie when she was leaving and he has put a clause into his will that Larry will be disowned unless he comes back to visit before Dad's death. . . .

"I'm getting gray hair through my bangs. I guess I'll have to start dying it. Debs said your hair is completely white and it looks really cute that way. I can imagine that it would. Is there anything you need sent down? I'd be glad to get together a care package. I'll bring it with me when I visit. When can I visit you in Georgetown? Tom would like to visit too. How about just before Christmas?"

When Congressman Leo Ryan went on his fact-finding mission to Guyana in November, he took Annalisa's letter with him, promising to deliver it in person to Lisa Layton. Tom's letter to his mother was never sent. He had planned to mail it, but never did.

It was inevitable that Debbie's leaving would have a profound effect on Jim Jones, and therefore on the residents of Jonestown. To make sure that no one else would try to follow her, he tightened security even further. And he circulated a rumor that Debbie had stolen twenty-five thousand dollars to finance her drug habit back in the states and had fled the church because she was pregnant. Temple representatives visited both American and Guyanese officials in Georgetown, trying to find some way of forcing Debbie to return to Jonestown. Sharon Amos reported on one such meeting with Guyanese Police Commissioner Lloyd Barker.

"We talked to him about Debbie Blakey and what she did, stealing the $25,000 and returning to her prior drug pattern, her family being in Jonestown, etc.

"He said you would have to prove that she physically took the money out, it isn't enough to have affidavits or statements against her or a lie detector test. If there is no evidence whatsoever there is no way to do anything.

"If we knew she took it before she left, she could have been searched at the airport. They wait until the last declaration, until the person is on the way up to the plane and then take them off and search them."

By this time, the American embassy was not in a particularly helpful mood either. When Temple representatives met with embassy official Richard Dwyer, to ask him to let them know if any more Temple members wanted to leave the country, they were not pleased with his response.

"May 24, 1978—2 meetings with Dwyer: Basically—he said he cannot inform us if one of our people came to him as they are leaving because the 'Secrecy Act' prevents him from doing so. We made it clear we felt we're getting the shaft & unequal treatment. We used the escort to the airport [when Debbie left the country] as an example. He said they would do that for anybody. We said, 'But you don't do it for everybody, therefore you showed her favoritism.' He didn't respond. . . . We didn't get much of anything out of Dwyer. McCoy seems somewhat human because he at least answers questions. With Dwyer it's like dealing with a robot that gives the safest answer possible."

At this point, Jim Jones and Peoples Temple had a lot to be worried about besides Debbie Blakey's apostasy, convinced as they were that they stood alone against the world, and that the world was gathering its forces to attack. Their main link with the outside had been Charles Garry, the Temple's lawyer in San Francisco; but Jones no longer entirely trusted Garry. He told his aides that Garry was too cautious, that he was too much inclined to sit back and wait rather than take action.

In September 1978 the Temple gained a powerful new friend and supporter, one who believed as they did that all of the agencies and forces of the U. S. government and its intelligence establishment were conspiring to destroy the Jonestown settlement because it was an embarrassment and a threat to the racist capitalist system. Mark Lane had come to Jonestown.

Jones had invited Lane ostensibly to give a lecture on the assassination of Dr. Martin Luther King; but as soon as Lane returned to the Bay Area from a long weekend at the jungle settlement, he was ready to call a press conference to announce plans to file a multimillion-dollar suit charging a heavily financed and concerted effort by the United States intelligence establishment to destroy Jonestown. Named as defendants in the suit were the FBI, CIA, Department of State, Internal Revenue Service, Treasury Department, Postal Service, Federal

Communications Commission, and their agents and employees.

Lane also accepted more than ten thousand dollars in fees and expenses to finance a "counteroffensive" program. As outlined in a memo to Jones, Lane projected a nationwide campaign that would include legal measures such as the proposed lawsuit; public relations and community fund-raising events; and congressional lobbying.

Jones and Lane were well matched, and the result was predictable: the paranoid "victim" of a conspiracy and the nation's foremost conspiracy buff each confirmed the other's suspicions about the nature of the world. It was exactly what Jonestown did not need; an outside figure of international fame seconding Jones' fears could only provoke even more irrational behavior. Not that it really made much difference—by this time too much else was fueling that same blaze of fear and paranoia.

For one thing, the Organization of Concerned Relatives was beginning to make its voice heard in the United States and in Guyana as well. They didn't actually get much press coverage, and the government was not receptive to their accusations, but the group was vocal, and they were beginning to draw some attention. The Temple, at least, was well aware of their activities.

One of the leaders of the organization was Tim Stoen, still determined to get his son out of Jonestown. A petition, signed by fifty-seven relatives of Temple members in Guyana, had been sent in April to Secretary of State Cyrus Vance and to Guyanese Prime Minister Forbes Burnham. Addressed to the Reverend James Warren Jones and titled "Accusation of Human Rights Violations By Rev. James Warren Jones Against Our Children and Relatives at the Peoples Temple Jungle Encampment in Guyana, South America," the petition outlined the alleged human rights violations and demanded, among other things, that Jonestown residents be encouraged to return to the United States for visits, at their relatives' expense. Like Debbie Blakey's affidavit, this petition also came to the attention of Congressman Leo Ryan.

During the first week of November another heavy blow fell: Terri Buford, perhaps Jones' most trusted aide, defected from the Temple, taking with her information about the organization's finances that could bring down the whole structure if she chose to make it public—and if she could get anybody to listen to her. From San Francisco, where she had flown from Guyana on Temple business, Terri made her way to New York and Mark Lane. She had met Lane in Guyana, and felt that she could trust his advice about her next moves. Jones didn't know where she'd gone; a Temple member in San Francisco called Lane to say that Jones was very concerned about her, and please to let them know at once if he heard from her.

And finally, something did seem to be happening in Washington. Temple members in San Francisco had heard alarming reports about the ongoing investigation by Congressman Leo Ryan into Temple activities in both San Francisco and Jonestown.

Leo Ryan's attention had first been brought to the Peoples Temple in November 1977, when he had read the San Francisco *Examiner* account of the death of Temple member Bob Houston on the day after he left the church. It happened that Sam Houston, the father of the young man, was Ryan's old friend; and Bob had been Ryan's student in high school. The congressman paid a sympathy call on the Houstons, and what he learned from them sparked his professional as well as his personal interest. Ryan began to follow more closely the news accounts of Jim Jones and the activities of Peoples Temple. And he began to receive mail from his constituents about the Temple. Particularly disturbing were the pleas for help from parents whose children had disappeared into the interior of Guyana.

From the beginning, he took the matter seriously and felt that it warranted investigation on behalf of his constituents. Leo Ryan was one legislator who believed in checking things out for himself. As a state assemblyman, he had taught for two anonymous weeks in a high school in the Los Angeles ghetto of Watts; and he had spent a week as a volunteer prisoner in Folsom prison. After his election to Congress in 1972, Ryan continued his policy of gaining understanding through first-hand experience. In March of 1978, while researching a wildlife preservation bill, he had traveled to Newfoundland to witness the slaughter of baby harp seals for their pelts.

So it wasn't out of character for Ryan to contact Debbie Blakey after reading in the San Francisco *Chronicle* about her affidavit regarding conditions in Jonestown.

By that time the pieces of Debbie's life were beginning to come together. She had found a job in the financial district of San Francisco, and her friendship with John Collins had developed into the first serious and satisfying relationship of her life. When Ryan called her she said she was anxious to meet with him, but she didn't want to jeopardize her job by taking time off during office hours. After Ryan talked with her supervisor's boss, however, there was no problem with Debbie taking the afternoon off. Debbie had the feeling that Ryan enjoyed exercising his power.

They met for the first time on a San Francisco street corner in early September. Attorney Jacqueline Speier, Ryan's aide, was with him. Ryan was more than a foot taller than Debbie, and his manner toward her was so reassuring that she immediately felt safe with him. For that initial interview, Ryan borrowed a friend's office in the Wells Fargo Bank Building. They talked for about two hours. At first Debbie was worried about speaking freely because her lawyer wasn't present and the discussion was being taped. Ryan promised her that he would keep the tapes in his safe, and that no one would ever hear them without his approval. Debbie told him everything she knew.

Toward the end of the interview Ryan's tone suddenly changed. He leaned forward and said angrily, "Do you expect me to believe that sane people would stand in line to take poison?"

Debbie was frightened by Ryan's abrupt change of manner, and shatteringly disappointed; he hadn't believed anything she had told him. She answered the question carefully, however, explaining once again how such a thing could happen. Then she asked, "You don't believe me, do you?"

"Yes, Debbie," he said, "I do believe you. I wanted to see how you would hold up under questioning by someone who didn't. This"—indicating the tape recorder—"is for unbelieving ears."

Ryan's interview with Debbie was only one part of his investigation. He also met with members of the Organization of Concerned Relatives, and as it became known that he was interested in the Temple and its affairs, more ex-members contacted him with their personal versions of the Jonestown horror story.

On the other hand, for every tale of horror and deprivation, Ryan heard some glowing report—from Temple members, public figures, independent observers—of the jungle paradise called Jonestown. Ryan was soon convinced that, as a member of the House Committee on Foreign Affairs, he would have to travel to Guyana to find out for himself the truth of the matter.

In preparation for his trip, Ryan and his staff met with State Department officials for briefings on what he might expect to find. They weren't very helpful. Ryan already knew more than the State Department about what was going on in Jonestown— or at least more than they seemed willing to tell him. The State Department felt that there was "no reason to anticipate the possibility" of violence. Potential danger was assessed as "unlikely." The warnings that Ryan did receive came mostly from Debbie, the concerned relatives group, and from his own staff. Jacqueline Speier had such strong premonitions of danger that she got her own will in order before the trip, and insisted that Ryan do the same.

Once Ryan had made up his mind to see Jonestown for himself, he moved quickly. On October 4 he wrote to Congressman Clement J. Zablocki, chairman of the International Relations Committee, requesting official permission to carry his investigation to South America. He wrote in part, "It has come to my attention that a community of some 1400 Americans are presently living in Guyana under somewhat bizarre conditions. There is conflicting information regarding whether or not the U. S. citizens are being held there against their will. If you agree, I would like to travel to Guyana during the week of November 12–18 to review the situation first hand."

Chairman Zablocki agreed. The next step was for Ryan to let Jones know that he was coming. On November 1 he telegraphed Jones:

IN AN EFFORT TO BE RESPONSIVE TO [MY] CONSTITUENTS WITH DIFFERING PERSPECTIVES AND TO LEARN MORE ABOUT YOUR CHURCH AND ITS WORK, I INTEND TO VISIT GUYANA AND TALK WITH APPROPRIATE GOVERNMENT OFFICIALS....

WHILE WE ARE IN GUYANA, I HAVE ASKED OUR AMBASSADOR,
JOHN BURKE, TO MAKE ARRANGEMENTS FOR TRANSPORTATION TO
VISIT YOUR CHURCH AND AGRICULTURAL STATION AT JONESTOWN.
IT GOES WITHOUT SAYING THAT I AM MOST INTERESTED IN A VISIT
TO JONESTOWN, AND WOULD APPRECIATE WHATEVER COURTESIES
YOU CAN EXTEND TO OUR CONGRESSIONAL DELEGATION.

Jones never responded directly to Ryan's telegram. Instead,
Ryan received a letter from Mark Lane announcing that Jones
had asked Lane to be present in Jonestown for the congressman's visit, but that since the scheduled time was inconvenient
for him, "a date which would be convenient to all of us should
be arrived at through discussion."

"You should be informed," Lane's letter continued, "that
various agencies of the U.S. Government have somewhat con-
sistently oppressed the Peoples Temple institution. I am now
exploring that matter fully in order to bring an action against
those agencies of the U.S. Government that have violated the
rights of my client. Some of the members of the Peoples Temple
have had to flee from the U. S. in order to experience a fuller
opportunity to enjoy rights which were not available to them
within the U.S. You should know that two different countries,
neither one of which has entirely friendly relations with the
U.S., have offered refuge to the 1200 Americans now residing
in Jonestown. Thus far the Peoples Temple has not accepted
either of those offers but it is their position that if religious
persecution continues and if it is furthered through a witch hunt
conducted by any branch of the U.S. Government, that they
will be constrained to consider accepting either of the offers.
You may judge, therefore, the important consequences which
may flow from further persecution of Peoples Temple and
which might very well result in the creation of a most embarrassing situation for the U.S. Government."

In response to Lane's thinly veiled threats, Ryan assured
the lawyer that his intention was to talk to "certain persons in
that community whose mothers, fathers, brothers, sisters, hus-
bands and wives have asked me to inquire on their behalf,"
and especially to allow Jones and the residents of Jonestown
to speak freely on their own behalf.

"No 'persecution,' as you put it, is intended, Mr. Lane," Ryan wrote, "but your vague reference to 'the creation of a most embarrassing situation for the American government' does not impress me at all. If the comment is intended as a threat, I believe it reveals more than may have been intended. I presume Mr. Jones would not be supportive of such a comment."

Shortly before this hostile exchange of letters, the Peoples Temple in Guyana had informed the American embassy that the congressional delegation would be allowed to visit Jonestown on three conditions: that the group be racially balanced and include some representatives sympathetic to Peoples Temple; that there be no media coverage of the trip; and that Mark Lane be present throughout the visit.

Ryan had originally intended to travel to Guyana with a very small official contingent. But as word of the trip spread, reporters and members of the concerned relatives group expressed their desire to accompany him, and on November 14, nine newspaper and television reporters and photographers and eighteen relatives boarded the same plane as Ryan and the other two official members of his group, Jacqueline Speier and James Schollaert, staff consultant for the House Foreign Affairs Committee. In fact, Tom Layton had been invited by Tim Stoen to join the concerned relatives on this trip. He decided not to because he felt that association with Ryan and the Stoens would hurt his chances of getting into Jonestown in December.

A few days before the congressional delegation left for South America, Debbie, Grace Stoen, and Steven Katsaris, another member of the Concerned Relatives group, flew to Washington at their own expense to meet with Ryan and to try once more to inform State Department officials of the conditions and dangers of Jonestown. On the evening of November 2, as they waited for their flight, Debbie and Grace were interviewed at the San Francisco airport by four of the newsmen who planned to accompany Ryan to Guyana—Don Harris, Bob Brown, and Steve Sung of NBC, and Greg Robinson of the San Francisco *Examiner*. Of the four, only Steve Sung survived the trip, and he was seriously wounded at the Port Kaituma airstrip.

The reporters interviewed Debbie and Grace separately,

each for more than an hour. Debbie cautioned them about the dangers they faced in Jonestown, and told them what to watch out for. At 11 P.M. the two women boarded the plane for Washington.

Their reception in Washington was not what they had been led to expect. Arrangements for meetings with State Department officials were haphazard, their appointments were not firm. Ryan had asked several people to meet with Grace, Debbie, and Steven Katsaris, but Ryan himself was in California, and of the people he had asked to be there, only Jackie Speier and Jim Schollaert showed up. Debbie was quite upset that they had flown three thousand miles to tell their story to only one person (Speier having already heard it). But as long as they were there they might as well get on with it, so they spent four hours once more going over the details of their experiences with Peoples Temple.

In the middle of their presentation Ryan called, and he and Jackie had a long and animated conversation. Ryan had just received Mark Lane's letter, and he was furious at its implied threats. It was Debbie's impression that Ryan had a hot temper, and that Speier was trying to cool him off.

Debbie was still upset when she left Ryan's office. She felt that she had wasted her time and jeopardized her new job for nothing. She and Grace were ready to fly home that evening, but Jackie Speier asked them to stay through the weekend because Ryan would be back in Washington on Monday. They finally agreed to stay, despite their misgivings about the disorganization and lack of response they had faced so far.

On Monday morning, when he heard about Friday's fiasco, Ryan was furious. He got on the phone and demanded that representatives of a dozen different State Department offices be assembled in twenty minutes because, he said, "I want them to hear something." He slammed the phone down and turned to his audience, grinning. "They damn well better jump," he said. "We pay their salary."

This meeting proved more satisfactory than the events of Friday. A dozen people sat around a long conference table. Debbie sat at the head of the table, with Ryan and Speier on either side. Ryan introduced Debbie and told the assembled State Department officials, "I want you to listen carefully and take notes as she explains her involvement and how she escaped from Peoples Temple." Debbie spoke for over an hour, and then her audience questioned her for another hour. It was obvious that they were completely uninformed about Jonestown and Peoples Temple, and that they had not read her affidavit or any of the other material that had been sent to them by the concerned relatives group.

When Debbie had finished, one of the men commented that there was really nothing they could do because all of this was occurring within the jurisdiction of a foreign country. He did suggest, however, that the same group should meet again after Ryan's return from Guyana to "receive an update on the situation."

Debbie was depressed by the meeting, but Ryan and Speier felt that it had gone just fine. As Ryan said, "Now that you have spoken to them and they have taken notes, they will never be able to deny that they heard it."

As Debbie and the others left the building after the meeting, they walked right into Mark Lane and Terri Buford coming down the street. Debbie had no idea that Terri had left the Temple. If they had been alone, the two women would surely have stopped and spoken; they had traveled a long way together. As it was, they glanced at each other, just a moment of eye contact, and kept going, each in her own direction.

Months later, Debbie would find out that Terri Buford might have had reason to snub her that day in Washington. "We were really good friends, considering what was possible in the church, and Jim knew I was close to Terri. So early on he asked me to write her up. One thing I wrote was that Terri had privately questioned his orders to send guns down to Guyana. After I escaped from Guyana he showed that report to Terri to break down the trust we had shared, so that she would hate me. But had we not said things against each other, neither of us would have been trusted to leave the interior and position ourselves in Georgetown. So that trust we fostered in Jim by reporting on each other eventually gave us both the freedom to make a break out of the Temple."

Ryan drove Debbie, Grace, and Jackie Speier back to the House Office Building. He was on his way to another meeting, so he said good-bye to them in the parking garage. He left Debbie with a reassuring hug. "Don't worry," he said, "everything is going to be all right."

The three women walked up the stairs from the garage and through the echoing hallways back to Ryan's office. They talked for several minutes, clearing up some details of the trip to Guyana. Debbie advised Jackie on what to take with her, and how to dress in Jonestown—no makeup, no jewelry, no short skirts. If she wanted people to trust her, the plainer the better. Debbie also gave Jackie the Layton family letters to be read to Lisa, and a list of the names of people who she thought might want to leave Jonestown if they were approached privately.

Grace Stoen and Steven Katsaris were to stay in Washington for their trip to Guyana as members of the Concerned Relatives group. Their good-byes were heartfelt but restrained; they all had at least some idea of the dangers that lay ahead.

On the drive to the airport Debbie tried to rest, but the images that crowded her mind gave her no peace. When John picked her up at the San Francisco airport she was exhausted and depressed.

At eight o'clock on the morning of November 14, Debbie was back at her desk in a financial district high-rise office building.

That same afternoon Congressman Leo Ryan and his delegation of reporters, photographers, and concerned relatives landed in Guyana.

11

The Tragic Fulfillment

In Georgetown, the tin-roofed capital city of Guyana, government officials were apprehensive about the American congressman's visit. For weeks the Temple representatives in the city had been clearly and emphatically stating their position: Ryan and his entourage of journalists and concerned relatives would not be welcomed at Jonestown. Temple members had succeeded to the point of making it difficult for the journalists even to enter the country.

On his first evening in Georgetown Ryan paid a surprise visit to the Temple headquarters. He knocked on the door, and when Sharon Amos answered it he said, "Hello, I'm Leo Ryan. I'm the bad guy." Amos seemed prepared for the congressman's visit; she presented him with a long scroll that bore the signatures of hundreds of Jonestown residents. The scroll read, in part, "Many of us have been visited by friends and relatives. However, we have not invited, nor do we care to see, Congressman Ryan." Besides, Amos added, the Reverend Jones was ill and wouldn't be able to see the congressman in any case.

Ryan, however, was undeterred. He announced that he would go to Jonestown with or without Jones' permission. The congressman would at least have the satisfaction of being turned away at the gates to Jonestown with television cameras filming and reporters taking notes. He had come this far and he was not going to turn around or back down now.

Ryan had a strong personal reason for continuing. Not only was he the last hope for the hundreds of relatives and friends who were worried about their loved ones in Jonestown, he was also on a mission for his good friend Sam Houston. Houston's son, Bob, had died under mysterious circumstances after leaving the Temple in California, and now Sam was concerned about his two granddaughters, Patricia, fifteen, and Judy, fourteen, presently living in Jonestown. In fact, Sam's wife, Nadine, had traveled to Guyana with Ryan.

For two days, Jim Jones remained adamant in his refusal to allow Ryan entry to Jonestown. Ryan was equally adamant in his decision to visit the jungle community. On Friday morning, November 17, Ryan informed Mark Lane and Charles Garry, the two Temple attorneys who had arrived from the United States the previous evening, that he had chartered an airplane and would be departing for the Port Kaituma airstrip within the hour. The lawyers, Ryan added, were welcome to come along.

The attorneys asked for a delay of two hours so they could confer with Jones by radio, and the congressman agreed. When Garry and Lane reached Jones and informed him of Ryan's imminent departure, Jones moaned, "This is terrible. It's terrible." The Temple leader wanted to know which relatives would be on the plane. The lawyers said they did not know, Ryan had refused to divulge the information. The chartered plane, they said, could seat eighteen passengers.

"You have two alternatives," Garry told Jones. "You can tell the Congress of the United States, the press, and the relatives to go fuck themselves. If you do that, it's the end of the ball game. The other alternative is to let them in—and prove to the world that these people criticizing you are crazy." Jones was reminded that if he wanted the attorneys on the same plane, he would have to decide quickly. Ryan would not wait beyond the deadline. "All right, Charles," Jones sighed, "they can come in. Will you both be with them?" Garry said they would, and the two lawyers dashed for the airport.

At 4 P.M., the chartered twin-engine Otter arched over the small fishing village of Port Kaituma and glided onto the landing strip that had been cut from the thick surrounding jungle six miles north of Jonestown. When the entourage alighted they were confronted by an angry contingent of Temple members led by Johnny Jones, one of Jones' adopted sons. Only Ryan, his administrative assistant, Jackie Speier, the two attorneys, Deputy Chief of Mission Richard Dwyer, and Neville Annibourne, a Guyanese information officer, would be allowed to continue to Jonestown, Johnny Jones told the group. The six boarded the truck for the slow and bumpy six-mile ride, and the rest of Ryan's party remained at Port Kaituma.

Marceline Jones met the congressman and his party. She greeted Ryan warmly and offered to take him on a tour of the settlement's nursery, school, and health center. Ryan demurred, saying that he'd like to see the facilities later but that his first order of business was to conduct private talks with specific people. He handed Marceline Jones a list of names.

While Ryan and Speier were interviewing residents, Jones decided to relent and allow the nine journalists and four concerned relatives still at Port Kaituma to enter the settlement. The truck was sent back for them, and when the group arrived Marceline led them to the corrugated tin-roof pavilion. "You must be hungry," she said. "The food is waiting." Jones was also waiting at the pavilion. He was perspiring profusely and appeared ill. Joined by Ryan, Speier, and the attorneys, the visitors sat down to a meal of barbecued pork, collard greens, salad, and coffee. After dinner, Jones treated his guests to a two-hour program of music. An eight-man band played old-fashioned blues, modern soul, and contemporary rock songs. The show ended at 10 P.M. During the course of the meal and the entertainment, the reporters had been casually interviewing Jones and various Temple members. After the entertainment, Ryan strode to the microphone and addressed the throng. "For some of you, for a lot of you that I talked to, Jonestown is the best thing that ever happened to you in your lives." The congressman received a thunderous response that lasted a full three minutes.

Sometime during the evening a Temple member passed a note to NBC correspondent Don Harris indicating that he wanted to leave Jonestown. Another member whispered to Richard Dwyer that he wanted to leave "immediately." Dwyer later passed the request on to Ryan.

Ryan, Speier, Dwyer, Annibourne, Lane, and Garry were allowed to spend the night in Jonestown. Although the reporters also wanted to stay overnight in the settlement, Jones refused. "Get them out of here," he whispered to his wife. "I will not have them staying here overnight." And back to Port Kaituma they went.

Saturday morning, November 18, began on a cheerful note. Jones seemed in good spirits, providing his overnight guests with a hearty breakfast of pancakes and bacon. Following breakfast Ryan and Speier continued their rounds of interviews. The dump truck returned to Port Kaituma to bring back the newsmen. During the night, however, the newsmen had been getting other views of Jonestown. Three local Guyanese, including one who said he was a police official, had told the journalists about beatings in Jonestown and had complained that Guyanese officials were denied entry to the jungle community. They also described a "torture hole" inside the compound, and warned that Jones had registered at least one automatic weapon with authorities.

When the newsmen returned, several set out on a tour of the compound. Charles Krause, a reporter for the Washington *Post*, discovered four barnlike buildings that turned out to be dormitories. When he tried to enter one—called Jane Pittman Place—he was turned away. He and other newsmen who had joined him protested. After Lane and Garry mediated and gained entry for the reporters, the group found about five dozen elderly women jammed into a small, cramped room with long rows of bunk beds. As Lane later told the press, "It was like a slave ship."

The atmosphere was already beginning to sour when Jones agreed to sit for an interview with NBC correspondent Don Harris. For forty-five minutes Jones sat implacably in front of a minicamera while Harris fired off one hard question after another, questions about drugs, corporal punishment, weapons.

When Harris asked about the automatic weapon that the Guyanese had told him about at Port Kaituma, Jones shot back, "A bold-faced lie." Then Harris pulled out a crumpled note that a Jonestown resident had furtively passed to him at dinner the night before. Jones' jaw became taut, his eyes narrowed. "People play games, friend," he said coldly. "They lie. What can I do with liars? Are you people going to leave us? I just beg you, please leave us. Anybody that wants to can get out of here. They come and go all the time."

After the interview, Ryan told Jones that a family of six had asked for his help in leaving. Jones became furious. "I feel betrayed," he shouted. "It never stops." Jones began ranting about liars and traitors, and Garry tried to calm the Temple leader down. "Let them go," he said to Jones. "Who gives a shit if six leave or sixty? It won't change what you've done here." Jones said he'd been stabbed in the back. "He just freaked out," Garry said later.

At 3 P.M., Ryan was called to the pavilion. An American Indian named Al Simon wanted to leave with his three children, but his wife was refusing to let the children go. With Ryan present, Garry and Lane persuaded both parents to let a court decide the matter. The entire family decided to stay, at least for another week.

Within minutes, a group of some fifteen Temple members gathered and indicated their desire to leave Jonestown. A late joiner was Larry Layton. His wife, Karen, expressed surprise that Larry was among the defectors. She berated him for wanting to leave and accused him of being a traitor to the cause. Larry shrugged and boarded the truck that would take Ryan's party, now more than doubled, to the Port Kaituma airstrip. The defectors appeared uneasy that there might be violence.

Ryan himself had planned to stay in Jonestown one more night with Garry and Lane. As the truck was being loaded, he stood in conversation with the two attorneys. Suddenly, without warning, a Jones lieutenant named Don Sly grabbed the congressman around the throat and put a six-inch fishing knife to his chest. "Congressman Ryan, you are a motherfucker," Sly yelled. Lane and Garry quickly grappled with Sly and freed Ryan. In the commotion Sly's hand was cut and blood splattered all over Ryan's shirt. Dazed, Ryan did not know whether the blood was his own or someone else's. Jones stood watching quietly. "Does this change everything?" he asked Ryan. "It doesn't change everything, but it changes some things," Ryan answered.

Despite the knife attack, Ryan stuck by his intention to remain in Jonestown for another night. He finally agreed to leave only after being virtually ordered to do so by Deputy Chief of Mission Richard Dwyer.

After the truck left, Jones summoned Garry. "This is terrible, terrible, terrible," he told his San Francisco attorney. "There are things you don't know. Those men who left a little while ago to go into the city are not going there. They love me and they may do something that will reflect badly on me. They're going to shoot at the people and their plane."

Near the airstrip, five members of the Parks family caught up with the truck. They had only been in Jonestown a few months, but earlier in the day the father, Dale Parks, had whispered to Ryan, "We've got to get out of here. This is hell." But his wife had refused to leave with him—until just after the truck left, when she saw Temple members hauling out some automatic weapons. "They started getting out the big stuff, and she finally knew it was coming down on us," Dale Parks said.

When Parks saw Larry Layton, however, he was alarmed. "He's not really going," he told one reporter. "This is a plot—something's going to happen." Other defectors nodded in agreement.

The Ryan entourage arrived at the Port Kaituma airstrip about 4:30 P.M. The planes that had been scheduled to be there on the group's arrival did not land until about thirty or forty minutes later. A white Cessna six-seater touched down first. It was followed ten minutes later by the twin-engine Otter.

The white Cessna was loaded first and began taxiing down the runway. After it had taxied about a quarter of a mile from the Otter and the remaining members of the Ryan group, a tractor-trailer pulled onto the runway. Climbing and jumping off it were Temple members armed with automatic pistols, semiautomatic rifles, and shotguns. Gerry Parks had also seen the tractor-trailer pull up. "Now we're going to get it," he said to no one in particular.

Gerry's wife, Patricia, had been standing in the doorway of the Otter. One of the first shots shattered her head. Tom and Juanita Bogue, two other defectors who were on the Otter with their parents, ran to the aircraft's door and slammed it shut. Both were slightly wounded in the next hail of gunfire, but the door remained shut.

Ryan and the newsmen were still on the ground outside. The assassins bore down on the two planes, firing as they came. Charles Krause was wounded in the hip. Ron Javers, a reporter for the San Francisco *Chronicle*, was shot in the shoulder. Tim Reiterman, reporter for the San Francisco *Examiner,* took a bullet in his left arm; another bullet fractured his wrist, blowing off his watch. Richard Dwyer was wounded in the thigh. All four managed to sprint for cover into the jungle.

The gunmen cut down NBC cameraman Bob Brown at the tail of the plane. *Examiner* photographer Greg Robinson died near the port engine, his body riddled with bullets. Ryan and Don Harris had dived behind the plane's starboard wheel when the firing started, but the tractor-trailer pulled around to that side of the aircraft and the assassins shot both men. Although Brown was wounded in the leg and could not run, he continued filming, aiming his camera at the gunmen as they advanced, until they were right up to him. One placed a shotgun next to Brown's head and pulled the trigger.

Steven Sung, the NBC sound man, was connected to Brown by a cable. He put his arm over his head and pretended he was dead. "The next thing I know," Sung recalls, "I feel tremendous pressure, an explosion right next to my head, and my arm feels like it's falling apart." The gunmen then walked up to Ryan and Harris, both still alive, and Robinson, already dead, and fired point-blank at their heads.

Bob Flick, the NBC field producer, was not wounded. He ran over to where a squad of Guyanese soldiers stood guarding a government plane. "We need guns," he shouted. The guards turned away.

Meanwhile at the Cessna, someone began firing a gun. At the time it was reported in the press that Larry Layton had pulled out a pistol and quickly fired three shots, wounding two of the other defectors before his gun jammed. These press reports said Dale Parks and Vernon Gosney wrestled the gun from his hands, and Larry ran out of the plane.*

---

*At Larry's eventual trial in Guyana, Gosney testified to this, and the jury voted to acquit Larry.

The shooting had lasted four or five minutes. When it was over, the gunmen boarded the tractor-trailer and drove away.

Dwyer and the newsmen who had taken cover returned. Larry Layton also wandered back to the airstrip. He was arrested by Guyanese authorities. The living, many of them wounded, had to wait until morning for help to arrive from Georgetown. They spent the night still unarmed in a cantina near the airstrip, terrified the gunmen would return.

At the Jonestown settlement, the camp loudspeaker summoned everyone to the pavilion. Garry and Lane were walking over when they were stopped by Jones. "Feeling is running very high against you," Jones calmly told them. "I can't say what might happen at this meeting." He then instructed the two lawyers to wait at the guest house. There, they were guarded by a pair of young Temple members, standing by the door with rifles at the ready. "We all going to die," one said. "It's a great moment— we all die."

The two youths explained to the stunned attorneys that Jones had ordered a revolutionary suicide. It would be a protest against racism and fascism. "Isn't there any other alternative?" Lane asked. The two said no. "Then Charles and I will write about what you do," Lane assured them. That idea seemed to sit well with the guards, and they started off for the pavilion. "How do we get out of here?" Lane called after them. One youth pointed toward the jungle. Garry and Lane ran in that direction.

At the pavilion, Jones was addressing his flock. "We're sitting here," he said, "waiting on a powder keg...for the catastrophe that's going to happen on that airplane—it's going to be a catastrophe. It almost happened here when the congressman was nearly killed. You can't take off with people's children without expecting a violent reaction. We have been so betrayed. We have been so terribly betrayed.

"What's going to happen here in a matter of a few minutes is that one of those people on the plane is going to shoot the pilot. I know that. I didn't plan it, but I know it's going to happen. And we better not have any of our children left when it's over. Because they'll parachute in here on us.

"So you be kind to the children and be kind to seniors, and take the potion like they used to take in ancient Greece, and step over quietly, because we are not committing suicide—it's a revolutionary act."

Jones' death decree was met with resistance as well as fatal acquiescence.

"Is it too late for Russia?" Christine Miller, a sixty-one-year- old member, asked.

"It's too late," Jones answered. "I can't control these people. They've gone with the guns. And it's too late."

Jones went on about what had to be done, but Christine Miller came back to the question of the defectors. "I think," she said, "that there were too few who left for twelve hundred people to give their lives . . ."

"Do you know how many left?" Jones asked her.

"Oh, twenty-odd. That's small compared to what's here."

"Twenty-odd," Jones said. "But what's gonna happen when they don't leave? When they get on the plane and the plane goes down? That plane'll come out of the air. There's no way you fly a plane without a pilot. You think Russia's gonna want us with all this stigma? We had some value, but now we don't have any value."

"Well," said Miller, "I don't see it like that. I mean, I feel like that as long as there's life there's hope."

"Well," said Jones, "everybody dies. I haven't seen anybody yet didn't die. And I'd like to choose my own kind of death for a change. I'm tired of being tormented to hell. Tired of it."

The congregation applauded.

"But I look at all the babies," Miller implored, "and I think they deserve to live."

"But don't they deserve much more?" Jones asked her. "They deserve peace."

As a final statement, Miller said: "I think we all have a right to our own destiny as individuals. And I have a right to choose mine, and everybody else has a right to choose theirs."

"The best testimony we can make," Jones declared, "is to leave this goddam world."

The congregation applauded once more, but now arguments broke out among Temple members. Jones' voice, which had been remarkably controlled up to this point, began to rise.

"Everybody hold it!" he shouted. "Hold it! Hold it! Lay down your burdens. Down by the riverside. Shall we lay them down here by the side of Guyana? When they start parachuting out of the air, they'll shoot some of our innocent babies. Can you let them take your child?"

The congregation chanted, "No! No! No!"

"I'm ready to go," one man shouted. "If you tell us we have to give our lives now, we're ready. All the rest of the sisters and brothers are with me."

"I've tried to keep this thing from happening," Jones said, more quietly. "But I now see it's the will of the Sovereign Being that we lay down our lives in protest against what's been done. If they come after our children, and we give them our children, then our children will suffer forever."

At this point, the gunmen returned from the airstrip. They told Jones that Congressman Ryan and several of the journalists had been shot and killed.

"Please get us some medication," Jones asked. "It's simple, there's no convulsions with it. Just, please get it. Before it's too late. Get movin'. Get movin'. Don't be afraid to die. Are you going to separate yourself from whoever shot the congressman? I don't know who shot him."

"No! No! No!" the crowd shouted.

"How many are dead?" Jones asked one of the gunmen. He was told that several had been killed.

"Aw, God, Almighty God," Jones cried. "It's too late. They're all laying out there dead. Please, can we hasten our medication?"

A woman's voice rose above the confusion of the crowd: "Okay, there's nothing to worry about. Everybody keep calm and try and keep your children calm. Let the little children in and reassure them. They're not crying from pain. It's just a little bitter-tasting."

"It's hard only at first," Jones added. "Living is much, much more difficult. Rising in the morning and not knowing what the night's bringing."

"This is nothing to cry about," the woman continued. "This is something we could all rejoice about. I'm looking at so many people crying. I wish you would not cry."

The crowd applauded these remarks.

"Please," Jones implored, "for God's sake, let's get on with it. We've lived as no other people lived and loved. We've had as much of this world as you're gonna get. Let's just be done with it. I want to see you go. They can take me and do what they want, whatever they want to do. I don't want to see you go through this hell no more. No more."

A man remarked, "The way the children are laying there now, I'd rather see them lay like that than to have them have to die like the Jews did, which was pitiful. Like Dad [Jones] said, when they come in, they're going to massacre our children. And the ones that they take capture, they're gonna just let them grow up and be dummies. And not grow up to be a person like the one and only Jim Jones."

Again the crowd applauded.

"Let's get gone," said Jones. "Let's get gone. We tried to find a new beginning. But it's too late. I don't know who killed the congressman. But as far as I'm concerned I killed him. He had no business coming. I told him not to come.

"Lay down your life with dignity. Don't lay down with tears and agony. It's just stepping over into another plane."

The crowd was crying. Some members were screaming.

"Stop this hysterics," Jones shouted. "This is not the way for people who are socialistic communists to die. Children, it's just something to put you to rest. Oh, God."

When all the bodies at Jonestown were counted, they totaled 908. Carolyn and Karen Layton and Carolyn's son, Kimo, were among the dead. Each had taken poison. Jim Jones was found with a bullet in his head. Just before he died, Jones had cried, "Mother, mother, please."

On November 18, 1978, at approximately seven P.M. San Francisco time, about seven hours after the shootings at the Port Kaituma airstrip, Annalisa phoned Debbie to say that she had heard from a neighbor that Congressman Ryan had been shot and was believed dead. Annalisa told Debbie that she would find a place in Davis for her and John to hide. Debbie too had heard the news, but she didn't want to go into hiding again until she had more details. Besides, Debbie added, she and John were expecting company for dinner that evening.

Agreeing that Debbie probably knew best how safe she was, Annalisa hung up. She waited all of fifteen minutes before calling back. This time she insisted that Debbie leave, and tack a note on the door with an explanation for her dinner guests. Debbie said a friend was coming over to lend them a gun, and that she still wanted to wait for more news.

Five minutes later, Debbie called Annalisa and said, "We just heard on the radio that a lot of people have been shot. We're leaving in about five minutes." To elude possible Temple assassins, Annalisa suggested that Debbie call from a public phone once she reached Davis, and that a close friend would lead them to a safe house. Since Temple members knew where Annalisa lived, there was no refuge for Debbie at her sister's home.

"I was scared to death that night," says Annalisa. "I sat up the entire night in our loft, from which I could see the headlights of any car coming up our street. I listened to the radio as uncertain reports came in from Guyana. Before morning I heard the report that Sharon Amos and her three children had had their throats slashed, presumably a murder-suicide. Then came the first rumors of mass suicide. I knew then that my mother and brother were dead.

"That night I cried most for my mother. I let our dog sleep in the house that night. She had been sick and at about four in the morning she started vomiting on the downstairs rug. I was too scared to go and let her out of the house. I absolutely couldn't move. My eyes were glued to the curtains looking for oncoming headlights. Finally, at about six, as it started getting light, I woke my husband and told him that I was going to let the dog out and not to mistake me for someone else and shoot me. He didn't appreciate being awakened for that message. He slept with a loaded gun in the bedroom closet. That gun had been at the ready since Debbie's escape in May."

An hour later Laurence Layton called Annalisa; a friend had just telephoned him to say that the Sunday newspapers were reporting Larry as dead. Her father was grief-stricken. "God, what can I do?" he kept repeating. He finally said he would get into the tub and take a bath, and hung up. Annalisa was terrified that her father was going to commit suicide. It was cold and wintry early that Sunday morning; Davis was completely fogged in. It would take her hours just to settle her children and drive to Berkeley.

Frantically, she telephoned her brother Tom in Los Angeles and asked him to fly up. He had a San Jose State University car, however, and had to drive it back up to return it. Then she called Joe Corse, one of Dr. Layton's closest friends, who lived in Lafayette. She told Joe that her father needed someone with him as quickly as possible. Joe replied that he couldn't get over there for a couple of hours, until he had driven his wife to work. Annalisa tried another of her father's friends, Marge Cump, who lived in Walnut Creek, but Marge's line was busy. Moments later, Joe called back to say that his wife had found another ride, and that he was on his way.

Meanwhile, Tom had reached Marge and she had agreed to hurry to his father's house. Then Tom quickly telephoned his father and kept him on the phone while Marge was en route from Walnut Creek, twenty miles away. When Marge arrived, she found Dr. Layton curled up in the fetal position in the bathtub, the telephone receiver to his ear, listening to Tom. She couldn't get him out. He just wanted to curl up and die.

Debbie and John had spent the night with two of Annalisa's friends. After telling her children what she thought had happened in Guyana, Annalisa hurried to her friends' house, making certain that she was not being followed. She parked a block away and walked to the house, looking carefully all around her. As soon as Annalisa walked through the door, one of her friends put an arm around her. As she would discover over the next few weeks, when her friends didn't know what to say to her about the tragedy they said nothing. That was fine with Annalisa. A quiet hug, she felt, said it all.

Debbie and John were in a flurry of activity. There were constant telephone calls from their friends, from their lawyers, from the "Today" show, which wanted to fly a reporter in for a live interview. Annalisa listened and watched all this activity, consciously delaying the drive to her father's house in Berkeley. She knew he needed her, but she did not know if she could cope with his needs on top of all that she expected to transpire that day. Even before the news was out, she was certain that everyone in Jonestown had committed suicide, and that it was only a matter of time before they received official word.

She telephoned her father's house about 11 A.M. Debbie had suggested that Annalisa tell Marge not to let her father answer the phone, in case the State Department called with confirmation of Lisa's and Larry's deaths. When Annalisa told this to Marge, Marge burst into tears. She told Annalisa that Dr.

Jim Jones *(center)* being told by the Parks family that they wanted to leave Jonestown *(Courtesy Greg Robinson/San Francisco Examiner)*

That same last day at Jonestown, members of the colony looking on just moments after Leo Ryan was attacked by Sly *(Courtesy Greg Robinson/San Francisco Examiner)*

Defectors climbing aboard the airport truck, with Larry
Layton *(circled)* in the rear *(Courtesy Greg Robinson/San
Francisco Examiner)*

View from the truck leaving Jonestown *(Courtesy Greg
Robinson/San Francisco Examiner)*

Larry in Georgetown, under arrest (*Courtesy Eric Meskauskas/San Francisco Examiner*)

Larry at his first trial in Georgetown (*Courtesy Lee Romero/San Francisco Examiner*)

Christmas 1978, one month after the Jonestown holocaust

Layton needed his children with him. Annalisa reluctantly agreed, went home to pick up a frozen casserole, and drove to her father's house.

She walked into her father's living room about two hours later. He was lying on the couch. Dr. Phyllis Newman, an old family friend from Johns Hopkins who was also a psychologist, was sitting beside him, holding his hand. Marge and Joe were watching quietly. Annalisa said hello to everyone and reintroduced herself to Phyllis, whom she had not seen for twenty years. Annalisa launched into a discussion about a scientific project she was working on in her lab. This perked her father up and he started talking about projects he was working on. But after about forty-five minutes, he broke down in tears. "My God, my God, what am I going to do?" he cried.

The group decided that it would be best to take a walk. It was drizzling rain when they started out, and a downpour when they came back an hour later. Before entering the house, Phyllis and Annalisa talked privately for a few moments. Phyllis reported that Dr. Layton had mentioned many times that day that he knew the worst was yet to come, but he did not mention the possibility of Larry's death to Phyllis. Annalisa said that her father had mentioned it to her as early as seven that morning. Phyllis seemed amazed; she said that he had not mentioned it to her, and that she had been going on the assumption that he did not know. She asked Annalisa how she was, but Annalisa didn't know what she meant. It took her a while to realize that she had been so worried about her father that she had given no thought to her own feelings.

At a certain point everyone in the living room would be talking animatedly. Moments later, everyone would be asleep. At one point Annalisa left a calm room and returned in less than sixty seconds to a room full of tears. That day Dr. Layton received over fifty phone calls from his friends all over the United States. Annalisa took the calls. Each conveyed a message of love and sympathy. "I wish there was something that I could say or do to help," many of the callers said. After each, Annalisa would tell her father who had called. Often his reaction was: "Oh my God, he knows too. Everyone knows this terrible thing." Annalisa tried to tell him that these calls were out of love and friendship, but she believed that her father felt they were for gossip and finger-pointing.

Annalisa also talked at some length on the phone with Leah

Tow, Karen Layton's mother. Mrs. Tow cried and cried. She was alone at home, her husband and daughter having gone out for the day. She had already had at least one massive heart attack, and she seemed on the verge of another. Annalisa tried to calm her down by suggesting that Lisa and Karen were as close as any mother and daughter, and that she was certain that both had supported and helped each other to the end. Perhaps they could find some comfort in that, Annalisa said. Mrs. Tow cried some more, expressing her conviction that Karen was such a devoted follower of Jones that she had probably been the first to take the cyanide.

Tom arrived in the early evening. He took over the phone, and hooked up an answering machine. At about eight o'clock Marge's daughter called and said that she had just heard on the news that Larry had been arrested. Annalisa went to the living room with the news; she was so happy with this knowledge that Larry was alive she could barely contain herself. Her father's reaction was, "There are some things worse than death." Dr. Layton repeated that theme often in the next several weeks, but Annalisa responded with "He's alive and therefore there's hope for him. He may need a lot of help, but at least he's getting a second chance."

The family went to bed at about nine o'clock, drained, exhausted, but also somewhat relieved. Tom and Annalisa were to sleep downstairs. Dr. Layton was meticulous about getting them enough blankets, pillow cases, and sheets. Tom and Annalisa took the telephone, radio, and television into one of the downstairs bedrooms. As soon as their father went to bed, they turned on the television. They were both anxious to hear the news, since Dr. Layton had asked that the television and radio be kept off in the house that day.

The late news confirmed the fact that Larry had been arrested at the airstrip, and reported that he had injured some person or persons in the smaller of the two airplanes before a gun was wrestled away from him. Annalisa and Tom knew in their hearts that Larry was not responsible for Leo Ryan's death, or any other death. When the television news was over they turned on the radio to listen to a phone-in program on Jonestown and the Peoples Temple. They recognized John's voice calling in around midnight. When he tried to talk about his parents and his little sister who were probably dead in Jonestown, he broke down in tears.

"From what Debbie had told us over the past six months," Annalisa recalls, "we all knew that the suicide was so finely tuned and well rehearsed that there would be no survivors. We knew our mother and our relatives were dead well before the tally was final." Confirmation of the mass suicide would be reported the following day.

Annalisa was afraid again that night that someone from the Peoples Temple might try to murder them. She planned where she would hide in her father's house if she heard any unusual sounds. She and Tom listened to the radio late into the night. She finally ended up sleeping on the floor in Tom's room. It reminded her of her childhood, sharing a room with a sibling when she was scared.

The following day Annalisa returned to her home in Davis. During the next four days she visited with Debbie and John, but most of the time she stayed glued to the radio. Twice a day she telephoned the State Department to ask whether they could confirm her mother's or Phil Blakey's death. She also tried to get information on Larry, but as far as the State Department was concerned he did not exist. Phil, however, was reported alive: He had been in Trinidad on the *Marceline*, the Temple boat, at the time of the suicides.

The happy news of Phil was countered for Debbie by word that Annie Moore, John and Barbara Moore's youngest daughter, had died on November 18 with a bullet through her brain. Annie had been one of Debbie's closest friends during her Davis High School days. She had come to Jonestown as a nurse, and Debbie supposed that she had helped dispense the poisoned fruit drink before taking her own life.

A few days later, Annalisa heard on the radio that an old woman with white hair named Hyacinthia Prathke had been found alive; she had slept through it all. Annalisa had the dim hope that the person was her mother, that Lisa had not wanted anyone to know her name, and so had given this other name to the authorities. Annalisa spent three days sitting in her kitchen looking at the walls, waiting for some word that this last, faint hope might become a reality.

The day before Thanksgiving, Tom and his father were watching the news when Larry appeared on the screen, barefoot and handcuffed, being led to his arraignment. Dr. Layton broke down and started talking again about committing suicide. The image of his brother also affected Tom deeply. He wrote in his journal that day: "Seeing Larry I could no longer hold the events at arm's length. I felt tears coming on. I decided to break down, feeling that a show of emotion from me would tell Dad that I really needed him. He needs to feel wanted, and we kids while growing up did not show much overt affection to him because we were showered by too much concern/affection/interference/love from him. I tried to explain this to him in tears, shaking, and he seemed to snap out of his depressed daze. Later, I heard him tell a friend who phoned that he had to help Tom and the rest of us through this. The ploy—my controlled breakdown—seems to have worked, at least so far."

The family observed Thanksgiving at Dr. Layton's house. Around the table were Dr. Layton, Tom, Debbie, John, Annalisa and her husband, Ray, and their two children. The dinner was quiet and sad. Just before everyone sat down to eat, a television crew arrived to photograph the house as part of a news feature they were preparing on Larry. The family stayed away from the windows, but John went outside to tell the photographer that he hoped the man would be able to live with himself for what he was doing to the family's Thanksgiving dinner.

When the dinner was over, Annalisa and her family returned to Davis. Debbie and John stayed in hiding. Tom remained with his father until almost Christmas. He stayed because he was still worried that his father would commit suicide if he were left alone. Dr. Layton had been talking about it from the day he learned of the Jonestown suicides. Once, when he mentioned his intention to Annalisa, she reminded him that Larry had killed no one, but would face a long and difficult recovery from what he had gone through. If her father killed himself, then that would be one death on Larry's conscience, and a hindrance to his recovery. Her father seemed to agree. He said that although he would rather be dead, he would stay alive for Larry.

The day after Thanksgiving Debbie and John returned to Dr. Layton's house to say that they had learned from Grace Stoen that Lisa had not died in the Temple's mass suicide, but had succumbed to cancer two or three weeks earlier. For the family it was a relief to know that Lisa had died still believing that the Temple's social experiment was viable, and before the escalating insanity that marked the last weeks of Jonestown. Dr. Layton cried, "Poor Lisa. My poor little Lisa."

Afterword

In the fall of 1979, the courts annulled Debbie Layton's marriage to Phil Blakey. In March of 1980, Debbie married John Collins. Both are currently working in the San Francisco financial community.

On May 5, 1980, Larry Layton went on trial in Guyana on two counts of attempted murder. He was tried for discharging a loaded firearm at two of the Jonestown defectors in the Cessna, Vern Gosney and Monica Bagby, and wounding them, with intent to commit murder. Vern Gosney flew down to Guyana and testified against Layton; Monica Bagby did not. On May 23, Larry was found innocent on both charges. The jury, reflecting Guyana's ethnic diversity, included six blacks, four East Indians, one Chinese, and one white. After deliberating for two and a half hours, the jury voted 12 to 0 for acquittal on the charge of attempted murder of Bagby, and 10 to 2 for acquittal on the charge of attempted murder of Gosney.

Tom Layton went to Guyana in May to be with his brother during the trial.

At that trial, Larry was called to the witness stand by his

attorney, Rex McKay, but he was so overcome with emotion when he mentioned his wife, Karen, that he was excused and not recalled to testify.

For the next six months Larry remained indicted in Guyana for conspiracy to murder Leo Ryan and others at the airstrip, an indictment that had been held in abeyance awaiting the outcome of the first trial. Then, in November 1980, the Guyanese court dropped the conspiracy charges and simultaneously Larry was extradicted to the United States in the custody of U.S. marshalls. He was arraigned in U.S. District Court, San Francisco, for conspiracy to murder Leo Ryan, the murder of the congressman being the only crime at the Port Kaituma airstrip for which Larry could be charged under U.S. legal jurisdiction. At the present writing, his trial is scheduled to begin May 12, 1981.

In the summer and fall of 1980, the surviving members of the family reflected on their lives and relationships with each other, and on the issues and implications raised by this book. Their dictated or written statements follow. Larry is represented by a letter constructed from several letters to his family over the past year and a half; these passages have been reordered to create the letter, but they have not been rewritten, except for the same copy editing given the other statements.

DR. LAURENCE L. LAYTON

I never was a suspicious person. I never had occasion to question or doubt or mistrust any member of my family. On that basis I didn't worry about whether I was told the truth or not. I assumed that always I was being told the truth. I felt that Lisa was always totally honest, so for all of our lives I had no suspicions about how she might secretly feel. We talked often about things and were very good friends. In fact, all her life, until joining Peoples Temple, she told me how much she appreciated being married to me and how happy she was in our marriage. I do admit that the fact that I was not a passionate person did bother her a bit.

However, the impression of our marriage that one gets from this book is entirely from Lisa's introspective statements written to herself. She would sometimes have feelings of guilt and inadequacy, and she would write them out. And in so doing she projected them onto me. Although these letters were written to herself, they were to me also, and I saved them.

It was after she joined Peoples Temple that Lisa in a sense rewrote her emotional feelings about our marriage. Lisa did feel an inadequacy about her education, and she was very conscious of it when we were in university society. She did not have the formal education and degrees that the other faculty wives had, but in fact she was far better educated than most of them, and she read more than they. But Lisa seemed to feel most comfortable with women who were not highly educated.

I felt a great deal of affection for Lisa. Late in our marriage we had a lot of fun camping. We took walks together arm in arm. It was only later that she told the children and others that I was a terrible person, but this was revisionist history written to justify her divorce. Right up to the time she joined the Temple, Lisa always felt a great concern for divorced people: How unhappy they must be; how terrible their lives must be. She perceived divorced people to be unnatural and strange. Lisa remained gentle and open for about the first six months she was in the Temple. It was only after she decided to leave me that she became secretive, to have a secret bank account, and to hide money. It was then that she began telling others that she didn't trust me. I was hurt by this. In her whole life with me there was no reason why she shouldn't trust me.

It was I who invited Lisa's father, Hugo Philip, to visit in 1970, 1973, and 1974. I knew that Lisa did not want him around, but he was an old man, more than ninety years old, and I projected onto him the feelings I would have had if I were an old man and my children didn't like me. Lisa was angered at my invitation to Hugo, and this is one of the few things that bothered me about Lisa: her willingness to cast aside people and to have no feeling at all for them.

I've learned from my own grief that it is sometimes necessary to short-circuit grief. Lisa learned to do that when forced to leave Germany and when she lost her friends in Nazi concentration camps. I would have mourned for weeks and weeks, but she did not break down, she took it in her stride. She had learned to drop people from her life, as she was later to do with her father, and finally even with half of her family when she went to Guyana.

For Lisa I still feel great grief for a lovely, intelligent, and very loving person. She had sought her "Beloved," this ideal of hers, and as far as she was concerned she had found him, until Jim Jones came onto the scene. Lisa and I were dreaming of retirement and the purchase of a camper. She wanted to drive from Alaska to Honduras. She picked out the camper only a few months before she began attending Peoples Temple.

I must admit that early in our marriage I was shocked to learn of her relationships with two former lovers, and whenever the subject came up I felt very bad. Sometimes she would insult me about it, saying "Oh, it's just your ego." That was not the way to handle it with someone of my conservative upbringing. Late in the summer of 1942, she told me that she didn't want me to kiss her anymore; she said it turned her stomach. Six months later she decided that she did want me to kiss her, but by then I was uptight and embarrassed at showing affection openly. I was now reluctant to do it ... at least I didn't initiate it. Perhaps these were things she carried over from her German upbringing.

Early in our marriage there was another thing that concerned me. We would take walks, and I noticed that she would step on the ants. "My God, what do you do that for?" I asked. She said, "It's strange, but in Germany I learned to hate weak things. I can't help myself." Things like this shocked me. I did not hold them against Lisa because she became a loving, considerate, kind person and got over this attitude.

It troubles me that this book has lost sight of all the beautiful things that characterized our relationship for over thirty years. Lisa has been portrayed in one dimension as a happy free spirit captured and abused by me. We both had flaws, but only mine are described. At the end of our marriage it was I who tried for reconciliation. Her lawyer told her that she was supposed to attempt a reconciliation before a divorce would be granted. She came to me and said, "I'm supposed to ask you if you would like to call this off and start over. If so, would you object to my being totally in the Temple as I presently am?" "I wouldn't like that," I answered. "That's what I thought you'd say," she replied. That was her attempt at reconciliation. She simply went through the motions. Even that I didn't hold against her....I didn't appear in court, and in the settlement of the estate I didn't even get a lawyer. And during this whole time I thought that Lisa would probably change her mind. I didn't realize how poisoned my family was against me. When she wanted to marry me she told me, "I'll never let you down." I reminded her of this. "Well I never did," she answered. "After all, I didn't for thirty years," as if that absolved all commitments.

After this I still thought of reconciliation, and even of seduction and reconciliation by way of passion. . . . I tried, and the way I had been brought up, that was a pretty long way to go. Afterwards, she actually told people that I had tried to get her to go to bed with me; and she boasted to her friends that she didn't need men.

I wanted to at least remain her friend, but she wouldn't even allow that. I never questioned her goodness or her motives, and now after reading this book I am shocked beyond belief to learn the things that Lisa said about me, and to learn that she tried to take advantage of problems in Annalisa's marriage to bring Annalisa into the Temple. I cannot believe that that was the Lisa I knew. We now know that Lisa died ultimately of cancer of the brain; and we know that cancer of the lung does metastasize that way very early. Consequently, I believe that Lisa was the victim of three things. First, the cancer did affect her brain toward the end of our marriage, and this altered her thinking and her emotions. Second, she was afraid of loneliness and death. She repeatedly spoke of how the Temple took care of its old people. She wanted love; she wanted people to need her; and she needed to be constantly reassured of that. Meanwhile her fear of death was met by Jones' promise to cure her. Third, she believed that she could do a great deal of good through the Temple.

How does all this affect me today? Well, first it makes me very much afraid of any commitment, of any associations, and of becoming too emotionally dependent on my children or my grandchildren. I have the feeling that nobody cares anything about me except my mother, and that I must face up to this. I must not form dependencies in relationships, based on family, blood, or love. I fear these will force me to come up against things that I will be unable to cope with as I get older. So I am afraid now of intimate, close, or even loving relationships. I have decided to become a hedonist. All of the efforts that I have made in my past life to be straight and honorable have come to nothing. My grandfather once said that "A good name is to be chosen rather than great riches." Well, I chose a good name, and look what has happened to it. My own children are ashamed to say, "Oh, my dad is Laurence Layton." Up to the time of Peoples Temple this was a very honorable name, respected in West Virginia, in the Departments of Defense and Agriculture and Public Health, in the Academy of Allergy, and in science. It's as if everything I have done that was right in my life has been ridiculed by a generation that has values completely different from mine. I don't know what to do about it except to honor my responsibilities. I feel that I have but a short time to live. My brother and sister, both younger than I, died within one month in 1980. My mother is dying. My family has rejected me. My wife is gone. My life has been destroyed. The only thing left for me is to try to enjoy the time I have; to attend parties, to dance, to travel, to seek love. These are things through which I can forget. I will try to drown my sorrow in activity, and I can only hope that I will die in my sleep. I will attempt to write, to do scientific work, and to philosophize, but Peoples Temple has effectively destroyed me. I don't even have a family. The Temple has left me with nothing.

As for the children, it seems that a lot of the dislike toward me that they express in this book is really hatred toward parents who were trying to block, stop, or hold back the tide of the collapse of our traditional morality during the 1960s and 1970s. And this is probably characteristic of any father or mother brought up in the times and in the situation in which I was brought up. Most such parents would make the attempt as I did, and it was truly an honorable attempt. Throughout history parents have controlled their children and attempted to mold them to get them into society as the next generation. But today we have allowed an aberration of this process to take over. We have allowed peer-group pressure to become more powerful than any other force of society. During the 1960s and 1970s, ten-year-olds came to have more influence on other ten-year-olds, and those younger, than did all other elements of society combined. The only salvation, it seemed to me, was to physically remove one's children from this urban media-bolstered peer group. I lost out because I trusted my kids. I waited too long before sending Debbie to Quaker school in England. I never suspected that Debbie and Larry were getting into the mischief that they were. I felt that we were a communicating family, that our Quaker upbringing would carry us over. For that reason I didn't protect myself. I knew that Larry had problems, but I thought that the love and support that I had given him were self-evident. He knew that I cared for him. But I could not overcome the drug-induced fantasies or memories of things that never happened that came to fill his mind. I was helpless to communicate any further with Larry. He dreamed of things in his acid-head that I had done to him that I would never have dreamed of doing. He projected onto me his own insane fantasies. Then Jim Jones appeared and encouraged those fantasies. Larry drew Debbie into the Temple not because he was evil, but because he was convinced that Jim Jones was real. But that Larry would put up with a man like Jones, doing the things that Jones did, is a shock to me. Larry had role models. None of the men or boys that Larry knew while growing up would ever have dreamed of doing the things that Jones did to his so-called flock. I cannot understand why Larry and Debbie did not face up to Jones for what he was.

I believe that no one in this family has ever thought that anything done to me was unfair or something to feel bad about. I was the lowest man on the whole totem pole. Mistakes that I made were held against me even after I corrected them. I went with the Army and became involved in chemical warfare, but no one seems to realize that I got out of the Defense Department, that I did go back into medicine and did achieve the greater part of my reputation from my career in medical research. So in this book I appear as the *scheitpoke*—the scapegoat—the fool. But really, at the final end, what do we have? Their world collapses and I'm the only person left to support and to defend this family . . . and nobody admits it. I'm still the ridiculous figure, and that's the way I come out in this book. Whatever good I have done in my life has been ridiculed, and the evil I have done through my own ignorance is all that comes through. To my family I am still a fool. I am the one person who does not matter. They can take my documents, they can take my words and their mother's letters to me; they can take innuendo, and they can take gossip. They can take anything and turn it against me. I become sort of a goddamn fool. In some way I am made to appear as the culprit of this whole ugly story.

As for Laurence John, of course I love him, and I will do everything in my power to defend him and to save him from a useless life of remorse by whatever means I can work out. Perhaps this book will help. I will allow it to be published so that my family will not look at me and say, "If only our dad had done thus and so." . . . I will give them that, but apparently nothing else I have matters: not my love, my character, the reputation that I have personally earned. Nothing matters to my family. They can write a book and imagine things about me and suddenly these things stand as fact when they don't represent me at all.

So, how do I feel about all of this? I feel that I wish I could run away; if only I could die before I wake up some morning. Anything to escape from a generation that has turned itself against decency. I feel that Larry and I are the real prisoners of Guyana. Hopefully he may pull through. . .

In retrospect, I can't say that I would have done anything differently if I were to relive the past forty years. I did what I did because that was the way I was brought up. I was true to my values. I do, however, think that I would have demonstrated more affection. But, you know, my children are inconsistent in their criticisms of me. On the one hand they say I smothered them with affection, and on the other they say I was a dictator. Their inconsistency is that on the one hand they say that I really didn't care about them while at the same time they admit that I overwhelmed them with affection.

There are other possible interpretations that have gone undiscussed in this book. Perhaps you should reread Lisa's early diary musings in which she questioned whether she was fit to be a mother. Maybe she wasn't. . . I don't agree with that interpretation, but I was uneasy throughout our marriage that she might not be strong enough to hold out for the eternal values against the negative forces of society in raising our children. Perhaps she did break. Perhaps the family would have run to destruction irrespective of anything that I might have done, and in some way perhaps I sensed it very early. The thought frightens me. Perhaps I was frightened from the beginning that given her values, her situation ethics, she might compromise. . . . And in the end that is what she did.

How do I see my children, as they were and as they are now? I see in my son Tom a boy who has been happy, who has been able to do things, and who certainly felt himself loved by all members of the family, friends, neighbors. As a consequence he has always felt very secure. He has always been able to do anything he has wanted to do. He trained himself to use his hands as a carpenter, a mechanic, and a musician. He had the right role model at home, the right intellectual life, the right books, the right ideas, the right discussions. All of my children had these, but Tom picked them up and went with them on his own. I really didn't want him to take a Ph.D. I thought it was too difficult a course. I wanted him to take a medical degree, with which he could be very useful, happy, and successful financially. He didn't want to go that way. He went his own way and he did it on his own. I feel that at times he has been near the breaking point, but his dad has tried to help him through those situations. The boy takes the credit for everything—of course. Kids do that. On the other hand he deserves credit for a lot. He could have sat back because it was possible to have an easier life than he chose. He has matured greatly. Perhaps this Peoples Temple interlude has matured him more than anything else. He visited the Temple, but he could not become involved because of a defect in his personality: he *couldn't subordinate himself*. That's considered a defect in modern society. Maybe that was the defect that saved him . . . just like the sickle-cell defect makes black Africans immune to malaria.

I am shocked at Annalisa. I feel that Annalisa doesn't seem to have as much wisdom about people as I thought she had. She has scientific ability similar to other scientists, but the kinds of things she said about herself and about the family and the lack of insight into how people were really thinking and feeling surprises me. I am happy that she was willing to help Debbie to get out of Guyana and disappointed that she isn't more interested in helping Larry. Yet I can see that she is married to a brilliant man who wishes to hell that his family was not involved in any of this. So she really can't do very much about it. In the long term I think that Annalisa will be far more cautious than she might have been about allowing her kids to come under the influence of peers, particularly in seeing how easily she was swayed herself. I had always thought that Annalisa was more cool and scientific in things. And I look at Lisa's behavior in all of this with amazement, that she would try to seduce Annalisa into that cult when she knew that it would destroy Annalisa's marriage. That is not the Lisa I knew. The description of the woman of Peoples Temple is not of Lisa Philip.

I think that Larry will come out of all of this as a liberal person. He will always remain interested in the problems of out-of-luck, hard-up people. He has become much more introspective, more philosophical, and he has become a reader, whereas before he was a listener to Jones. I believe that he will become more critical in the future . . . he will never again be as easily swayed as he once was. Should he ever get through with the charges against him he will have other problems, but I doubt that he will ever be tempted again by a cult. As for his relations with the rest of the family, I think there is really nothing left for him but family, particularly at this time. We must be careful not to overwhelm him with family, but for him that is the only place to start. It's as if he must grow up again. As for me, I'm still resentful, and I must be careful to control that resentment.

As for Larry's future, I see difficulties because of things that he has created and things that the Temple has created for him. I believe that for him the tragedy has to be a growth situation. He has learned a great deal about human nature and his own gullibility, and about faith in people. He will be far more critical in the future, though I think that the mark against him is so great that he will face terrible obstacles; and his own feeling of guilt may come back to haunt him. Certainly I must be careful not to add to it in any way. I will have to assume that I have a child who is somewhat crippled—who has an impediment, an emotional impediment. For him I can only pray that he will pull through with understanding and love . . . and if he is not guilty, with that knowledge to fortify him. I love him very much, and I have always identified with him, more so than the other children, mostly because he had emotional troubles as a child just as I had. He suffered much as I did, and I feel a special empathy bond with him.

Debbie received so much attention as a little girl that she developed a need for attention as an adult. Lisa was concerned about Debbie when she got her first job in 1958. She was quite uneasy about the hour that Debbie would be alone, but she took the job anyway. The job meant very little economically, but Lisa needed to get out of the house. Eventually, after the older children left, Debbie sought attention by erratic behavior—anything for attention. Lisa and I suspected nothing until Debbie was fourteen, when Lisa claimed that Debbie was lying. I remember once saying to Lisa in Debbie's presence that I couldn't believe that Debbie would deliberately lie . . . and Debbie chimed in "Well, maybe I might," letting me in on the secret that she might already be off on the wrong track.

Debbie is now in control of her own life, and I think it was this need to have that control that brought her out of Peoples Temple . . . in a sense she is much like Tom and me. She can't submit to someone else. She will always be a rebel. Lisa was a rebel too, but in a different way from me. I think that Debbie will be a conservative upper-middle-class homemaker . . . and I think that someday she too will be as frightened as her father was, but Debbie will know what to watch for and what to expect from her own children.

Often I can't help but think about John and Barbara Moore. They were a part of our extended family; they are victims just as I am. But there is a great contrast between them and me. Under no circumstances could I have allowed Jim Jones and my daughter to live together under my roof. There you have the Christlike Reverend John Moore and the puritan, Laurence Layton. They coped very differently. Perhaps John coped better than I did. I know that John Moore's involvement in Peoples Temple impressed Lisa. She would often tell me that John approved of this or that Temple action and that he had fully investigated the organization. John Moore's vocal and written support gave Jim Jones both credibility and protection from attack. After all, "Would Doctor John Moore knowingly support the Antichrist?" I remain troubled that John has never publicly acknowledged that Debbie was not a liar when she described Jonestown in her affidavit to the State Department, as I remain troubled that Charles Garry's letter to the San Francisco *Chronicle*, vilifying Debbie and quoting from both John and Barbara on the wonderful "truth" about Jim Jones and Jonestown, is still unretracted.

My hope is that from all of this the kids will learn that there must be communication, there must be expressed love. It must be shown. And this is especially true for little ones who don't know. They look at the big people as gods, and whatever these big creatures say stands. Adults can feed you, they can clean you, they can move you around. They can mold you pretty much as they want you to be irrespective of your genes. And a parent must realize that this is the attitude of the child. I never realized that as I grew up. I was not brought up by a father. I look at my family and I look at myself and I see that part of my trouble has been that I have tried to give my children what I lacked in my own childhood. I was an "eight-year-old's father." That was my age when my father, my role model, died. So when my children were about eight I was a pretty good father, but when they got to be twelve, I was still an eight-year-old's father. I had never known a father after I was eight. From that age on I was deprived of any close interaction with a man. My grandfather, my uncles, they all looked down their noses at me, and I grew up with a tremendous inferiority complex which I was determined to overcome. So I overcompensated. But what I never learned was how a child should feel toward a parent—because I never had one. Perhaps, had my father lived, I would have learned to anticipate rejection by my children because I myself might have broken with the beliefs and attitudes of my own father. But that was not to be, and I was unprepared for my own children's rejection of me.

My father was not upset by many things. He overcame problems by being ahead of them. But my grandfather held on to the old ideas. He brought me up to see the old ways as the only ways. "There are eternal verities," he would say. These were industry, commitment, loyalty, honesty, chastity. Even if there were no people left in the world, these other values would sit out there in the universe. So that when the fishing worms would evolve into primates a billion years from now, those same truths would be there for them to be governed by. My grandfather believed in a Creator with absolute values. And whatever is created must accept those values, be he a fishing worm or a man. I have not abandoned these old values, though I have abandoned an uptight attitude about rather trivial matters, such as whether unmarried people make love or not.

Today sometimes I feel like the Rock of Gibraltar. Storms, waves, and currents beat against my feet; birds and monkeys defecate on me, they tunnel through me. But I'm still there. There is no value judgment—it's not good, it's not bad. Gibraltar is just there. I happened to have been born; I happened to have a wife and four children, and I'm just that "thing" that had "those things." So after they sail off into the ocean on their ships, and weather the storms, they come back and park on me and say "Well, one thing's certain, it's not going to blow away."

I functioned in the only way that I knew how to function— as husband, parent, scientist, wage earner, taxpayer, and law-abiding citizen. My family reacted not against me, but against all of the old traditionalist things that I represented. As far as I'm concerned I am an anachronism. I'm out of the seventeenth and eighteenth centuries. I am more Sarah Beirne's child than I am her great-grandchild.

ANNALISA LAYTON VALENTINE

What effect has this ten-year involvement with Peoples Temple had on me? When only Larry was in the group I just ignored the situation. From his description it seemed to be no more than an encounter group where problems were worked out publicly and the members were devoted to a common liberal cause.

When Debbie joined she seemed to find something that made her want to get her life into order. It pulled her out of her nose dive. I knew then about the healing aspects. I didn't even begin to believe any of it, but I figured that for Debbie it was doing more good than harm.

It was only with Mom's conversion that the Temple had a profound influence on my life. During her and my involvement I could not accept what I was hearing, yet I couldn't fully reject it either. I had no "neutral" party to discuss it with; besides, I'm not at all good at discussing emotional or sensitive issues.

I felt a tremendous emotional release when I made my break from Peoples Temple after a four- to six-month involvement, yet I still carried a lot of strain and uncertainty. I knew I'd never go near the group again, but I feared they would do something to harm my life, or my family's life. I was physically but not psychologically free from the Jim Jones charisma (or curse). This fear faded with time. It was three years between my involvement and the suicides. However, I never felt truly free until Debbie's escape from Guyana and her confirmation of the fact that Jones was a crazy criminal. My mother's un-wavering belief and persuasive arguments were what kept a seed of belief alive in my mind. I saw only fear and intimidation in the Temple, but for her to want so desperately for me to be in it I felt I must have, in some way, misread Jim Jones.

So, it all ended, and the question is, where did it leave me?

I'd say I have a great disillusionment with "causes." I was what you would call a "knee-jerk liberal." Anything for the poor, the oppressed was worth my vote. I still feel that time, effort, and resources are needed to go in this direction, but I distrust any leader whose strength comes from his causes.

"Question authority" is a rule I have for both myself and my children. If I tell them to do something, or not to do something, and they can convince me I'm wrong, I'll change my mind. The answer "because I said so" can be used only on rare and necessary occasions. I look at how Jim Jones ruled lives autocratically, and I look at children who are taught they must always obey their parents' demands, and I shudder. Children must be taught that we all make a lot of mistakes, even parents, even ministers. And even the youngest child has the right to make some of his own decisions.

The effect Peoples Temple has had upon me personally is less than what it has done to my marriage. An affair would have been far more easily forgiven. My involvement with this book is seen by my husband as a continuation of my Temple involvement. He wants it out of our lives 100 percent. With this book, and Larry's predicament, I worry if that will ever happen. My husband was the major force that kept me from getting more than marginally involved in Peoples Temple back in 1975; he wouldn't let me just up and leave with the children. But still now during many arguments, Peoples Temple, like an ex-lover, will rear its ugly head. Ray and I have yet to discuss the hows and whys of my involvement, although I'm sure he has a pretty clear idea of what was happening. Again, perhaps this book will serve that purpose.

Peoples Temple hasn't had too great an effect on my relationship with Tom, Debbie, and Larry. It has made Dad less able to handle criticism, and me more critical, so that hasn't jibed too well. He phoned me yesterday to tell me that tomorrow, July 14, is Mom's birthday. I said, it "would have been" her birthday. He said it "is," and so it went. For me she is dead and I have lovely memories of the fine mother and human being she was. Dad dwells so much in the past, on his losses and lack of any future, that I am at a total loss to deal with him. On one hand I feel like I have a responsibility to help him through it, yet I also know that he is the only one who can do it, and it will take a great deal of effort on his part. Debbie is the one who can cope with his moods and crying without any criticism. I am thankful that she is living near him (and that she is living).

Tom and I were quite close through college, but were both poor correspondents when we moved to different areas. Since my March 1978 letter from Debbie, stating her intention to escape, Tom and I have stayed in very close contact, to the point of knowing each other's day-to-day activities. I have watched and understood Tom's academic and personal interest in pursuing the Layton-Philip family roots and watching the family evolve through this crisis. I know that many people will look upon this book as a selling of privacy, or money made on people's interest in gossip and perversion. I know that it was conceived well before the November 18 tragedy as an anthropological study, a personal probe, and a literary foray. I hope the quality of the book will reflect such a concern.

I still feel the same solidarity with Tom that I felt in our youth. I know that Dad sees Tom as cold and calculating (Tom's description). This description stems from Tom's taking notes (keeping a diary) on events and relationships since Debbie's escape. I see it as Tom, typically Tom, immersed in a project. I see it going from arrowheads to sharks' teeth to coins, cars, instruments, archaeological digs, teaching, and now to "who am I and why am I?" He is collecting raw data and hoping for the answer to appear when it is collated.

Also, I think it is asking a lot for a father and thirty-seven-year-old son to be friends, real friends. I'm sure it happens in some families, but there are too many negative factors in existence in most cases. The Oedipal complex is a force to be reckoned with, to say nothing of parental respect, adult-child relationships, expectations, and so on. A child starts very early sorting out what he wants his parents to know about his personal life and feelings. That attitude does not change. By the same token, a child does not want to know the depths of the parent's soul—at age ten, twenty, or forty (perhaps at fifty). Mom used to tell me that the person least capable of handling a teenager is the parent. There are too many emotional undercurrents.

These, I think, are some of the undercurrents that make real adult friendships between parents and children so difficult. However, the less authoritarian the parent, I would guess, the greater the chance of adult friendship. I would like to see some statistics on the matter.

Back to my relationships, now with Debbie. Being eight years older, I filled that nonauthoritarian role described above, and we have remained close friends. We can now interact as equals (not big sister–little sister). Her life with John in the world of money and finance is leading her in quite a different direction from mine in science and homemaking, but there is a strong bond of love that will keep us close.

Debbie has had a lot of rough realities to live with since her teen years. Her mind saw one set of values, but her life portrayed another. She was uncomfortable about Peoples Temple when she was in the group, and even more uncomfortable about exposing her role once she came out. She was somewhat naïve in undertaking this book to believe that she could maintain her privacy, something which she has come to value quite highly. I respect the difficult decisions she has had to make in allowing so much of her personal life to be exposed. Her strong desire to keep her present married life away from public scrutiny has met with harsh criticism from Min and Tom, who see it as a necessary conclusion to the story. It's at the point now where the writing of this book is having a greater effect on our lives than Peoples Temple ever did. It is actively changing personal relationships within the family. It's forcing honest feelings and hitherto unfelt feelings to the surface. Whether this is for the good or bad of each of us is yet to be seen.

Any change in my relationship with Larry would be hard to define. I was not close to him during the Temple years. My letters to him during his imprisonment show a no-holds-barred catharsis on my part. This was because I felt that he needed to feel in touch with some human life, to know that normal occurrences were going on in the outside world, and perhaps someday he too could be satisfied to fill his mind with mundane things like when the Swiss chard would bolt to seed or actual versus estimated mileage on a VW van. I don't think I could show the same candor with Larry in person that I showed in my letters. That has just never been our relationship.

Any real help Larry gets with his problems, whatever they are, must come from outside the family. We, the family, can only be supportive of Larry the person, but in that support I think we all have to step back and let him make his own decisions and get control over his own life. We can't "send" him to a psychiatrist. We have to hope that he realizes the need and will pursue it himself. Or perhaps he believes that he can cope with his past on his own by getting back into the mainstream. A firm belief is what it will take.

LAURENCE J. LAYTON

Dear Family,

I find the most therapeutic thing in my case (after good food) is interest in things and people other than myself. Therefore, please expect no histories. At the moment food plays a more important role in my mental life. I do, however, hope that the following will help you in your writing effort.

Having failed the third grade, I was always tormented with feelings of inferiority as a child. Despite this, once I learned to read in the third grade I became very much interested in the news, current events, politics, and race relations. I was an outcast among the children at Indian Head and this furthered identification with blacks, peasants in South America, and so on. I thought I might become a great political reformer. I admired men like FDR and Stevenson. I followed the civil rights movement avidly. By the time we reached Berkeley I was involved in politics and hoped someday to run for office. But with the assassination of Kennedy and the events that followed I lost hope, little by little, in the ability of politics to right the world's wrongs which weighed so heavily on my prematurely adult mind.

I was always in competition with Tom who, alas, could always do everything better than I could with the exception of talking, an area in which I have always been a champ. Why the hell I always thought it was my duty to save the world would be better answered by a psychiatrist—perhaps a Jesus complex.

As a child in Indian Head the reformer Methodist pastor Reverend Gunn was a favorite of mine. At BHS [Berkeley High School] besides being president of the Young Democrats I also wrote much of our paper called *The Liberal*. I was very shy around girls and had only one girl friend in high school, she being a political nut like myself.

I publicly debated in favor of a fair housing bill while at BHS. I always enjoyed being around animals and nature and spent much time in the Sierras camping and hiking, but always with a certain loneliness that permeated most of my youth.

I admired Dad but was also afraid of him, and in a sense for him because I knew Dad had problems of his own and I tended to feel sorry for him. I often felt I was a great disappointment to him. It seemed he had me cut out to be a scientist which was not my forte. Through my youth Dad didn't really know me because he was blinded by great visions of what I was to become.

Also as a child I had great fear that people would discover I was insane and put me in an insane asylum. This fear reappeared when I entered college. With college came alcohol, an interest in psychology, sociology, and unfortunate experimentation with pharmacology. That caused me to see pot and LSD as the answers to my problems. I became further separated from straight society with its race for money, its power, and its lack of brotherhood. The draft was on my heels so I always had to study enough to stay in school, but I really was looking for a happy existence, and this after graduation led me and Carolyn, whom I loved very deeply, to head to Ukiah in search for utopia.

Getting to the subject of Peoples Temple and the family history, I really grew up a lot in terms of self-confidence after getting married to Carolyn. During the Peoples Temple years at one point I was working two jobs and still putting in time at Peoples Temple. Being in Peoples Temple wasn't always pleasant, but one had the feeling he was really doing something to advance society. Also there was a strong feeling of community—people of all races who really cared about each other.

Where did things go wrong? First, when discipline became so austere that people were afraid to speak their minds. Second, religious states of mind and politics don't mix well. The advance of democracy has coincided with increased secularization of religion. Third, power corrupts absolutely.

Peoples Temple was a paranoid scene, and most former members still suffer from the problem. They really shouldn't be made to feel harassed—history, I think, will confirm this. This is a time for healing, not revenge.

There is a lot I will never know about Peoples Temple. The only thing I can say is that it started out looking like a civil rights movement, and Jim Jones started out looking like Martin Luther King. Obviously things turned out differently.

I was a fool to leave California, but then I was a fool long before that.

If I had the recent past to live over again, I would have stayed in the United States, but now I am faced by an entirely different set of variables. I really don't know what to expect on my return to the States. It would be nice to be back in California and talk things over with you. Prison teaches one to grow up fast and discard many delusions, and face life as it is. And yet, knowing people such as you are concerned gives me the hope to continue on.

Needless to say I am homesick and look forward to seeing all of you, but I am sure this experience will make me stronger and wiser.

Tonight it is cool and cloudy, and it will probably rain. Rainy weather reminds me of my Berkeley High School days, running to catch a bus at Palmer's Drug Store. All that I have gone through teaches me greater appreciation for the simple things in life too many people take for granted. I am especially fond of rain because it helps to keep down the mosquito population. Just now I am sitting on my mattress in my cell warring with the world's most intelligent mosquitoes. Perhaps they have ESP. They anticipate my every move.

I want to thank you all for the boxes of books. I certainly won't have any excuse for leaving here ignorant. Knowing that you are standing with me gives me great strength. I have no doubt that whatever happens I will leave here stronger in the areas that count.

I am doing well and am looking forward to living a life free from the influences of the past ten years. If there is one thing that jail teaches you, it is appreciation for freedom. If there is one thing that being vilified and deserted teaches you, it is appreciation for those who stand by your side when it appears the world has turned against you. So much for my paranoia.

As for the future, this is what I often picture in my mind: how I would enjoy seeing once more a pine forest, a mountain stream, or ocean beach. I am so tired of being indoors all the time. I must find a job that enables me to be out of doors for a while to get back to normal functioning.

Eventually I would like to do a little traveling. One really can't begin to understand a place or thing until one has seen it firsthand.

You may be surprised to know I am not the only Layton in this prison. There is a Scotsman named Leighton here awaiting deportation after running away from the French Foreign Legion, a very brutal organization used mainly to put down rebellions in Francophone Africa.

I want to thank you for your constant love and support through the most difficult circumstances imaginable.

You must forgive me for my short letters. They result from a combination of factors: lack of imagination; lack of events; rarely lack of space.

In the meantime take good care of yourselves. I enjoy your letters a lot.

Your Son and Brother,
Larry

DEBORAH LAYTON

I now look back on myself as a rebellious child and on my parents as wanting to do right by me, but confused. I believe that my parents responded to me in the only way they could.

I have fond memories of my childhood and of my parents, and I do not believe that I was brought up or treated any differently by them than were my brothers and sister. The difference was merely one of timing: Being so much younger than my siblings, it was unavoidable that the nature of my childhood would be different in some ways from theirs.

The source of my need to rebel against my parents can be traced to my early childhood, when I was "darling Debbie" and my much older brothers and sister showered me with love and attention; I was the "baby," the "star," and I became quite dependent upon being the constant center of attention.

When I was ten I suddenly became an only child. Tom and Annalisa were away at school; Larry was still home, but he had discovered "girls" and his attentions were more likely to be focused upon the older girls who lived on our block, than upon me. Sure, he was still my older brother and he still took me for walks, but he could not possibly hope to fill the gap left by the departure of the others.

When Larry was gone too I was forced to find other sources of attention. So, I turned to the neighborhood and to my classmates. I soon discovered that if the neighbors and my friends were otherwise occupied and had no time for me, I could attract their attention by making up some outrageous lie that would force them to listen. That was when I began to lie.

I began to spend more and more time entertaining and thus holding the attention of my audience, and less and less time occupied with the normal activities of a preteenager such as going to school, studying, piano practice, etc. My parents were finally forced to exercise some control, and when I was thirteen they told me that I would not be allowed to go out as frequently. That was when I began to dislike them. They were attempting to cut me off from the activities which I had come to depend on as a substitute for my missing brothers and sister.

So, I connived both to punish my parents and to regain the lost attention of Tom, Annalisa, and Larry. My facility for lying served me well. I began to write to them of the mistreatment I was suffering at home and my great desire to be with them at college. This strategy worked splendidly. Soon I began to receive letters from them and was allowed to feel important once again.

By the time I reached the ninth grade at West Campus I was on a roller coaster that was dangerously out of control. I no longer knew how to behave in other than a delinquent fashion; it was easier for me to lie than to tell the truth. I was on a one-way road to juvenile hall when my parents finally decided that more unusual measures would have to be taken if the tide of my rebellion were ever to be stopped. When they enrolled me in an English Quaker boarding school I welcomed it. I was relieved to have some structure introduced into the endless free-for-all that had become my life. I was happy no longer to have to be a rebel. A few years later I joined Peoples Temple because that too gave structure to my life. But then I came to realize that I wanted a life of my own, that contrary to Jim's pronouncements it was possible to have a happy and productive life outside of the Temple. Jim's growing insanity was one of the reasons for my defection, but another was that I wanted to settle down with a husband in a house of our own and raise a family.

I am now twenty-seven and I've thought a good bit about the kind of future I want to experience. Ten years from now in 1990 I'll be thirty-seven, and by then I will want to have two children aged five and seven. Remembering my own loneliness when my brothers and sister went off to college, I will want my children closely spaced. Life can be difficult for an only child. A child deserves a brother or sister. Although on the one hand I want to maintain a career through child rearing, ideally I would like to be home until each child is three. That would take six years out of my early thirties. I hope that my husband will earn enough to make that possible, but I suspect that it will take two incomes for us to own our own home and enjoy a comfortable life-style . . . and I suppose that I will always feel the need to be self-sufficient—to be able to make it on my own. In Peoples Temple I learned to trust no one and to count on nothing. I still feel that need to be self-sufficient and to have an escape route . . . but those feelings are much diminished. Our apartment is my first real nest since I was a little girl in Berkeley. John and I worry and anguish over whether we can afford a lamp . . . or whether we should save for a coffee table. We don't worry much about saving the world. We talk more about our own futures.

Perhaps because of my Temple experience, I have become more conservative than I might otherwise have become. A number of associates in the business world smoke marijuana, but I do not. I want to be in control of my body and my life. I will never again relinquish control over my mind, my body, or my future—not to drugs, alcohol, to another person. Perhaps I still overreact to anything that requires blind faith or allegiance, or that involves altered states of consciousness. I become angry when others try to influence me by laying on a guilt trip. I have nothing to feel guilty about. I have paid my debt.

I do worry about my own children. If I raise them in San Francisco, I will send them to private schools because the educational system has become so poor here in the urban parts of the Bay Area. When Tom, Annalisa, and Larry went to Berkeley High School it was one of the best schools in the country. By the time I got there the earlier academic rigor was lost to social experimentation and permissiveness. Although my formal education has not yet been completed I do feel that

I am perceptive because of the things that I have gone through.

I love Larry and it troubles me to see him as the scapegoat for all of Peoples Temple. The U.S. government will do its best to convict him . . . and I worry that he may have to do time in prison in this country. But I think Larry will come through all of this in his own quiet, philosophical way. For him, I think the most important thing will be to find a wife and to raise a family. I think that he would be a good father. But I suspect that he will need to be encouraged. He may feel that he should not have children who might have to suffer with his name and reputation. Larry's adolescent alienation from the family is finished. I believe that he will emerge from all of this as a strong and committed member of this family. I think that Larry will miss Karen until he makes a good bond with someone else. He loved her deeply. Larry has been in physical and social isolation for the past two years. I think that it will be important for him to talk with Temple defectors to learn the other side of the story about things that happened in the church. When I returned from Guyana I learned a lot about how I was influenced and held in the Temple when I spoke with other defectors and heard their stories. None of us knew more than a little bit of what was really happening. Larry needs to talk with others in order to put his own life into perspective.

Although Tom and Annalisa see Larry's problems as growing out of the family, I see them beginning when he met and then married Carolyn Moore. I think it was Carolyn who influenced Larry into drugs. She was an extremely dominant person. She was a hard girl. There was no way that Larry could influence her. And Carolyn was very negative towards our family. I think that Larry's real problems began with Carolyn's drug-taking and her negativity. Karen on the other hand was very positive towards the family, and Larry's relations with Mom and Dad improved markedly when he married her.

I remember the relationship between Mom and Dad as a happy one. My teenage rebellion put a strain on that relationship because I would play them one against the other. Mom went into the Temple because Larry and I were in the Temple. I don't think she attended because of any problems in her relationship with Dad. She would never have joined had we not been members . . . never! Often she would tell me that she felt guilty that the main reason for her membership was that Larry and I were there. She felt guilt because she was there for the wrong reasons. It wasn't that that was the place she wanted her family to be; she just wanted everybody to be together. That's the reason she tried to get Annalisa to join . . . and to get Tom to attend—which would have been a disaster.

I think that Dad is in far better shape now than he is willing to admit. Perhaps Annalisa and Tom like to perceive of him as an unhappy hermit. But he dates women all the time. He seems to be adjusting to singlehood with more ease than any of us would have expected. Because of his puritanical up-bringing he doesn't want his children to think that he no longer follows the moral code that he wants his children to follow. It's not as if he had a double standard, but he does worry about what the children think of him. Anytime I visit his house two or three women telephone. He must be doing something right. With Dad it's what he thinks we think of him that most concerns him, and for that reason he has been very discreet in his relations with his lady friends.

I think Mom had a pretty full life, but an insecure one. I think that there were parts of her past that she didn't want to face. She had the opportunity to go to Germany with Dad but she didn't want to go. Having been taught by the Nazis that she was inferior, perhaps she came to believe it. She went through life concerned that she had a hook nose . . . and she didn't have one at all. She thought she had kinky hair when she only had a natural wave. She didn't want us to know of our Jewish background because she didn't want us to feel un-comfortable if a Jewish joke was told. She wanted to protect us.

If Mom were looking at the family today, she would be proud and pleased that Annalisa is a mother, a family person, with a garden. She would be pleased that Tom is happier now as a professor and living closer to the rest of the family. I think she would be pleased with the way I have turned out. I know that she didn't believe the awful things that Jim told her about me after my escape, but I do wish she could see me today. I know that she would be happy to see Dad dating. I think her only real source of unhappiness would be Larry and his pre-dicament . . . and that this book has so upset and held the family up to the scrutiny of outsiders. She would have wanted this book to express the more positive side of the family. As for my opinion of this book, I think it is unfortunate that it was ever written. I would rather the family be remembered by what we choose to pass on to our own children . . . and not what they can read in a library. This family has gone through a lot of turmoil, but I also think we are resilient. I think all of us are living normal lives and only once in a while do we think about how our mother died, and why . . . and where. I don't think that this book is a fair or sympathetic interpretation of the family. I don't think that the problems between Mom and Dad—if there were any—affected any of us children in any way.

I worry that when others who don't know and understand this family read this book, the family's name and reputation will be damaged. It worries me that my child can go to the library, pick up this book, and read something that is not a fair picture of me and the other members of my family. I love Tom and Annalisa but I believe that they may have used this opportunity unwittingly to purge themselves of some of the resentment that has built up in them over the years. Perhaps if they had rebelled against our father when they were young they would not feel this need so strongly now.

THOMAS N. LAYTON

Where have the Laytons been? Where are we now? And where are we going? I suppose I should start with Dad. For all of us he has been the most dominant member of the family.

It seems to me that Dad has been unhappy all of his life. First he strove to escape West Virginia, then to achieve scientific recognition and to build a home and happy family. Eventually he had it all but he never realized it. He lived a dream deferred, of delayed gratification. He visualized noble goals but never savored the small triumphs in their pursuit. And in eventually achieving those goals he found them empty, and replaced them with even more distant goals.

Dad was happiest when the children were small and dependent. As we grew older and increasingly involved with our peer groups, he took this to be a rejection of him. Self-doubt, insecurity, and a sense of failure then began to dominate his world view. As a consequence we children assumed a sense of guilt that we were somehow responsible for our father's unhappiness. In 1962 I felt major misgivings about going away to college because I would be breaking up the family ... and the family, I believed, was the only thing my unhappy father lived for. Even today Debbie feels personally responsible for Dad's ulcers and heart attacks.

I see in Dad a brilliant and sensitive man who lived a life of insecurity and self-doubt. The real tragedy of Dad's life is that he had it all, but he never realized it.

Yet with all of Dad's problems I love him very much, and a major theme of my own life has been to win the approval of my father, to prove to him that really I'm an OK person, not cold and self-centered, and that my behavior should not be the cause of his unhappiness. But after all is said and done, if there is any moral in this book, it is that Dad has remained true to his values throughout. And in the end it has been the family bonds that he fostered which have lasted. Those bonds rescued Debbie and now bolster Larry, and Dad is still picking up the tab.

Debbie . . .

I was eleven when Debbie was born. Annalisa and I treated her like a mascot. We were proud of her and we spoiled her. She could do no wrong. When we left home for college, Debbie's problems began. Without her sibling support structure Debbie's self-image was damaged. By 1967 she had become a loser. She found support from other counterculture losers who were into drugs, alcohol, and truancy.

Having both strict parents and unacceptable counterculture friends, Debbie developed new skills. She learned to fabricate elaborate stories and explanations to justify her behavior. She learned to lie with a straight face. She became adaptable like a weed. She learned to rapidly assume the values, the dress, and the vocabulary of whomever she was with. In short, she developed the cunning street-wise survival skills that eventually enabled her to escape from Guyana and the clutches of Jim Jones.

In many ways I think the Temple tragedy has affected Debbie less than the rest of the family. Debbie has moved easily from a conservative upbringing, to the street, to the Temple, and now into a career in the San Francisco finance community. She has moved from the revolutionary Third World rhetoric of the Temple into a business-world appreciation of Ronald Reagan. Although Debbie is intelligent and perceptive, she is not yet wise. She has become trained, but she is essentially uneducated.

She still sees things in simplistic terms of black and white. She worries about whether specific incidents of her past will make her appear good or bad in the book. A case in point is her recent marriage. She has objected to any reference to it in the book. She has married a fine young man who was raised by parents who joined the Temple during its beginnings in Indiana. John, as he is called here, grew up in the Temple, and throughout his childhood related to Jones as one would to a father, eventually marrying Jones' adopted Korean daughter. John, however, was able to recognize Jones' growing insanity and quit the Temple long before the mass exodus to Guyana. When a love relationship developed between John and Debbie following her escape in 1978, my father summed up his own feelings when he told me, "How can this work? They have one thing in common—one disaster!" I strongly disagree with his view, but Debbie fears that the public will judge her marriage harshly... she imagines people saying under their breath, "Why, she never left the Temple at all. Just look at who she married!" Frankly I believe that she has married a man whose wisdom, sensitivity, sophistication, and education far exceed her own. I hope that she will grow to be a good wife to him. The fact that the Reverend James Warren Jones and Dr. Laurence Laird Layton will have shared the same son-in-law tells us nothing about them. Rather it demonstrates that two women independently recognized the fine qualities of a very courageous young man.

Larry...

In many ways I hardly know Larry. He grew up a loner. Annalisa and I interacted with our precocious little sister, Debbie. Larry, two years younger than Annalisa, was perceived rather as a wimp. Whereas Debbie, in her rebellion, learned street-wise survival skills, Larry was always open, trusting, and obedient. Larry was the most Quakerly member of our family. His opinions and actions were based on moral and ethical principles. Perhaps being an underdog he developed a sympathy for the downtrodden of the world.

Larry's Quaker upbringing fostered the kind of guilt that drives the white, liberal, middle-class do-gooder. When Jones offered Larry a program to create a better world, Larry was already preadapted to make any sacrifice toward that noble objective. Like so many young people of the middle 1960s, Larry was seeking purpose and a cause. Jones supplied both ready-made, and Larry saw in Peoples Temple a truly New Testament Christian community.

My father and Jim Jones were both demanding and absolute. Larry rejected one only to become obedient to the other.

Larry is still an unknown quantity to me. During my month-long stay in Guyana for his trial I spoke with him, but we never really communicated.

In a strange way I believe that Larry's sensitivity and vulnerability may be responsible for his being alive today. Larry watched Mom die very slowly of cancer. He sat next to her for weeks as she cried out in pain, sometimes coherent and sometimes not. As the weeks passed he became frantic to help her. He begged and pleaded with the Temple physician to give her pain suppressants and sedatives. Mom finally died on October 30 in Jonestown. Larry was at her side. Larry underwent a progressive breakdown as he witnessed Mom wasting away. He was given increasing doses of drugs to counteract his own deepening depression. Larry spent the two and a half weeks between Mom's death and November 18 drugged, and in deep grief. He went to the airport in a nonfunctioning state. Had he remained in Jonestown, he would have taken the potion. It was through a drugged, grief-broken mind that Larry was able to survive the airport massacre, the mass suicide, the scapegoat's role in an intricate frame-up, and finally a murder trial.

Larry has not had an opportunity to deal with his recent past. At the trial, when he mentioned Karen's name during his first few minutes of testimony, he broke down in tears, unable to speak. He will need help from a professional psychiatrist as he attempts to deal with a still-closed past, which like a Pandora's box is filled with ghosts of loved ones and memories of committed sacrifice for a noble and good cause that today lies in ruins, transformed into an ugly symbol of all that is evil.

Emotional support for Larry will come from the family, but the real help must come from outsiders. We, his family, are part of his problem. Laying our own trips on him will not contribute to his rehabilitation. Larry and Dad will both need considerable counseling before they spend much time together reviewing their convergent past. I'm afraid that deep down,

Dad still feels anger and may subconsciously blame Larry for some responsibility in the destruction of our family. Larry must not be made to carry that kind of guilt if he is to recover. Larry is a pathetic victim just like all the others; he deserves sympathetic understanding and not blame.

What do I see ahead for Larry? First, should he ever return to this country there will be another trial. I hope that he will return, for he is innocent and will be found so. Beyond that I think that Larry will feel grateful to the family for standing by him, but I wonder if he will ever feel truly close to any of us. He has always kept himself just a little outside the family. And I suspect, at least in his attitudes toward Annalisa and me, he will always remain there.

Annalisa . . .

Annalisa and I have always been close, and I have always thought her to be a bit miraculous. When I was eight and she was six she used to regale me and the other little neighborhood children with the continuing story of Mrs. Pickelpuss and her mile-long penis. As Annalisa told it, that poor old woman had it borrowed by the fire department and unrolled down the streets of Baltimore. Later Annalisa became an expert in finding lost belongings. No one suspected her abilities until she began finding things in places where they could never have been lost.

It finally took Annalisa with all her miraculous powers and her inspired storytelling to pluck Debbie from Guyana. Annalisa and I have worked as partners for a long time. As undergraduates we dated each other's friends. At twenty-one I bought booze for her girl friends and boyfriends, and she was always a willing hand in smuggling my date back into the girls' dorm after lockup. We likewise worked together in choreographing Debbie's escape.

I remain closer to Annalisa than to my other siblings.

Tom . . .

After I went off to college in the spring of 1962, I was never again a permanent resident of the family. I left California for the Harvard graduate program in anthropology in 1966, two years before Larry joined Peoples Temple. During succeeding doctoral research, foreign expeditions, and employment in faraway parts of the country, I was able to discern the growth of the Temple's hold on the family only dimly from letters and during short visits home. My contact with the Temple and knowledge of it were minimal until Debbie's escape from Guyana on May 13, 1978. Up to that time I had the impression of a strange but vital organization that was engaged in good works. Mom, Larry, and Debbie seemed happy and busy, and that pleased me. That they seemed to believe uncritically in all kinds of conspiracy theories disturbed me, so I avoided talking politics with them. That they believed in healings and miracles disturbed me somewhat more. It smacked of an Oral Roberts Southern fundamentalism that I considered to be beneath the dignity of an educated upper-middle-class family. I saw that Dad's aggressive questioning of Temple beliefs had isolated him from Larry, Debbie, and eventually Mom. I wanted to maintain my ties, so I kept my mouth shut. At the same time I had had a long-simmering idea that after years of archaeological projects and studying extinct peoples I would like to attempt to write an ethnography of living people. I thought the Temple was a sufficiently good example of a utopian cult to be an ideal candidate for study. Moreover, if I could maintain the trust of my mother, brother, and sister, I would have an entrée into the workings of the group unavailable to any other anthropologist.

Having for several years played with the idea of studying the Temple, I was mentally prepared to formally interview Debbie and record her story within days of her escape. On hearing her story, my interest in studying the organization was replaced by the more immediate concerns of hiding Debbie, reaching Larry, and freeing Mom. The family was faced with a hideous situation. Mom and Larry were being held hostage by Jim Jones and our government refused to do anything to secure their release. In fact, Debbie's story was so fantastic that telling it to the State Department resulted in disbelief by them and loss of credibility for me. As I talked with State Department personnel trying to arrange "welfare-whereabouts" checks on Mom and Larry, I sensed that they took me for a kook. So I began to take notes on telephone calls and to dutifully document our efforts to secure Mom's release. With the murders and suicides of November 18, 1978, I began a diary. I felt that what was happening to our family was of sufficient importance that it should be recorded. As the days passed, what had begun as a notion to do an ethnography, and during the succeeding months had transmuted into a legal documentation of efforts to free Mom, finally became a diary in which I sublimated my anguish by forced daily recording of the tragedy as it unfolded from the vantage point of my father's living room.

By the morning of November 19, 1978, my father was emotionally devastated. He had ceased to function. He spoke repeatedly of suicide. I watched him constantly to prevent it. With Dad's breakdown came the realization that I would have to take responsibility for everything. I became the father, Annalisa the mother, and Dad one of the children: dependent and vulnerable.

Because of Dad's negative interpretation of each unfolding event, Annalisa and I were thrust into the opposite position of trying to demonstrate why things were not as bad as they seemed on the surface. At the times when we felt least hope we never revealed our misgivings to Dad. Annalisa and I have always been close, but we are far closer now. As Dad approached each day with a deepening attitude of defeat, I put a smile on my face and assumed a positive stance. In retrospect, I see that this positive attitude was usually rewarded with positive outcomes, even out of what seemed at the time to be the most hopeless situations. For me that attitude has become a habit, one of the better aftereffects of the tragedy.

One by-product of a tragedy is the self-examination and introspection that come in its wake. As I cared for Dad during the weeks following November 18, I came for the first time to see him without the armor of the dominant father. Rather I saw a broken old man, cognizant only of his own dashed hopes, unable and unwilling to face the future. I questioned him about his life, his relationship with Mom, and other topics. I felt that he didn't have long to live, and I wanted to record as much as I could about our family while that was still possible. Mom had died in Jonestown. I had wanted to get to know her as an adult, and to hear her story. I bear no grudges, but I suppose if there is anything that I hate Jim Jones for, it is that he made it impossible for me to talk with my mother before she died.

As I became aware that I knew nothing of my mother's roots and had been told only a revisionist glorification of my father's, I got out all the old family photographs and enlisted Dad's help in labeling them. I tried to locate family documents

in the vast pile of disintegrating cardboard boxes in the basement. I tried to find letters and diaries that would contribute
to a family history. Our family is remarkable in that we have
saved so many documents over the years. Dad, Debbie, and
I were the worst pack rats. But Mom saved many documents
from her youth in Germany. Only Larry and Annalisa discarded
correspondence. Dad had a sense of family—of dynasty—and
for that reason saved letters. I also saved letters for that reason,
but there was an underlying psychological motivation as well.
For years my father had told me that I was self-centered and
cared nothing for the family, and I felt guilty for somehow
being responsible for his consequent unhappiness. For this reason I saved every letter written to me by family members. I
was physically unable to throw away a family letter, unable
to execute the symbolic act of rejecting the family and proving
my father's judgment of me correct. So we Laytons live with
a vast baggage of paper, and some of that paper has found its
way into this book. But this book is not the family history for
which I have been collecting data for years. Rather it is an
interim effort that I hope will pay some of Larry's legal bills.

By assuming a leadership role in the family and at the same
time attempting to interpret the major psychological trends in
its evolution, I have become a focus of Dad's anger. He feels
betrayed and stabbed in the back as he reads my interpretations
of his life. A book about a family can be cathartic. But this
is the first time that Dad has not felt in control of his life. He
feels helpless as myths of family origin are questioned. For me
the past two years have been a time of great stress. First I had
to act strong at a time when I didn't feel particularly strong.
Then I had to face the anger of Dad and Debbie, as the book
revealed more and more about their lives. But there have been
joys as well. I have been able to make contact with Jewish
relatives of my mother scattered around the world from São
Paulo to Capetown, and from Houston to Cologne. I currently
feel great satisfaction as I research a history of Mom's family
from 1820 to 1945. Ancestors, I find, are far easier to write
about than living relatives.

I was a very young thirty-five in May 1978 when Debbie
reappeared in my life, bearing her horrible story. Now almost
thirty-eight, I am beginning to feel my age both physically and
emotionally. But if I have ever felt guilt, I don't now. I've

donated the last two years to the family. I've paid my dues. Now I want to get on with my own life. Dad once told me that "He who takes a wife and raises a family gives hostages to fate." But in spite of all that has happened—or perhaps because of it—I now want very much to marry and start a family of my own.

Tears still come to my eyes when I remember Mom. But I have laid most of my ghosts to rest. Late one night as I slept in the Pegasus Hotel while attending Larry's trial in Guyana, I dreamed my mom was in the room with me. I awoke with a start. I imagined she was sitting in the overstuffed chair facing my bed. I thanked her for all the love and concern she gave to me from babyhood to manhood. Tears cloud my eyes as I try to type these sentences.

A few days later, at Larry's trial, a Hindu psychiatrist testified that people under the influence of drugs and suffering from malnutrition and stress often forget what they have done. He spoke of the Hindu goddess Kali Mai whose devotees under the influence of drums pass into an altered state of consciousness, remembering nothing of their trance state when the drums stop. I silently promised Kali Mai that if she spared Larry, I would be her devotee. I promised to throw coins into the ocean. I promised to raise a Jandi flag in her honor. The flag flies in my backyard, the coins were cast where the Demerara River flows into the Caribbean.

I see a great deal to be thankful for in this tragedy. First I am thankful that Mom died of cancer eighteen days before the final holocaust. I am thankful for being spared the horrible thought of my mother who loved life so much being forced to drink the cyanide potion. Again, I am thankful that Larry has had a year and a half to read and think and reflect on his past in the Temple. I believe that had he been released immediately as was Mike Prokes, he too would have taken his life. Finally, I am thankful that Larry had the good fortune to be defended by Rex McKay. McKay could have put up a perfunctory fight for a lost cause but he did not. He put on a magnificent defense that rivaled the best of Perry Mason.

It seems a miracle to me that the Layton family is still relatively whole having weathered a tragedy that was so brutally complete. What other family in Jonestown had the good fortune that ours did?

AFFIDAVIT OF DEBORAH LAYTON BLAKEY
RE THE THREAT AND POSSIBILITY OF MASS SUICIDE
BY MEMBERS OF THE PEOPLE'S TEMPLE

I, DEBORAH LAYTON BLAKEY, declare the following under penalty of perjury:

1. The purpose of this affidavit is to call to the attention of the United States government the existence of a situation which threatens the lives of United States citizens living in Jonestown, Guyana.

2. From August, 1971 until May 13, 1978, I was a member of the People's Temple. For a substantial period of time prior to my departure for Guyana in December, 1977, I held the position of Financial Secretary of the People's Temple.

3. I was 18 years old when I joined the People's Temple. I had grown up in affluent circumstances in the permissive atmosphere of Berkley, California. By joining the People's Temple, I hoped to help others and in the process to bring structure and self-discipline to my own life.

4. During the years I was a member of the People's Temple, I watched the organization depart with increasing frequency from its professed dedication to social change and participatory democracy. The Rev. Jim Jones gradually assumed a tyrannical hold over the lives of Temple members.

5. Any disagreement with his dictates came to be regarded as "treason." The Rev. Jones labelled any person who left the organization a "traitor" and "fair game." He steadfastly and convincingly maintained that the punishment for defection was death. The fact that severe corporal punishment was frequently administered to Temple members gave the threats a frightening air of reality.

6. The Rev. Jones saw himself as the center of a conspiracy. The identity of the conspirators changed from day to day along with his erratic world vision. He induced the fear in others that, through their contact with him, they had become targets of the conspiracy. He convinced black Temple members that if they did not follow him to Guyana, they would be put into concentration camps and killed. White members were instilled with the belief that their names appeared on a secret list of enemies of the state that was kept by the C.I.A. and that they would be tracked down, tortured, imprisoned, and subsequently killed if they did not flee to Guyana.

7. Frequently, at Temple meetings, Rev. Jones would talk non-

stop for hours. At various times, he claimed that he was the reincarnation of either Lenin, Jesus Christ, or one of a variety of other religious or political figures. He claimed that he had divine powers and could heal the sick. He stated that he had extrasensory perception and could tell what everyone was thinking. He said that he had powerful connections the world over, including the Mafia, Idi Amin, and the Soviet government.

8. When I first joined the Temple, Rev. Jones seemed to make clear distinctions between fantasy and reality. I believed that most of the time when he said irrational things, he was aware that they were irrational, but that they served as a tool of his leadership. His theory was that the end justified the means. At other times, he appeared to be deluded by a paranoid vision of the world. He would not sleep for days at a time and talk compulsively about the conspiracies against him. However, as time went on, he appeared to become genuinely irrational.

9. Rev. Jones insisted that Temple members work long hours and completely give up all semblance of a personal life. Proof of loyalty to Jones was confirmed by actions showing that a member had given up everything, even basic necessities. The most loyal were in the worst physical condition. Dark circles under one's eyes or extreme loss of weight were considered signs of loyalty.

10. The primary emotions I came to experience were exhaustion and fear. I knew that Rev. Jones was in some sense ''sick,'' but that did not make me any less afraid of him.

11. Rev. Jones fled the United States in June, 1977 amidst growing public criticism of the practices of the Temple. He informed members of the Temple that he would be imprisoned for life if he did not leave immediately.

12. Between June, 1977 and December, 1977, when I was ordered to depart for Guyana, I had access to coded radio broadcasts from Rev. Jones in Guyana to the People's Temple headquarters in San Francisco.

13. In September, 1977, an event which Rev. James viewed as a major crisis occurred. Through listening to coded radio broadcasts and conversations with other members of the Temple staff, I learned that an attorney for former Temple member Grace Stoen had arrived in Guyana, seeking the return of her son, John Victor Stoen.

14. Rev. James had expressed particular bitterness toward Grace Stoen. She had been Chief Counselor, a position of great responsibility within the Temple. Her personal qualities of generosity and compassion made her very popular with the membership. Her departure posed a threat to Rev. Jones' absolute control. Rev. Jones

delivered a number of public tirades against her. He said that her kindness was faked and that she was a C.I.A. agent. He swore that he would never return her son to her.

15. I am informed that Rev. Jones believed that he would be able to stop Timothy Stoen, husband of Grace Stoen and father of John Victor Stoen, from speaking against the Temple as long as the child was being held in Guyana. Timothy Stoen, a former Assistant District Attorney in Mendocino and San Francisco counties, had been one of Rev. Jones' most trusted advisors. It was rumored that Stoen was critical of the use of physical force and other forms of intimidation against Temple members. I am further informed that Rev. Jones believed that a public statement by Timothy Stoen would increase the tarnish on his public image.

16. When the Temple lost track of Timothy Stoen, I was assigned to track him down and offer him a large sum of money in return for his silence. Initially, I was to offer him $5,000. I was authorized to pay him up to $10,000. I was not able to locate him and did not see him again until on or about October 6, 1977. On that date, the Temple received information that he would be joining Grace in a San Francisco Superior Court action to determine the custody of John. I was one of a group of Temple members assigned to meet him outside the court and attempt to intimidate him to prevent him from going inside.

17. The September, 1977 crisis concerning John Stoen reached major proportions. The radio messages from Guyana were frenzied and hysterical. One morning, Terry J. Buford, public relations advisor to Rev. Jones, and myself were instructed to place a telephone call to a high-ranking Guyanese official who was visiting the United States and deliver the following threat: unless the government of Guyana took immediate steps to stall the Guyanese court action regarding John Stoen's custody, the entire population of Jonestown would extinguish itself in a mass suicide by 5:30 P.M. that day. I was later informed that Temple members in Guyana placed similar calls to other Guyanese officials.

18. We later received radio communication to the effect that the court case had been stalled and that the suicide threat was called off.

19. I arrived in Guyana in December, 1977. I spent a week in Georgetown and then, pursuant to orders, traveled to Jonestown.

20. Conditions at Jonestown were even worse than I had feared they would be. The settlement was swarming with armed guards. No one was permitted to leave unless on a special assignment and these assignments were given only to the most trusted. We were

allowed to associate with Guyanese people only while on a "mission."

21. The vast majority of the Temple members were required to work in the fields from 7 A.M. to 6 P.M. six days per week and on Sunday from 7 A.M. to 2 P.M. We were allowed one hour for lunch. Most of this hour was spent walking back to lunch and standing in line for our food. Taking any other breaks during the workday was severely frowned upon.

22. The food was woefully inadequate. There was rice for breakfast, rice water soup for lunch, and rice and beans for dinner. On Sunday, we each received an egg and a cookie. Two or three times a week we had vegetables. Some very weak and elderly members received one egg per day. However, the food did improve markedly on the few occasions when there were outside visitors.

23. In contrast, Rev. Jones, claiming problems with his blood sugar, dined separately and ate meat regularly. He had his own refrigerator which was stocked with food. The two women with whom he resided, Maria Katsaris and Carolyn Layton, and the two small boys who lived with him, Kimo Prokes and John Stoen, dined with the membership. However, they were in much better physical shape than everyone else since they were also allowed to eat the food in Rev. Jones' refrigerator.

24. In February, 1978, conditions had become so bad that half of Jonestown was ill with severe diarrhea and high fevers. I was seriously ill for two weeks. Like most of the other sick people, I was not given any nourishing foods to help recover. I was given water and a tea drink until I was well enough to return to the basic rice and beans diet.

25. As the former financial secretary, I was aware that the Temple received over $65,000 in Social Security checks per month. It made me angry to see that only a fraction of the income of the senior citizens in the care of the Temple was being used for their benefit. Some of the money was being used to build a settlement that would earn Rev. Jones the place in history with which he was so obsessed. The balance was being held in "reserve." Although I felt terrible about what was happening, I was afraid to say anything because I knew that anyone with a differing opinion gained the wrath of Jones and other members.

26. Rev. Jones' thoughts were made known to the population of Jonestown by means of broadcasts over the loudspeaker system. He broadcast an average of six hours per day. When the Reverend was particularly agitated, he would broadcast for hours on end. He would talk on and on while we worked in the fields or tried to sleep.

In addition to the daily broadcasts, there were marathon meetings six nights per week.

27. The tenor of the broadcasts revealed that Rev. Jones' paranoia had reached an all-time high. He was irate at the light in which he had been portrayed by the media. He felt that as a consequence of having been ridiculed and maligned, he would be denied a place in history. His obsession with his place in history was maniacal. When pondering the loss of what he considered his rightful place in history, he would grow despondent and say that all was lost.

28. Visitors were infrequently permitted access to Jonestown. The entire community was required to put on a performance when a visitor arrived. Before the visitor arrived, Rev. Jones would instruct us on the image we were to project. The workday would be shortened. The food would be better. Sometimes there would be music and dancing. Aside from these performances, there was little joy or hope in any of our lives. An air of despondency prevailed.

29. There was constant talk of death. In the early days of the People's Temple, general rhetoric about dying for principles was sometimes heard. In Jonestown, the concept of mass suicide for socialism arose. Because our lives were so wretched anyway and because we were so afraid to contradict Rev. Jones, the concept was not challenged.

30. An event which transpired shortly after I reached Jonestown convinced me that Rev. Jones had sufficient control over the minds of the residents that it would be possible for him to effect a mass suicide.

31. At least once a week, Rev. Jones would declare a "white night," or state of emergency. The entire population of Jonestown would be awakened by blaring sirens. Designated persons, approximately fifty in number, would arm themselves with rifles, move from cabin to cabin, and make certain that all members were responding. A mass meeting would ensue. Frequently during these crises, we would be told that the jungle was swarming with mercenaries and that death could be expected at any minute.

32. During one "white night," we were informed that our situation had become hopeless and that the only course of action open to us was a mass suicide for the glory of socialism. We were told that we would be tortured by mercenaries if we were taken alive. Everyone, including the children, was told to line up. As we passed through the line, we were given a small glass of red liquid to drink. We were told that the liquid contained poison and that we would die within 45 minutes. We all did as we were told. When the time came when we should have dropped dead, Rev. Jones ex-

plained that the poison was not real and that we had just been through a loyalty test. He warned us that the time was not far off when it would become necessary for us to die by our own hands.

33. Life at Jonestown was so miserable and the physical pain of exhaustion was so great that this event was not traumatic for me. I had become indifferent as to whether I lived or died.

34. During another "white night," I watched Carolyn Layton, my former sister-in-law, give sleeping pills to two young children in her care, John Victor Stoen and Kimo Prokes, her own son. Carolyn said to me that Rev. Jones had told her that everyone was going to have to die that night. She said that she would probably have to shoot John and Kimo and that it would be easier for them if she did it while they were asleep.

35. In April, 1978, I was reassigned to Georgetown. I became determined to escape or die trying. I surreptitiously contacted my sister, who wired me a plane ticket. After I received the ticket, I sought the assistance of the United States Embassy in arranging to leave Guyana. Rev. Jones had instructed us that he had a spy working in the United States Embassy and that he would know if anyone went to the embassy for help. For this reason, I was very fearful.

36. I am most grateful to the United States government and Richard McCoy and Daniel Weber, in particular, for the assistance they gave me. However, the efforts made to investigate conditions in Jonestown are inadequate for the following reasons. The infrequent visits are always announced and arranged. Acting in fear for their lives, Temple members respond as they are told. The members appear to speak freely to American representatives, but in fact they are drilled thoroughly prior to each visit on what questions to expect and how to respond. Members are afraid of retaliation if they speak their true feelings in public.

37. On behalf of the population of Jonestown, I urge that the United States Government take adequate steps to safeguard their rights. I believe that their lives are in danger.

I declare under penalty of perjury that the foregoing is true and correct, except as to those matters stated on information and belief and as to those I believe them to be true.

Executed this 15 day of June, 1978 at San Francisco, California.

5

Deborah Layton Blakey

DEBORAH LAYTON BLAKEY

Deborah Layton Blakey

Bestsellers from Berkley
The books you've been hearing about—and want to read